COMPLETE TAEKWONDO POOMSAE

*THE OFFICIAL TAEGEUK, PALGWAE
AND BLACK BELT FORMS OF TAEKWONDO*

COMPLETE TAEKWONDO POOMSAE

*THE OFFICIAL TAEGEUK, PALGWAE
AND BLACK BELT FORMS OF TAEKWONDO*

BY

KYU HYUNG LEE   *SANG H. KIM*

TURTLE PRESS   SANTA FE

COMPLETE TAEKWONDO POOMSAE: THE OFFICIAL TAEGEUK, PALGWAE AND BLACK BELT FORMS OF TAEKWONDO Copyright © 2007 Sang H. Kim, Kyu Hyung Lee. All rights reserved. Printed in the United States of America. No part of this book may be reproduced without written permission except in the case of brief quotations embodied in articles or reviews. For information, address Turtle Press, PO Box 34010, Santa Fe NM 87594-4010.

To contact the author or to order additional copies of this book:
    Turtle Press
    PO Box 34010
    Santa Fe NM 87594-4010
    1-800-77-TURTL
    www.TurtlePress.com

Editor: Cynthia A. Kim
Photos by Marc Yves Regis
Calligraphy by Sang H. Kim
Chapter One translation by Ju-Young Kim
Photo models: Carlos Sanchez and Marco Correia

ISBN 9781880336922
LCCN 2006039085
Printed in the United States of America

10 9 8 7 6 5 4 3 2 1 0

Library of Congress Cataloguing in Publication Data

Kim, Sang H.
  Complete taekwondo poomsae : the official taegeuk, palgwae, and black belt forms of taekwondo / by Sang H. Kim, Kyu Hyung Lee ; [photos by Marc Yves Regis].
      p. cm.
  ISBN-13: 978-1-880336-92-2
  ISBN-10: 1-880336-92-8
  1. Tae kwon do. 2. Tae kwon do--Pictorial works. I. Yi, Kyu-hyong, 1948- II. Regis, Marc Yves. III. Title.
  GV1114.9.K538 2007
  796.815'3--dc22
                            2006039085

Contents

POOMSAE FUNDAMENTALS 19
   Common Qualities of All Poomsae 21
   Characteristics of Poomsae 23
   Strengths and Limitations of Poomsae Techniques in Actual Combat 25
   Fundamental Techniques of Taekwondo 26
      How to Form a Fist Correctly 28
      How to Form a Knifehand Correctly 30
      Rules of Poomsae Practice 31
      Junbiseogi: Ready Stance 32
      Juchumseo Momtong Jireugi: Horseriding Stance Middle Punch 34
      Araemakki: Low Section Block 36
      Momtong Bandae Jireugi: Reverse Middle Punch 38
      Apchagi: Front Kick 40
      Sonnal Bakkatchigi: Outward Knifehand Strike 42
      Momtongmakki: Middle Section Block 44
      Yopchagi: Side Kick 46
      Sonnal Momtongmakki: Double Knifehand Block 48
      Olgulmakki: High Section Block 50
      Sonnal Mokchigi: Knifehand Neck Strike 52
      Dollyochagi: Roundhouse Kick 54
      Momtong Barojireugi: Straight Middle Punch 56
   Stance 58
   Blocking 60
   Evasion 60
   Gupso: Vital Targets 61
   Bodily Weapons 62
   Attacking Techniques 64
   The Structural Principles and Types of Poomsae 68
   Principles of Poomsae Creation 69
   Movement Principles of Poomsae 70
   Tips for Effective Poomsae Practice 72
   Emphasis in Poomsae Training 73
   Mastery of Poomsae 80

POOMSAE TERMINOLOGY 83

POOMSAE WARM-UP 91

TAEGEUK POOMSAE 101
- What is Taegeuk? 103
- Origin of Taegeuk 103
- Nature of Um and Yang 103
- Principles of Poomsae Practice 104
- Palgwae Trigrams from Taegeuk 104
- Symbols for Eight Taegeuk Poomsae 105

- Poomsae Taegeuk Il Jang 107
- Poomsae Taegeuk Ee Jang 117
- Poomsae Taegeuk Sam Jang 127
- Poomsae Taegeuk Sah Jang 139
- Poomsae Taegeuk Oh Jang 151
- Poomsae Taegeuk Yuk Jang 165
- Poomsae Taegeuk Chil Jang 177
- Poomsae Taegeuk Pal Jang 193

PALGWAE POOMSAE 209
- What is Palgwae Poomsae? 211
- Palgwae Trigrams from Palgwae Poomsae 211
- Palgwae Diagram 211
- Symbols for Eight Palgwae Poomsae 212

- Poomsae Palgwae Il Jang 213
- Poomsae Palgwae Ee Jang 223
- Poomsae Palgwae Sam Jang 235
- Poomsae Palgwae Sah Jang 245
- Poomsae Palgwae Oh Jang 259
- Poomsae Palgwae Yuk Jang 273
- Poomsae Palgwae Chil Jang 285
- Poomsae Palgwae Pal Jang 297

BLACK BELT POOMSAE 315

- Poomsae Koryo 317
- Poomsae Keumgang 337
- Poomsae Taebaek 349
- Poomsae Pyongwon 363
- Poomsae Sipjin 377
- Poomsae Jitae 395
- Poomsae Cheonkwon 409
- Poomsae Hansoo 427
- Poomse Ilyeo 441

*This book is dedicated to Taekwondo instructors
and students who believe in this art.*

PREFACE

By Dr. Kyu Hyung Lee

Everyone is born with the instinct for self-protection. It enables us to cope with crises with a positive attitude rather than negative. There is no doubt that it is you who are responsible for your own safety in life. In order to survive, you need more power and better techniques. Thus, we can witness a rich martial culture at a variety of levels in every nation in the world. Taekwondo is one of those leading martial arts.

Taekwondo was chosen as an official medal event for the 2000 Summer Olympic Games in Sydney at the 103rd General Assembly of the International Olympic Committee. Taekwondo will also be an official event at the 2008 Beijing Summer Olympic Games and the 2012 London Summer Olympic Games. The World Taekwondo Federation as the official governing body has 192 member nations with over 5 million practitioners. Taekwondo is by far the most popular martial sport in the world.

This global sports phenomenon of Taekwondo, however, cannot fulfill the need for a complete martial arts system for personal self-protection. This is where Taekwondo Poomsae plays an important role in combining diverse offensive and defensive techniques that are not used in Sport Taekwondo. Poomsae techniques are valuable for self-defense due to their economy of the usage of power: with minimum power you can generate maximum effect.

Poomsae is a scientifically synthesized form of martial practice that utilizes mental and physical elements to maximum capacity to defeat an opponent with defensive and offensive techniques. Poomsae movement lines are pre-determined according to principles and practical applications.

In order to promote the benefits and importance of Poomsae practice, The World Taekwondo Federation successfully held the 1st World Taekwondo Poomsae Championships in Seoul, Korea in 2006. The need for a quality Taekwondo Poomsae text book, therefore, is increasingly demanded.

As the Head of the Kukkiwon and Korean National Taekwondo Demonstration Team and Korean National Junior Taekwondo Demonstration Team, I have traveled the world teaching and performing at major national and international events. As the Team manager for the Korean National Team for the 1st World Taekwondo Poomsae Championships, I witnessed all 26 team members receiving gold medals. Hence I hope my experience and knowledge in various fields of Taekwondo can serve for you to enhance and standardize your techniques.

I often ask myself "what is Taekwondo?"

My conclusion is that Taekwondo is a combat art to develop our senses for automatic responsive ability by repetitive practice against imaginary and actual opponents. In that respect, Poomsae is an essential tool to understand the principles and relationships of combat skills to be effective in an actual confrontation. Unlike sparring, you can practice Poomsae in a safe environment without any limitation of techniques. Known benefits of Poomsae practice are better circulation of the entire body, enhanced concentration and fitness and self-protection ability.

A teacher (leader) is one who helps his or her students attain self-actualization by guiding to higher goals and illuminating their weaknesses. The foremost mission of a Taekwondo instructor, in my opinion, is to develop the next generation of leaders by planned, intended and systemized education. This process continues the tradition of excellence of Taekwondo, which is the goal of publishing the *Complete Taekwondo Poomsae* book. The way of using this book is entirely up to each reader. My wish is that this book will help you move to the next level and beyond and a lot more talented masters will become leaders in our society. I believe that your dedication and passion will make our community a better place. In the echo of Taekwondo Kihap, you are always with me.

Finally, I would like to thank Dr. Sang H. Kim for jointly publishing this book with me. I have known and trained with him for decades and have a deep respect for his knowledge of martial arts. It has been truly pleasure to work with him and I hope it continues for more decades.

FORWARD

My first fight took place at the age of 4. An older boy from the neighbor wanted my favorite toy and I refused to give in. He scratched my face with his fingernails but I was defenseless. I was holding the toy so firmly that he took advantage of my wide-open face. I still have those scars on my face. Darker skin than the rest of the face. It was my first lesson in self-defense.

Since then, 45 years have passed. Taekwondo has been my daily companion. Many friends and senior masters have come and gone. Lots of changes have swept local, national and international Dojangs. It was called Korean fighting arts back then. We practiced forms whose names I no longer remember. Palgwae, then Taegeuk Poomsae were introduced. Kicking methods have changed significantly due to the popularity of competition. Taekwondo became an Olympic sport.

Nonetheless, the essence of Taekwondo has never changed: a mental and physical discipline that shapes the mind and body. Whether you win or lose, Taekwondo is an important part of life; more than that, it is a way of life for most of us. It is addictive. It has been so for nearly a half century for me.

Out of many students, masters and grandmasters with whom I trained with, I have had great reverence to Grandmaster Kyu Hyung Lee. In 1983, I was training at the Kukkiwon in Seoul. At the time, I often witnessed Master Lee's early training. Often, I saw him running along the Han River bank while I was riding a public bus in Seoul. In 1993, I was staying at the US Olympic Training Center in Colorado Springs. Very early one morning, after running a few miles, I sensed a person running toward me in the darkness. It was a humbling moment when I saw it was Grandmaster Kyu Hyung Lee. He was one of the lecturers sent by the World Taekwondo Federation to train Olympic officials and athletes in the US. He was sweating like he just got out of a sauna. We trained together all morning. It was the most joyful training day for me. From that time, I wished to write something with him to make Taekwondo more accessible to more people in the world.

In 2003, I visited Midong Elementary School in Seoul which is known worldwide for its superb demonstration of Taekwondo at the 1988 Olympic games and for her Excellency Queen Elizabeth II on her visit to Korea in 1999. Grandmaster Lee was teaching the class with over 200 children who literally never blinked while training. I witnessed the soul of Taekwondo at Midong. Their innocent spirit, so pure and ardent, echoes in my mind even after several years have passed.

My long cherished wish to write a good Taekwondo book finally came to be materialized. I invited Grandmaster Lee (by then Dr. Lee) to my home in Connecticut in 2005. We had long discussions for days on various subjects of Taekwondo training. Those discussions bore fruit in this *Complete Taekwondo Poomsae* book.

As my friendship with Dr. Lee has been long and mutual, I wish your friendship with Taekwondo is long and mutual. When you love Taekwondo, there is the way; No one can take it away from you.

My sincere thanks go to Dr. and Mrs. Kyu Hyung Lee and all the Taekwondo masters and students in this global village. When we become one in Taekwondo, the world will be a lot better place to live in.

In the journey to reach Taegeuk, we are always one in Taekwondo!

Sang H. Kim
Santa Fe, Winter 2006

Complete Taekwondo Poomsae

Dr. Kyu Hyung Lee with HM Queen Elizabeth II and Prince Phillip during the royal visit to Midong Elementary school in 1999, Seoul, Korea

Dr. Kyu Hyung Lee with Juan Antonio Samaranch, Former President of I.O.C.

Dr. Chungwon Choue, President of the World Taekwondo Federation, with Dr. Kyu Hyung Lee at the 1st World Taekwondo Poomsae Championships, Seoul, Korea

Authors Dr. Sang H. Kim and Dr. Kyu Hyung Lee during the photo session for *Complete Taekwondo Poomsae* in Hartford, Connecticut, 2005

Dr. Kyu Hyung Lee with the Korean Poomsae Team at the 1st World Taekwondo Poomsae Championships, Seoul

Dr. Kyu Hyung Lee with members of the Korean Poomsae Team at the 1st World Taekwondo Poomsae Championships

Dr. Kyu Hyung Lee receiving the World Peace Prize in 2004

Dr. Kyu Hyung Lee training Taekwondo masters at Kukkiwon, the World Taekwondo Headquarters

Dr. Kyu Hyung Lee demonstrating Creative Poomsae

Dr. Kyu Hyung Lee with the Korean National Demonstration Team to Africa in 2002

Dr. Kyu Hyung Lee with Taekwondo practitioners from the World Taekwondo Poomsae Championships

Sang H. Kim demonstrating a flying side kick at his 5th dan black belt promotion test in Daegu, Korea

Sang H. Kim with fellow black belts and instructors at Jung Moo Taekwondo Dojang in Daegu, Korea, 1977

Sang H. Kim practicing side kick during his military service, on the roof of the Military General Hospital in Seoul

Sang H. Kim training with a fellow special agent at a military base near the DMZ, in Kangwon Province, Korea, 1979

Sang H. Kim at the US Olympic Training Center in Colorado Springs, CO, 1993

Grandmaster Kyu Hyung Lee in Action

Master Sang H. Kim in Action

POOMSAE
FUNDAMENTALS

Common Qualities of All Poomsae

Although there are various types of Poomsae and their difficultly level varies greatly, all Poomsae have common qualities. These qualities fall into three categories: technical skills and applications, structure and emphasis.

Technical skills and applications

The technical principles of Poomsae apply to all types of Poomsae techniques. At its essence, Taekwondo is a combat art, therefore it is crucial to categorize techniques by their method of practical adaptation to actual fighting.

Technical Skills of Poomsae

In Taekwondo Poomsae there are more kicking and blocking techniques than is necessary in actual combat. Through training you can clarify which techniques are most practical.

Combat Skills of Poomsae

The actual combat skills of Poomsae only contain practical techniques. They are divided into kicking-centered Poomsae, defense-centered Poomsae and Poomsae that proportionately emphasize kicking and blocking.

Fundamental Skills of Poomsae

The fundamental skills of Poomsae have both beginner and advanced levels of performance. The advanced level introduces a Naegong (inner energy) method, which aims to strengthen inner power through breathing and is indirectly presented. Only through direct practice can you discover all of the variations of the fundamental skills of Taekwondo.

MASTER'S TIP

All of the Poomsae have both Waegong (external energy) and Naegong (internal energy) applications. After you have mastered the physical Waegong application of each movement, further practice and study can lead you to the Naegong applications.

Structure

The movement structure of Poomsae has a variety of styles, yet it is largely divided into form, method, hand techniques, foot techniques, stance and the directions and angles of the movements. In order to achieve balanced development of the body, Poomsae techniques are comprised of symmetrical action to the front and back or left side and right side except on special occasions. Therefore, the ratio of movements in each direction (front/rear or left/right) is identical in any given Poomsae. The stances and techniques are also generally symmetrical, for example a front stance low section block to the left will be repeated to the right. The movement structure of Poomsae is divided into foot techniques and hand techniques that clearly demonstrate the characteristics and uniqueness of Taekwondo.

Classifications of Poomsae based on the ratio of foot and hand skills:

- Poomsae emphasizing hand techniques
- Poomsae emphasizing foot techniques
- Poomsae balancing the emphasis on hand techniques and foot techniques

Emphasis

Taekwondo Poomsae is classified according to the emphasis of Taekwondo training elements including the application of power and the speed of movement. Slow powerful movements and quick light movements are equally important in the development of a well balanced Taekwondo practice. The qualities of Poomsae movements are classified as follows:

- Strong and slow Poomsae
- Quick and light Poomsae
- Poomsae with balanced power and speed

However, when the practitioner reaches the ultimate level, these classifications are not absolute.

Characteristics of Poomsae

Poomsae is system of solo practice of offensive and defensive techniques. There are five reasons why Taekwondo Poomsae training is different from Chinese and Japanese martial arts.

First, Taekwondo Poomsae is characterized by its **application of power and its technical principle of power usage**. Each Poomsae movement consists of two types of rhythm: the preparation for the movement and the actual or main movement. The preparation for the movement occurs when you move your legs using minimal power while simultaneously twisting your upper body in order to prepare for blocking, punching and kicking. The main movement concentrates all of your power on the blocking, striking or kicking action as your body simultaneously uncoils. Karate emphasizes intense focus throughout the whole body from start to finish of the movement, whereas in Taekwondo Poomsae the practitioner momentarily relaxes during the preparation for the movement then focuses power during the main movement. Taekwondo Poomsae is distinguished by its practical use of the body's energy and the momentary power exertion created by the speed of execution of a movement.

Here is an example of the application of power in Taekwondo techniques. In photo 1, the muscles are relaxed as the arms are chambered for the block. As the block is executed, in photo 2, full power is channeled into the movement.

MASTER'S TIP

One of the key characteristics of Taekwondo Poomsae techniques is their unique application of power. Each movement consists of two parts: a preparatory phase in which you relax your muscles as you chamber your body for the movement and then the movement itself in which you focus on applying full power to your block, strike or kick.

Second, the **stances of Taekwondo use a relatively narrow base** emphasizing quick body movement. Chinese martial arts and Karate utilize many low and wide stances whereas the walking stance, front stance and back stance of Taekwondo Poomsae are characterized by a distinctly narrow placement of the feet. Although this creates a disadvantage in the creation of power and maintenance of balance, it enables agile movements by allowing quick body maneuvers, enhancing the ability to skillfully confront the opponent's actions.

Notice how narrow the stances above are. The knees and feet are relatively close together, making the stances less stable but well suited to quick, agile movements.

MASTER'S TIP

The narrow stances of Taekwondo Poomsae, including front stance, back stance and walking stance, are less stable but they enable quick agile movements. The creation of power in Taekwondo Poomsae originates more from the speed of movements than from powerfully rooted stances.

Third, **Taekwondo Poomsae reflects the characteristics of Korean culture**. The color belt Poomsae, Taegeuk and Palgwae, are based on the principles of Um and Yang and the eight trigrams, which originate from the Taegeukki (Korean flag). The black belt forms (Koryo, Keumkang, Taebaek, Pyongwon, Sipjin, etc.) are based on traditional Korean philosophy and Taoist principles. The technical composition and the philosophical meaning of Poomsae Ilyeo (Oneness), the final black belt Poomsae, distinguish Taekwondo from other martial arts.

Fourth, the defensive and offensive techniques of Taekwondo consist of movements that take advantage of the **natural movement of the joints**.

Fifth, the defensive and offensive techniques of Taekwondo utilize the **elasticity and resilience of human body**.

Strengths and Limitations of Poomsae Techniques in Actual Combat

Poomsae (Kata in Karate, Taolu in Kung Fu) is a very important aspect of martial arts training. However, its usefulness is limited in actual combat situations. This limitation originates from the nonconfrontational nature of the practice, the lack of an opponent and the rigidness of the structure of each Poomsae.

Because Poomsae is learned individually and practiced against an imaginary opponent, it is far from the intense and urgent fighting situation of actual combat. In addition, Poomsae is a repetitive training system based on a rigid framework of offensive and defensive movements which creates doubt as to whether the practitioner can adapt to an ever-changing actual combat situation. In order to make Poomsae useful for combat, you have to visualize fighting against an opponent using your bodily weapons. That is why the principles and procedures of Poomsae are different from Kyorugi (sparring).

The strength of Taekwondo Poomsae's combat application is its adaptability in close distance fighting using the fists, knifehands, and elbows. Despite many weaknesses of Poomsae techniques as practical combat techniques, Poomsae has its own strengths in the structure of the overall Taekwondo system. Poomsae especially plays an important role in supplementing the limitations of Taekwondo Kyorugi, which focuses almost exclusively on kicking techniques under limited rules. The widely used official Poomsae is less useful for Kyorugi, as they lack the kicking techniques that are characteristic of Taekwondo. However, Kyorugi and Poomsae complement each other in terms of the general technical structure of taekwondo.

Finally, Poomsae is one of the required elements for official belt rank promotion testing run by the Kukkiwon (World Taekwondo Headquarters). Students and instructors should give the same attention to Poomsae practice as to other elements of training.

Limitations of Poomsae Training:
1. Because Poomsae is practiced alone, it lacks the urgency and intensity of actual combat.
2. The rigidness of Poomsae practice doesn't promote the ability to adapt that is required for actual combat.
3. Because Poomsae training is non-contact, it doesn't develop the practical skills of distance and timing necessary for combat.

Strengths of Poomsae Training:
1. Poomsae techniques are applicable to close distance combat situations.
2. Poomsae training emphasizes offensive and defensive hand skills, which are not emphasized in Taekwondo Kyorugi (sparring).
3. Poomsae techniques and stances are varied, making them complementary to the system of Kyorugi techniques.

Fundamental Techniques of Taekwondo

Presented here are the 13 representative movements fundamental to taekwondo Poomsae.

Korean Name	English Name
Junbiseogi	Ready Stance
Juchumseo Momtong Jireugi	Horseriding Stance Middle Punch
Araemakki	Low Section Block
Momtong Bandaejireugi	Reverse Middle Punch
Apchagi	Front Kick
Sonnal Bakkatchigi	Outward Knifehand Strike
Momtong Anmakki	Middle Section Inward Block
Yopchagi	Side Kick
Sonnal Momtongmakki	Double Knifehand Block
Olgulmakki	High Section Block
Sonnal Mokchigi	Knifehand Neck Strike
Dollyochagi	Roundhouse Kick
Momtong Barojireugi	Straight Middle Punch

The above movements are essential. Practice them diligently to achieve the precise execution of each movement. Often, and problematically, many instructors deviate from the correct performance of the fundamental movements and adopt a variety of changes. A good instructor will teach the basic concept of these fundamental techniques to help students perfect them prior to attaining Black Belt ranking.

Juchumseo Momtong Jireugi

Momtong Barojireugi

Poomsae Fundamentals 27

Apchagi

Yopchagi

Momtong Anmakki

Olgulmakki

Sonnal Mokchigi

Dollyochagi

Sonnal Momtongmakki

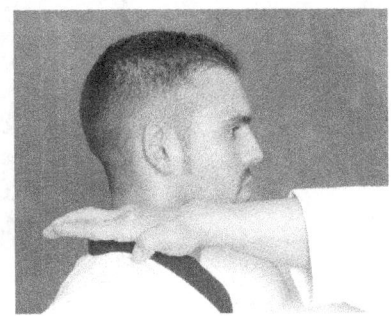
Sonnal Bakkatchigi

How to form a Fist correctly:

1. Hold your fingers tightly together.

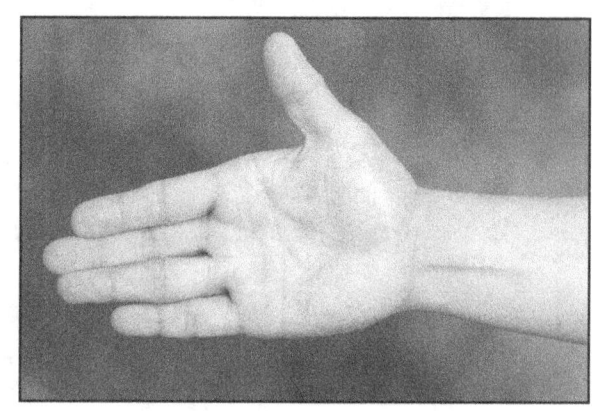

2. Start curling the fist from the center knuckles.

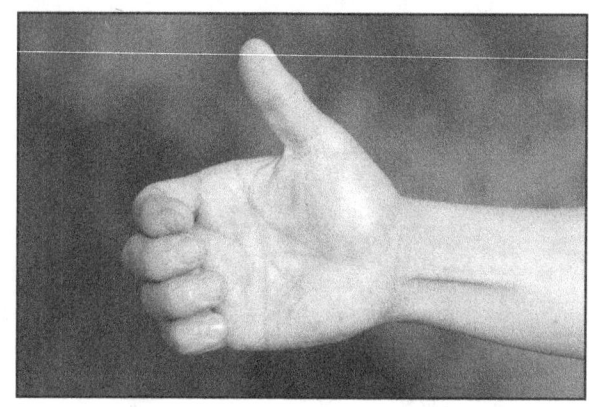

3. Grip the fingers tightly.

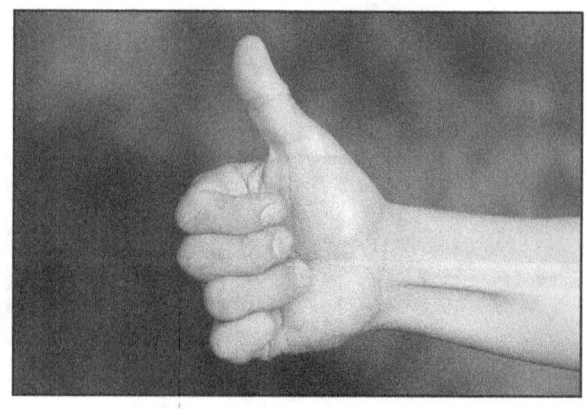

Poomsae Fundamentals

4. Rest your thumb between the first and second joint of your index finger.

5. Maintain proper alignment of your wrist.

Examples of Punches:

Vertical Punch:

Keep the wrist straight and hold your fist with the palm facing inward. With your first two knuckles, strike the target. This punch is effective for striking a narrow target such as the solar plexus or kidney.

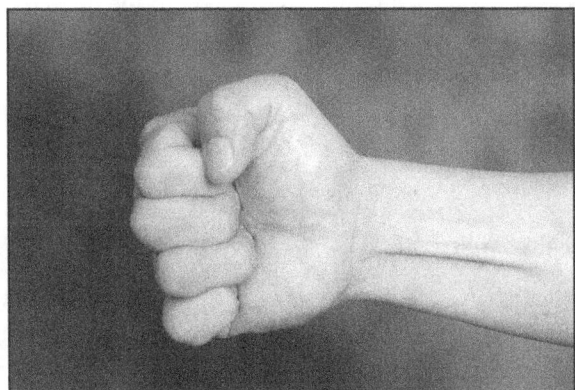

Straight Punch:

Keep your wrist straight and hold the fist with the palm facing downward. With your first two knuckles, strike the target. This punch is effective at striking a wide target such as the chest.

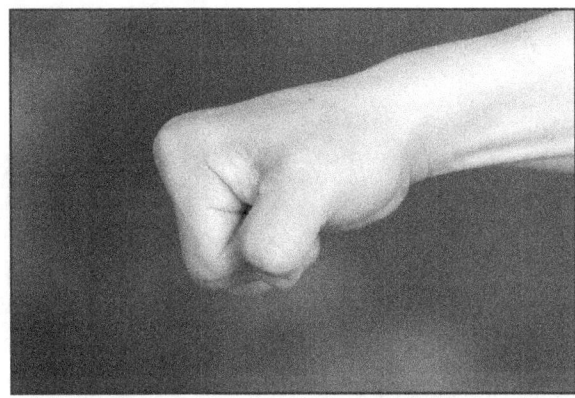

Hook Punch:

Strike with your fist in a circular motion to the side of the target. Keep your elbow bent to maximize power and safety. This technique is effective at striking a laterally exposed target such as the rib cage or temple.

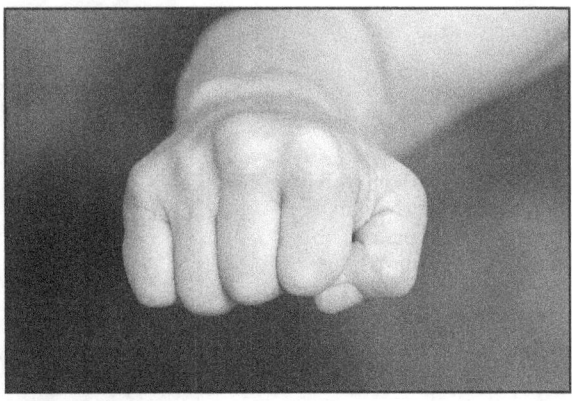

How to form a Knifehand correctly:

1. Press your fingers tightly together.
2. Focus the force firmly in your fingers to the degree that they bend slightly.
3. Curl your thumb downward on the ridge of your palm.
4. Use the knife blade, the ridgehand or the fingertips as a weapon.

Examples of Knifehand Strikes:

Vertical Thrust:

Align your fingers with your palm facing inward. With the fingertips of the middle and ring finger, thrust vertically. This technique is effective against narrow soft targets such as the solar plexus.

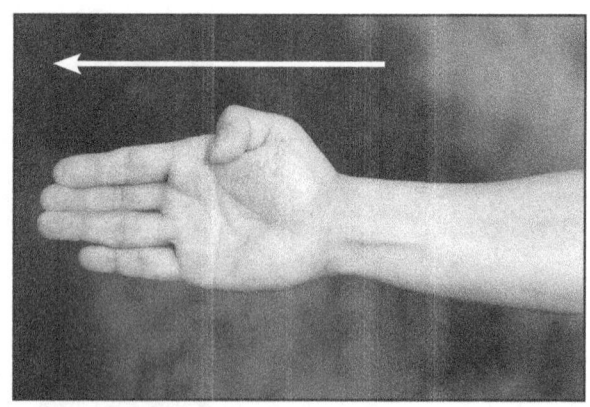

Vertical Strike:

Align your fingers with your palm facing inward. In a downward motion, strike with the blade of the hand. This technique is effective against horizontally exposed targets such as the bent back or the exposed wrist.

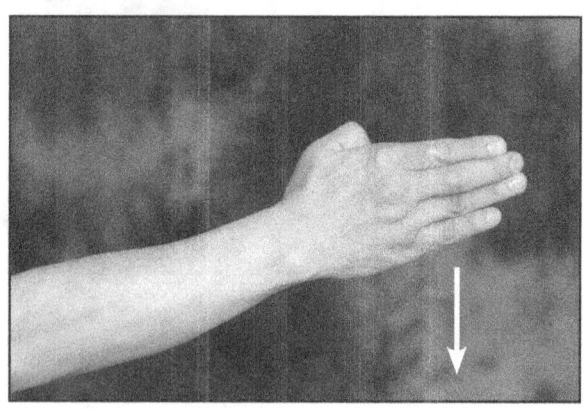

Inward Knife-hand Strike:

Align your fingers with your palm facing upward. From the outside, strike inward with the blade of your hand. This technique is effective against vertically exposed targets such as the neck or temple.

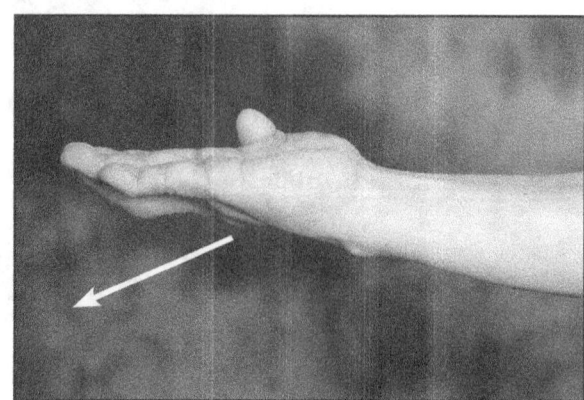

Rules of Poomsae Practice

1. Don't be in a hurry.

2. Never give up.

3. Be patient.

4. Be consistent.

5. When you encounter a difficult movement, practice persistently until you master it.

6. Understand the relationship between the individual techniques.

7. Practice the movements of each Poomsae in the prescribed order.

8. Follow the Poomsae line accurately so you begin and end in the same place.

9. Remember the three principles of Poomsae practice:

    • Poomsae must have beauty and power.
    • Rhythm is derived from softness and strength of force.
    • Technique is made of the slowness and rapidity of movement and the contraction and expansion of the body.

10. Poomsae begins and ends with etiquette.

Junbiseogi : Ready Stance

GENERAL POSTURE	Stand with your feet parallel about one foot apart, your legs straight and your chest open. Hold your fists in front of your Danjun (lower abdomen) with the backs of your hands facing forward.
EYESIGHT	Look straight ahead.
STANCE	• Stand with your feet about one foot apart. • Keep the inside of the soles of your feet parallel. • Straighten your knees.
POSTURE	• Hold your chest open and your torso erect. • Tuck your chin down. • Stand relaxed and alert, with confidence. • Square your chest to the front.
ARM POSITION	• Hold your fists in front of your Danjun (lower abdomen) with the backs of your fists facing forward. • The distance between the Danjun and two fists should be one fist. • The distance between the fists should be one vertical fist. • Keep your wrists straight.
CENTER of GRAVITY	• Equally distribute your weight on both legs. • The center of gravity is on the centerline of the body. • Focus your power in your Danjun.
BREATHING	• When you raise your fists to your solar plexus, inhale. • Slowly rotate your fists in front of the solar plexus and exhale about 2/3 then hold the breath. Focus your power in your Danjun and prepare to execute Junbiseogi.
APPLICATION	• Junbiseogi mentally focuses the mind and physically prepares the your prior to beginning the Poomsae. • Your mind should be alert and prepared to adapt to the opponent's movements. • Ready stance encompasses both the beginning and ending movements of the Poomsae. It is symbolic of each ending being another beginning. • Junbiseogi is the starting point for all of the Fundamental Techniques that follow in this section.
EMPHASIS	Look straight forward but use your peripheral vision to take in your surroundings. Synchronize the speed of your arm and leg movements.
COMMON ERRORS	**Hand Position:** Raise your hands only to the height of your solar plexus. **Foot Position:** Position your feet no wider than the width of the shoulders.

Poomsae Fundamentals

How to Perform Junbiseogi

STEP ONE
- Eyesight: Look straight forward.
- Left leg: Shift your weight onto your right leg while slowly moving your left leg one foot to the left.
- Trunk: Open your chest, erect your trunk and tuck in your chin.
- Hands: As you raise your hands to your solar plexus, slowly roll your fists so the back of the fists face downward.
- Breathing: When raising your hands, inhale.

STEP TWO
- Eyesight: Continue looking forward.
- Left leg: With your weight primarily on your right heel, set your left foot down one foot to the left.
- Hands: Rotating your fists, lower them to the front of your Danjun where the back of the fists face forward.
- Breathing: As you lower and rotate your fists, exhale about 2/3 then hold your breath. Focus your power in your Danjun, completing the Junbiseogi.

In the first and second steps, the movement of your eyes, feet and arms as well as your breathing should be synchronized throughout the technique.

Begin from close stance (moaseogi), with your feet together and your fists at your side.

Step your left leg one foot to the left. As you raise your hands to your solar plexus, slowly roll your fists so the back of the fists face downward.

Rotating your fists, lower them to the front of your Danjun where the back of the fists face forward. Focus your power in your Danjun.

Juchumseo Momtong Jireugi :
Horseriding Stance Middle Punch

GENERAL POSTURE	Stand with your feet about two feet apart. Lower your body by bending your knees to the degree that you can easily spring up at any time. Open your chest and hold your trunk erect. Place your right fist on your right side just above your belt with the back of the fist facing downward. Your left fist punches to the trunk.
EYESIGHT	In Juchumseogi, look straight forward.
STANCE	• Stand with your feet about two feet apart. • Position your feet with the inside of the soles parallel to each other. • Bend your knees, lowering the body. • When you bend your knees, your chest should be open and your torso erect. Your face, knees and toes should be on the same plane.
POSTURE	• Open your chest and straighten your torso. • Before punching, square your chest to the front. • When punching, angle your left shoulder about fifteen degrees to the front. • Tuck your chin and hold your head straight.
ARM POSITION	• Hold your right fist at your waist, just above your belt. • The back of the right fist faces downward. • With your left fist, punch to the opponent's trunk at solar plexus height.
CENTER of GRAVITY	• Distribute your weight equally on both legs. • The center of gravity is on the centerline of the body. • Squeeze the muscles of your knees and feet inward. • Focus your power in your Danjun.
BREATHING	• When you raise your fists to solar plexus level, fully extend your arms to the front and inhale. (This movement can vary depending on the instructor.) • Twist your fists in front of your solar plexus and pull them to your side, exhaling 2/3 of the way then stopping.
APPLICATION	• The wide distance between the feet makes this a secure posture. • This technique is utilized as a defensive or in-place attack since the center of gravity is low and the stance is stable. • While this stance is highly stable, flexibility is reduced, limiting the use of speed to create power. Therefore, this technique is largely utilized to develop force in basic movements.
EMPHASIS	• When shifting your weight, lift the left foot so it lightly touches the ground. Do not raise the left leg high. • When you raise your fists to the height of your solar plexus, relax your muscles. • Look straight forward. Synchronize the speed of your arm and leg movements and your breathing.

Poomsae Fundamentals

How to perform Juchumseo Momtong Jireugi

STEP ONE
- Eyesight: Look straight forward.
- Left leg: Shift your weight to your right leg, then lift your left foot.
- Trunk: Open your chest, straighten your trunk and tuck your chin.
- Hands: Raise your extended arms to solar plexus level. The backs of your fists face upward.
- Breathing: While raising your fists, inhale.

STEP TWO
- Eyesight: Look straight forward.
- Left leg: With your weight on your right leg, step your left foot two feet to the left.
- Hands: Pull your right fist to your right side just above your belt, with the back of the fist facing downward. Punch with your left fist at the height of your solar plexus.
- Breathing: When twisting your fists and punching, exhale 2/3 and hold your breath.

In the first and second steps, the movement of your eyes, feet and arms as well as your breathing should be synchronized throughout the technique.

COMMON ERRORS
Posture: Do not bend your torso forward or backward. Keep it erect.
Stance: Keep both knees facing forward. Do not turn your knees outward.

Step your left leg two feet to the left into horseriding stance. Squeeze your knees inward. Open your chest, tuck your chin and straighten your trunk.

Punch to the solar plexus. Align your face, knees and toes on the same plane.

Araemakki : Low Section Block

GENERAL POSTURE	In left front stance*, perform an Araemakki with the left arm. Place your right fist on your right side just above your belt with the back of the fist facing downward.
EYESIGHT	Look straight forward.
STANCE	**(Right leg)** • Placing your weight on the ball of your right foot, pivot your right heel 30° inward. • Keep your right knee straight. **(Left leg)** • With your weight centered on your right leg, step forward one and a half steps with your left leg. • Bend your left knee. Your left shin and knee face the front. • Bend your left knee to the degree where your face, knee and toes are on the same plane. Hold your torso erect.
POSTURE	• Open the chest and straighten the trunk. • Turn the shoulders 30° to the right.
ARM POSITION	• Your left wrist and elbow should be straight. Block with the outer left forearm. The back of your left fist faces upward. • Place your right fist by your right side just above the belt, where it is prepared to throw a punch if necessary.
CENTER of GRAVITY	• Put the same amount of power in each leg. • Place your center of gravity 2/3 to the front of the stance.
BREATHING	• Inhale when lifting your arms. • At the moment of twisting your fists and blocking, exhale 2/3 then hold the breath.
APPLICATION	This technique is mainly utilized for defense because it has great forward force.
EMPHASIS	Look straight forward. Synchronize the speed of your arm and leg movements and your breathing. By making the proper stance and posture, you can ensure your safety.
COMMON ERRORS	**Posture:** Do not lean your torso forward. Hold it upright. **Hand Position:** In step one, do not raise your hands higher than your shoulders. Place your blocking forearm right above your front thigh.

All of the movements in this section are described using left front stance or right back stance but can be performed from right front stance or left back stance by reversing the instructions.

Poomsae Fundamentals 37

How to perform Araemakki

STEP ONE
- Eyesight: Look forward toward the blocking side.
- Left leg: When you lift your left leg to step forward, shift your weight to your right leg.
- Trunk: Twist your trunk to the right, using your waist as the axis.
- Left hand: Raise your left fist to your right shoulder, with the palm turned toward your face.
- Right hand: Lift your right fist to position it under your left elbow. The back of your fist faces your elbow.
- Breathing: When raising your arms, inhale.

STEP TWO
- Eyesight: Continue looking in the direction of the block.
- Right leg: Placing your weight on the ball of your right foot, pivot your right heel 30° inward.
- Left leg: Moving your left foot, step forward one and a half steps.
- Trunk: Using your waist as the axis, uncoil your body to the left.
- Left hand: Initiate the block by unfolding your bent left elbow and executing a low section block using the outside of the left wrist.
- Right hand: Twisting the right fist, pull it back and place it on your right side just above the belt, with the back of the fist facing downward.
- Breathing: When twisting your trunk, exhale 2/3 then stop and complete the low section block.

In the first and second steps, the movement of the eyes, feet and arms as well as the breathing should be synchronized throughout the technique.

Pivot your right heel 30° inward. Raise your left fist to your right shoulder.

Place your weight 2/3 to the front of your stance. Using your waist as the axis, uncoil your body.

When blocking, keep your left wrist and elbow straight. Turn your shoulders about 30° to the right.

Momtong Bandaejireugi : Reverse Middle Punch

GENERAL POSTURE — Momtong Bandaejireugi is a left middle section punch to the solar plexus in left front stance. The left foot is forward. The wrist and elbow should be straightened and the back of the fist faces upward.

EYESIGHT — Look straight forward.

STANCE

(Right leg)
- Placing your weight on the sole of the right foot, pivot your right heel 30° inward.
- Stand firmly with the knee of your right leg straightened.

(Left leg:)
- Shifting your weight to your right leg, step your left foot forward by one and a half steps.
- Bend your left knee. Your left shin and knee face the front.
- Bend your left knee to the degree where your face, knee and toes are on the same plane. Hold your torso erect.

POSTURE
- Open your chest and hold your trunk erect.
- Turn your shoulders 30° to the right.

ARM POSITION
- With your left fist, punch to the solar plexus of the opponent.
- When the punch is completed, your wrist and elbow should be straight.
- The back of the punching (left) fist faces upward.
- The right fist is placed on the right side just above the belt.
- The back of the right fist faces downward.

CENTER of GRAVITY
- Stand firmly with equal power exerted by each leg.
- The center of gravity is placed 2/3 toward the front of the stance.

BREATHING
- Using your waist as the axis, turn your trunk to the left and inhale.
- When turning your trunk to the right, exhale 2/3 then stop and punch.

APPLICATION — Because the power of this technique moves in the forward direction, it is commonly used for attacking.

EMPHASIS
- With your weight centered on your right leg, move your left foot close to the ground. Do not raise your left leg too high when stepping forward.
- When shifting your weight, maintain your balance and do not vary the height of your body.

COMMON ERRORS

Posture: Keep your centerline firmly rooted vertically.
Hand Position: Aim your punch directly at the solar plexus. Keep your wrist straight.

How to perform Momtong Bandaejireugi

STEP ONE
- Eyesight: Look straight forward in the direction of the punch.
- Legs: Shift the weight to the right leg when lifting the left leg.
- Trunk: Open the chest and straighten the trunk while turning the trunk slightly to the left.
- Arms: Bring your left fist to just above your left hip bone.
- Breathing: When your left fist is at your left side, inhale.

STEP TWO
- Eyesight: Continue looking straight forward toward the target.
- Left leg: With your weight on your right leg, step your left leg forward by one and a half steps.
- Trunk: Using your waist as the axis, uncoil your trunk in the direction of the punch.
- Arms: When the wrist of the left fist passes close to your ribs, turn it over and punch.
- Breathing: As you uncoil your trunk in the direction of the punch, exhale 2/3 then stop and punch.

In the first and second steps, the movement of the eyes, feet and arms as well as the breathing should be synchronized throughout the technique.

Pivot your right heel 30° inward. Bend your left knee. Your left shin and knee face the front. Your left fist punches to the opponent's solar plexus.

Place your weight 2/3 to the front of your stance. Hold your right fist at your side, just above your belt. Turn your shoulders 30° to the right.

Apchagi : Front Kick

GENERAL POSTURE	From left front stance, shift the weight to the left leg and kick to the front at the target of the solar plexus with the right leg.
EYESIGHT	Look straight forward.
STANCE	**(Right leg)** • Placing the weight on the ball of the right foot, pivot the heel 30° inward. • Straighten the knee of the right leg. **(Left leg)** • Shifting the weight to the right leg, step the left leg forward by one and a half steps. • Bend your left knee. Your left shin and knee face the front. • Bend your left knee to the degree where your face, knee and toes are on the same plane. Hold your torso erect.
CENTER of GRAVITY	• Place equal power in both legs. • Place your center of gravity 2/3 toward the front of the stance.
BREATHING	• When shifting your balance to your left leg in order for your right leg to kick, inhale. • When your right leg slightly passes your left knee, exhale 2/3, stop and kick.
APPLICATION	Kick the opponent's trunk.
EMPHASIS	• When kicking, center your weight over your front foot. • Pull your toes back to expose the ball of your foot.
COMMON ERRORS	**Foot Position:** Keep your standing foot on the ground. Do not rise up on your toes. **Arm Position:** Hold your arms close to your body to maintain balance and protect your vital targets. Do not let your arms open wide or hang behind your body.

How to perform Apchagi:

- In left front stance, fold the knee of the right leg, drag and lift.
- When the right leg nears the inside of the left knee, straighten the folded knee and kick to the solar plexus.
- The foot travels from the starting point toward the target in a straight line.

All of your movements should be synchronized when executing Apchagi.

Fold your right knee and lift it so your right foot passes closely by your left knee.

Your foot should travel in a straight line to the target.

Center your weight over your left leg and pull the toes of your right foot back to expose the ball of your foot.

Sonnal Bakkatchigi : Outward Knifehand Strike

GENERAL POSTURE	Stand with your feet about two feet. Bend your knees to lower your body, open your chest, straighten your torso and execute a right knifehand outward strike.
EYESIGHT	Look straight forward.
STANCE	• Shift your weight to your left foot while moving your right foot to the right. • Stand with your feet about two feet. • The inside of the soles of your feet should be parallel. • Bend your knees to the degree that you can easily spring upward. • When you bend your knees, your chest should be open and your torso erect. Your face, knees and toes should be on the same plane.
POSTURE	• Open the chest and stand straight. • Square your chest to the front. • Tuck your chin and straighten your head.
ARM POSITION	• With your right hand, perform a right knifehand outward strike. • Hold your right wrist and knifehand straight. • Place your left fist by your left side just above the belt with the back of the left fist facing downward.
CENTER of GRAVITY	• Distribute your weight equally on both legs. • The center of gravity is on the centerline of the body. • Squeeze the muscles of your knees and feet inward. • Focus your power in your Danjun.
BREATHING	• When you extend your arm at the level of the solar plexus, straighten your elbow, wrist and knifehand, inhaling. (Although this may vary depending on the instructor, the fundamental principle is the same.) • When performing Sonnal Bakkatchigi, cross your arms in front of your solar plexus, exhaling 2/3 and then hold your breath while striking.
APPLICATION	• The wide distance between your feet makes this a secure posture. • Because this stance has a low center of gravity and good stability, it is utilized for in-place attacking. • While this stance is highly stable, flexibility is reduced, limiting the use of speed to create power. Therefore, this technique is largely utilized to develop force in basic movements. • This technique can be used to attack on both sides of the body.
EMPHASIS	• When you raise your hands to the height of your solar plexus, relax your muscles. • Look at the target. • Synchronize the speed of your arm and leg movements and your breathing.

Poomsae Fundamentals 43

How to perform Sonnal Bakkatchigi

STEP ONE
- Eyesight: Look in the direction you are striking (right).
- Left foot: Shift your weight to your left foot as you move your right foot two feet to the right.
- Trunk: Open your chest, straighten your trunk and tuck in your chin.
- Hands: Raise your right knifehand to above your left shoulder. Your right palm faces toward your face. Bring your left fist up under your right elbow, with the back of the left fist facing upward.
- Breathing: Inhale while raising your arms.

STEP TWO
- Eyesight: Continue looking to the right.
- Left foot: With your weight on your left foot, set your right foot down two feet from your left.
- Hands: Execute a Sonnal Bakkatchigi with your right hand. Place your left fist on your left side just above your belt with the back of your left fist facing downward.
- Breathing: While twisting your arms in front of your solar plexus and executing the Sonnal Bakkatchigi, exhale 2/3 and hold your breath.

In the first and second steps, the movement of the eyes, feet and arms as well as the breathing should be synchronized throughout the technique.

COMMON ERRORS
Eyesight: Look in the direction you are striking.
Hand Position: Aim for a specific target, i.e. rib cage, neck or temple.
Keep your hand and wrist straight.
Fold your thumb by the side of the hand. Do not extend it or place it under your palm.

Stand with your feet parallel and about two feet apart. Distribute your weight equally and place your center of gravity on your centerline. Keep your wrist and knifehand straight. Look in the direction of the strike.

Momtong Anmakki : Inward Middle Block

GENERAL POSTURE	In right back stance, execute an inward block using the left outer forearm.
EYESIGHT	Look straight forward.
STANCE	• Using your right heel as the axis, pivot your right foot 90° outward. • With your weight on your right foot, move your left foot forward by one step. • Bend your knees to lower your body. • Lower your body vertically so that your left knee and toes face the front and your right knee and toes face 90° to the right. • Place 2/3 of your weight and balance on your right foot. • Bend your knees to the degree where your face, left knee and left toes are on the same plane. Hold your torso erect.
POSTURE	• Open your chest and straighten your trunk. • Turn your left shoulder 45° away from your blocking arm.
ARM POSITION	• When your left fist blocks, it should be held at shoulder height. • The back of your blocking fist faces the front. • The interior angle of your left arm is about 110°. • The outside of your left wrist should be aligned vertically with your solar plexus. • Place your right fist just above your belt on your right side with the back of the fist facing downward.
CENTER of GRAVITY	Place your center of gravity 2/3 to the rear of your stance.
BREATHING	• While twisting your trunk to the left and simultaneously raising your arms, inhale. • When turning your trunk and arms to the right, exhale 2/3 then stop breathing as you block.
APPLICATION	• This block is used to protect your trunk against an opponent's attack with the fists or feet. • Because your weight is centered on the back leg, this is a defensive posture.
EMPHASIS	• Look toward the blocking direction. • Before blocking, when lifting your arms or shifting your weight, relax your muscles. • When blocking, twist your body and quickly transfer the power in your arm. • Synchronize the speed of your arm and leg movements and your breathing.

COMMON ERRORS	**Hand Position:** Bring the outer forearm beyond the centerline to block the attack.
	    Protect your body with your other arm when you prepare for the block.
	    Keep your wrist straight.
	Posture: Keep your body at a 45-degree angle. Do not turn it fully sideways or forward.

Poomsae Fundamentals 45

How to perform Momtong Anmakki

STEP ONE
- Eyesight: Look to the front in the direction of the block.
- Left leg: With your weight on your right foot, lift your left foot to step forward by one step.
- Trunk: Twist your trunk to the left, using your waist as the axis.
- Left hand: Raise your left fist to your left shoulder height, with the back of the fist facing the rear.
- Right hand: Raise your right fist in front of your chest with the back of the fist toward the rear.
- Breathing: When twisting your trunk to the left and simultaneously lifting your arms, inhale.

STEP TWO
- Eyesight: Continue looking to the front.
- Left foot: Step your left foot forward by one step into right back stance.
- Trunk: Uncoil your trunk to the right, using your waist as the axis.
- Left hand: The outside of your left forearm executes an inward block of the trunk.
- Right hand: When twisting your right fist and bringing it to your right side just above the belt. The back of the hand faces downward.
- Breathing: Uncoiling your trunk and bringing your arms to the right, exhale 2/3, then stop and execute a Momtong Anmakki.

In the first and second steps, the movement of the eyes, feet and arms as well as the breathing should be synchronized throughout the technique.

Twist your trunk to the left, using your waist as the axis. Raise your left fist to shoulder height.

Uncoil your trunk to the right while twisting your left fist into the block.

Block with your left fist at shoulder height. The outside of your fist should be aligned with your solar plexus.

Yopchagi : Side Kick

GENERAL POSTURE
From left front stance, kick with the blade and heel of your right foot aiming at the height of the solar plexus.

EYESIGHT
Look at the target.

STANCE
(Right foot)
- Placing the weight on the ball of the right foot, pivot the heel 30° inward.
- Straighten the knee of the right leg and stand firmly.

(Left foot)
- With your weight centered on your right leg, step forward one and a half steps with your left leg.
- Bend your left knee. Your left shin and knee face the front.
- Bend your left knee to the degree where your face, knee and toes are on the same plane. Hold your torso erect.

ARM POSITION
- With executing Yopchagi, hold your left hand in front of your solar plexus and keep your right arm folded at your right side. Hold your elbows slightly back and place all of your weight on your left leg in order to kick with your right foot.
- After kicking, step forward into right front stance, crossing your arms at shoulder height then executing a low section opening block.

CENTER of GRAVITY
- In left front stance, equally distribute your power in both legs to create a firm stance.
- Place your center of gravity 2/3 to the front of your stance.
- When kicking, the full weight of your body should be balanced on your left foot.

BREATHING
- When moving your left leg into front stance, inhale.
- When your right foot reaches the left knee at the beginning of the side kick, exhale by 2/3.
- When you have completely finished kicking, hold your breath briefly and collect your strength in your Danjun.

EMPHASIS
All of your movements should be synchronized when executing Yopchagi.

COMMON ERRORS
Posture: Keep your head up.
Eyesight: Look over your shoulder at the target.
Feet Position: Keep your toes lower than your heel to maximize the power of your kick by hitting the target with the entire blade of the foot.

Poomsae Fundamentals

How to perform Yopchagi

STEP ONE
- In left front stance, fold and lift your right knee.
- Bring your right foot to your left knee, twisting your trunk to the left with your weight balanced on the front of your left foot.

STEP TWO
- When your right foot passes your left knee, chamber your right knee.
- When kicking with your right foot, straighten your right leg and kick to your opponent's trunk.

When kicking, place your left arm in front of your solar plexus and fold your right arm by your side. Strike with the blade and heel of your right foot.

With your weight on your left leg, pivot on your left foot.

As your right foot passes your left knee, chamber your leg.

Sonnal Momtongmakki : Double Knifehand Block

GENERAL POSTURE	In right back stance, execute an outward middle block with the outside of the left knifehand. Hold the wrist of your right knifehand in front of your solar plexus to augment to the left arm block.
EYESIGHT	Look straight forward.
STANCE	• Using your right heel as the axis, pivot your right foot 90° outward. • With your weight on your right leg, step your left foot forward by one step. • Bending both knees, lower your body. • Bend your knees to the degree where your eyes, left knee and left toes are on the same plane and your right knee and right toes are on the same vertical plane. • Erect your torso. • Place 2/3 of your weight and balance on your right leg.
POSTURE	• Open your chest and straighten your trunk. • Turn your shoulders about 45° into your block.
ARM POSITION	• Hold the tips of your fingers of your left knifehand at shoulder height. • The palm of your left knifehand should face front, toward the blocking direction. • The inner angle of the left elbow is 110°. • Your outer right forearm faces your torso and your right wrist should be positioned in front of your solar plexus. • The palm of the right knifehand faces upward. • Leave a space the thickness of a finger between your right knifehand and chest, and between your right elbow and chest.
CENTER of GRAVITY	Place 2/3 of your weight and balance on your right foot.
BREATHING	• Using your waist as the axis, twist your torso to the rear and raise your arms backward on the right side of your body, inhaling. • Uncoiling your body to the left and bringing your knifehands forward, exhale by 2/3, stop and then block.
APPLICATION	• Because your weight and center of gravity is toward the rear of the stance, this technique is used for advancing forward (transitional movement) or defending. • When the opponent attacks the solar plexus, this position protects the trunk as the right knifehand supports and aids the block performed by the left knifehand. • Execute the knifehand as sharply as if cutting with a knife.
COMMON ERRORS	**Posture:** Align your shoulders horizontally. Do not raise one shoulder higher than the other. **Hand Position:** Keep your blocking wrist straight. Cover your solar plexus with the augmented knifehand, but do not let it touch your body.

Poomsae Fundamentals

How to perform Sonnal Momtongmakki

STEP ONE
- Eyesight: Look in the direction of the block.
- Left foot: Shift your weight to the right foot when you lift your left foot.
- Trunk: Using your waist as the axis, turn your shoulders to the right.
- Arms: Raise your arms to the right.
- Left hand: Raise your left knifehand to the front of your right shoulder with the palm turned toward the face.
- Right hand: Raise your right knifehand behind your body at solar plexus level with the palm turned toward the face.
- Breathing: When twisting your chest and shoulders to the right and lifting your arms, inhale.

STEP TWO
- Eyesight: Continue looking in the direction of the block.
- Left foot: With your weight on your right foot, step your left foot forward by one foot.
- Trunk: Using your waist as an axis, turn your chest to the left in the direction of the block.
- Arms: Bring your arms forward to execute Sonnal Momtongmakki.
- Left hand: With your left knifehand, block your trunk with your palm facing toward the front.
- Right hand: Place your right hand in front of your solar plexus with your palm facing upward.
- Breathing: Using your waist as an axis, uncoil your shoulders and chest. Exhale 2/3 while uncoiling then stop and complete the Sonnal Momtongmakki.

In the first and second steps, the movement of the eyes, feet and arms as well as the breathing should be synchronized throughout the technique.

Pivot your right foot 90° outward. Raise your left hand to your right shoulder and your right hand behind your body.

Place your weight 2/3 on your back leg. Turn your shoulders about 45°.

Place your right hand in front of your solar plexus and the tips of your left hand at shoulder height.

Olgulmakki : High Section Block

GENERAL POSTURE — In left front stance, Olgulmakki is executed to block the face area using the left outer forearm.

EYESIGHT — Look straight forward.

STANCE —
(Right foot)
- Placing the weight on the ball of the right foot, pivot the heel 30° inward.
- Straighten the knee of the right leg and stand firmly.

(Left foot)
- With your weight centered on your right leg, step forward one and a half steps with your left leg.
- Bend your left knee. Your left shin and knee face the front.
- Bend your left knee to the degree where your face, knee and toes are on the same plane. Hold your torso erect.

POSTURE
- Open the chest and straighten the trunk.
- Turn your shoulders about 30° toward the rear.

ARM POSITION
- Position your left arm just above your forehead.
- Leave a space of one fist between the wrist of your blocking arm and your forehead.
- Align your left wrist with the centerline of your body.
- The back of the left fist faces your forehead.
- Place your right fist on your right side just above the belt.
- The back of the right fist faces downward.

CENTER of GRAVITY
- Distribute your power equally between both legs.
- Place your center of gravity 2/3 to the front of your stance.

BREATHING
- Inhale as you turn toward the right, lifting your arms and rotating your body from the waist.
- As you uncoil your body and move your arms to the left to block, exhale 2/3 then stop and block.

APPLICATION — This block protects your face using your left outer forearm when the opponent makes a frontal attack toward the face.

EMPHASIS
- To avoid being struck in the head, judge the situation quickly then execute the high section block precisely and forcefully.
- No matter how strong and fast the attack may be, confront it bravely and proactively.
- Defense should be transformed into offense. Therefore defensive techniques should be practiced diligently to make them as effective as offensive techniques.
- Because blocking is not an initiative attack, it represents the true intention of the self-defense spirit of Taekwondo.

Poomsae Fundamentals

How to perform Olgulmakki

STEP ONE
- Eyesight: Look straight ahead in the direction of the block.
- Left foot: Shift your weight to your right foot, when you lift your left foot.
- Trunk: Using your waist as the axis, turn your chest to the right.
- Arms: Bring your right fist up in front of your left chest and bring your left fist below your right elbow with the back of the fist facing downward.
- Breathing: Inhale when lifting your arms.

STEP TWO
- Eyesight: Continue looking in the direction of the block.
- Left foot: With your weight on your right foot, step your left foot forward by one and a half feet.
- Trunk: Using your waist as the axis, turn your torso into the high section block.
- Arms: Rotate your left arm to block your face using your outer forearm. The back of your left fist faces your forehead. Place your right fist at your right side, just above your belt level.
- Breathing: When twisting your chest and arms, exhale by 2/3 then stop and block.

In the first and second steps, the movement of the eyes, feet and arms as well as the breathing should be synchronized throughout the technique.

COMMON ERRORS   **Arm Position:** Begin your blocking arm movement from outside of the other arm. Keep your blocking arm angled outward, not parallel to the floor.

Bring your right fist up to your left chest and your left fist under your right elbow.

Rotate your left arm as you raise it to block.

Position your left arm above your forehead, aligning your wrist with your centerline.

Sonnal Mokchigi : Knifehand Neck Strike

GENERAL POSTURE — This technique is an inward left knifehand strike to the neck in left front stance. The left palm faces upward and the wrist and elbow should be straight.

EYESIGHT — Look straight forward.

STANCE

(Right foot)
- Placing the weight on the ball of the right foot, pivot the heel 30° inward.
- Straighten the knee of the right leg and stand firmly.

(Left foot)
- With your weight centered on your right leg, step forward one and a half steps with your left leg.
- Bend your left knee. Your left shin and knee face the front.
- Bend your left knee to the degree where your face, knee and toes are on the same plane. Hold your torso erect.

POSTURE
- Open the chest and straighten the trunk.
- Turn your shoulders about 30° inward to the right.

ARM POSITION
- Align your wrist and elbow at your neck height.
- The left palm faces upward.
- Hold your left knifehand at your opponent's neck level.
- Place your right fist at your right side just above your belt.
- The back of the right fist faces downward.

CENTER of GRAVITY
- Distribute your power equally between both legs.
- Place your center of gravity 2/3 to the front of your stance.

BREATHING
- Inhale when turning your shoulders to the left (rear) after lifting your knifehands.
- As you uncoil your body and return your hands to the front, exhale 2/3 then stop and execute Sonnal Mokchigi.

COMMON ERRORS

Arm Position: In step one, keep your striking hand at shoulder level.
Hand Position: Keep your hand and wrist straight.
  Fold your thumb by the side of the hand. Do not extend it or place it under your palm.
Posture: Keep your centerline perpendicular to the ground and do not lean forward.

Poomsae Fundamentals

How to perform Sonnal Mokchigi

STEP ONE
- Eyesight: Look straight ahead in the direction of the Sonnal Mokchigi.
- Left foot: Shift your weight to your right foot when moving your left foot.
- Trunk: Open your chest and straighten your trunk, turning your shoulders to the left.
- Left hand: Bring your left knifehand up so your left wrist is at the level of your left shoulder. The back of the hand should face toward your face.
- Right hand: Clench your right fist and raise it to the level of your chest with the back of the hand facing the rear.
- Breathing: Inhale when turning your shoulders to the left and lifting your hands.

STEP TWO
- Eyesight: Continue looking in the direction of the Sonnal Mokchigi.
- Left foot: With your weight on your right foot, step the left foot forward by one and a half steps.
- Trunk: From your left shoulder uncoil your trunk in the direction of the Sonnal Mokchigi.
- Left hand: Execute a neck strike by twisting your wrist and elbow.
- Right hand: Twist your right fist downward to rest at your right side, just above your belt level.
- Breathing: When you uncoil your shoulders, exhale 2/3 then stop and complete the Sonnal Mokchigi.

In the first and second steps, the movement of the eyes, feet and arms as well as the breathing should be synchronized throughout the technique.

Turn your shoulders to the left and raise your left hand to shoulder level. Step your left foot forward while rotating your trunk into your strike.

Strike to your opponent's neck level with your palm facing upward.

Dollyochagi : Roundhouse Kick

GENERAL POSTURE
From left front stance, this technique is a roundhouse kick to the solar plexus with the ball of the right foot. All of the weight is placed on the left foot when kicking.

EYESIGHT
Look straight forward.

STANCE
(Right foot)
- Placing the weight on the ball of the right foot, pivot the heel 30° inward.
- Straighten the knee of the right leg and stand firmly.

(Left foot)
- With your weight centered on your right leg, step forward one and a half steps with your left leg.
- Bend your left knee. Your left shin and knee face the front.
- Bend your left knee to the degree where your face, knee and toes are on the same plane. Hold your torso erect.

POSTURE
- Distribute your power equally between both legs.
- Place your center of gravity 2/3 to the front of your stance.
- When turning and kicking, place your body weight entirely on your left leg.

BREATHING
- Inhale when shifting your balance to your left leg.
- When pivoting on the left foot, exhale by 2/3. When you complete the roundhouse kick, hold your breath momentarily and collect your strength in your Danjun.

COMMON ERRORS
Posture: Keep your head up while kicking.
Foot Position: Pivot your standing foot as you transfer your body weight.
Hip position: Rotate your hip fully to align your body with the target line.
Arm Position: Relax your shoulders so that your arms freely move around your torso. Keep your elbows close to your body. Don't drop or open your arms.

How to perform Dollyochagi

STEP ONE From left front stance low section opening block, clench your fists and shift your weight to your left foot to kick with your right foot. At this moment, place your left hand in front of your solar plexus. Your right arm is bent and your right elbow should be positioned slightly behind the body to maintain your balance.

STEP TWO When turning and kicking, the pelvis and shoulder turn 180°.

All of your movements should be synchronized when executing Dollyochagi.

When kicking, turn your pelvis and shoulders 180°.

With your weight on your left leg, pivot on your left foot. Place your left arm in front of your solar plexus and fold your right arm by your side.

Raising your right leg, bring your right foot close to your left knee.

Momtong Barojireugi : Straight Middle Punch

GENERAL POSTURE	Momtong Barojireugi is the process of executing a right hand punch when your opposite (left) leg is positioned forward in left front stance. The punching target is the solar plexus. The wrist and elbow of the right arm should be straightened and the back of the right fist faces upward.
EYESIGHT	Look straight forward.
STANCE	**(Right foot)** • Placing the weight on the ball of the right foot, pivot the heel 30° inward. • Straighten the knee of the right leg and stand firmly. **(Left foot)** • With your weight centered on your right leg, step forward one and a half steps with your left leg. • Bend your left knee. Your left shin and knee face the front. • Bend your left knee to the degree where your face, knee and toes are on the same plane. Hold your torso erect.
POSTURE	• Open the chest and straighten the trunk. • Your chest faces toward the front (punching direction).
ARM POSITION	• Your right fist aims at the solar plexus, with the wrist and elbow straightened. • The back of the right fist faces upward. • Place your left fist on your left side just above the belt. • The back of the left fist faces downward.
CENTER of GRAVITY	• Distribute your power equally between both legs. • Place your center of gravity 2/3 to the front of your stance.
BREATHING	• Using your waist as the axis, raise your right fist to the side and twist your shoulders to the right, inhaling. • When uncoiling your shoulders and punching, exhale 2/3 then stop and punch.
APPLICATION	• The fist is only utilized for punching techniques. • The target for Momtong Jireugi is the trunk (both sides of the solar plexus).
EMPHASIS	• Clench your punching fist firmly. Only the knuckle of the index and middle fingers should be utilized for punching. • Keep your wrist straight. • Align your wrist and the back of your hand when punching. • The front of the fist and the top of the fist should form a right angle.
COMMON ERRORS	**Posture:** Center yourself. Shift your weight forward to generate power rather than leaning forward. **Hand Position:** Punch to the centerline of the solar plexus to maximize force.

How to perform Momtong Barojireugi

STEP ONE
- Eyesight: Look straight ahead in the direction of the punch.
- Left foot: Shift your weight to your right leg when lifting your left leg.
- Trunk: Using your waist as the axis, twist your shoulders to the right.
- Arms: Raise your right fist on your right side with the back of the fist facing downward.
- Breathing: When twisting your shoulders and lifting your right fist to the side, inhale.

STEP TWO
- Eyesight: Continue looking in the direction of the punch.
- Left foot: With your weight on your right foot, step your left foot forward by one and a half steps.
- Trunk: Uncoil your shoulders in the direction of the punch.
- Arms: Rotating your right fist, bring it forward from your side until your wrist and elbow are straightened, punching hard to the solar plexus.
- Breathing: When you bring the fist forward, exhale by 2/3 then stop and complete the punch.

In the first and second steps, the movement of the eyes, feet and arms as well as the breathing should be synchronized throughout the technique.

Place your weight 2/3 to the front of your stance. Your right leg is straight and your left knee is bent, with the knee and shin facing forward.

Punch to the solar plexus with your hand opposite from your lead leg. Look straight ahead.

Stance

Understanding how to perform Taekwondo stances is essential to understanding how to execute Poomsae techniques. There are 28 types of stances: 15 wide stances, 8 narrow stances and 5 special Poom stances.

Stance is defined as a technique in which the only parts of the body that touch the ground are one or both feet. While your upper body and arms may move, your trunk should remain erect (vertically). Within this framework, there are many variations in stances according to where your center of gravity is placed and where the centerline of your body is positioned as well as the position and movement of your feet.

Stances can also vary in their application. For example there are heavy powerful stances which are meant to defend with the strength of a mountain. There are also unstable stances that promote the flexibility and agility needed to explosively counter an attack.

Stances can be distinguished by the placement of your feet, either side by side or with one foot in front and the other in the rear, and to what degree your knees are bent or straightened. When your feet are closer together, the centerline of your body is more stable. When your knees are bent and your body is lowered, your center of gravity is lowered, creating a very strong, firm posture. However, when your stance is lower, the centerline of your body is much harder to maneuver making it difficult to move quickly and reducing the explosiveness of your movements.

Walking stance
Higher center of gravity

Horseriding stance
Lower center of gravity

Horseriding stance has a low center of gravity which makes it difficult to move quickly to another position. From walking stance, your feet are close together and your centerline is very stable so you can easily move quickly in any direction.

THEORY

Stance can be categorized by:
1. Center of gravity placement
2. Centerline placement
3. Stability
4. Foot placement
5. Foot angle

Poomsae Fundamentals

Just as the distance between your feet affects the stability of your stance, it also impacts your ability to maintain your balance. When it comes to the human body, there are many variations: long legs, short legs, large feet, small feet, and various body proportions. Because of these variations, it is unfair to specify a fixed width or length of any stance. Therefore, the distance between the feet is relative depending on your body size. The units of measurement used are the length of your natural step and the size of your foot. For example, when stepping forward, you will take "one step," "one and a half steps" or "two steps." When placing your feet side by side, you will place them the distance of one foot apart or two feet apart. This will ensure that your stance is executed in proportion to your body size.

It is also important to consider the angle of your feet as part of your stance. For each stance, the angle of your left foot and right foot is described individually. For example, in left front stance your left foot faces directly forward and your right heel is turned 30° inward. Your eye direction and body angle for each stance are based on the placement of your feet. Again using left front stance as an example, your eyes and body face forward in the direction of your left foot.

FRONT STANCE

In left front stance your left (front) foot faces directly forward and your right (rear) heel is turned 30° inward. Your upper body angle is aligned to your foot placement; in this case the chest, like the feet, faces almost fully forward.

BACK STANCE

In left back stance your right (front) foot faces directly forward and your left (rear) foot is turned 90° outward. Your upper body angle is aligned to your foot placement; in this case your chest is rotated toward the rear to align with the open rear foot.

Blocking

Blocking is used to protect yourself from an opponent's attack. In Taekwondo defending well is as important as attacking. The defensive techniques of Taekwondo are not just simple blocks, but involve conditioning certain parts of your body including your knifehand and wrist to impact your opponent's arms or legs and disable them to prevent further attacks.

In other words, the goal is to transform defensive techniques into the attacks. A true master controls his opponent not by initiating an attack but by defending with only the necessary force against his opponent's attack. Therefore, Taekwondo movements emphasize blocking first then attacking to promote this spirit of self-defense.

When blocking, your block can double as an attack. Above, this inward knifehand block can also be an attack to the opponent's wrist using the bony part of the forearm.

Evasion

Evasion is a new technique that has been developed in Taekwondo Kyorugi (sparring) competition. There are many instances during Kyorugi when you can evade your opponent with quick footwork while simultaneously executing a counterattack rather than blocking your opponent's attack. Instead of blocking, this technique takes advantage of the opportunity presented by your opponent to execute a counterattack. For example, when your opponent attacks with a Dollyochagi (roundhouse kick), rather than blocking you can counterattack with a back kick. Or when your opponent attacks with Tzigeochagi (axe kick), you can defend by leaning your upper body slightly backward, avoiding the kick and simultaneously counterattacking with Dollyochagi.

In Kyorugi, blocking is used sparingly in crisis situations where you cannot evade your opponent's attack. When this happens, block quickly and without hard impact to your opponent's leg. The secret of contemporary Taekwondo Kyorugi techniques is to evade and counterattack rather than block.

Evasion is used frequently in Kyorugi. For example, when your opponent attacks with a Dollyochagi (roundhouse kick), evading the kick by moving your body and then counterattacking with a back kick or roundhouse kick is much more effective than blocking.

Gupso: Vital Target

Taekwondo is a martial art to develop self-discipline. By practicing techniques with speed and power you can develop your Ki (inner energy) and improve your mental focus. Diligent Taekwondo practice results not only in improved physical fitness but increased patience and willpower as a result of overcoming the physical challenges in training. As you progress in Taekwondo, you will gain self-control and the ability to assess a situation and respond appropriately. Without these higher goals, Taekwondo is simply another form of exercise.

In life, if you don't have a goal, you are like a boat drifting in the ocean. So setting daily goals in your Taekwondo practice eventually leads you to the higher goals of training. Each time you train, you should have a specific goal in mind and practice every movement with maximum precision and focus. Having goals beyond your physical training will help you achieve a sense of oneness of your mind and body.

Just as you need specific goals in your training, you need a specific target for every striking and kicking technique. These targets are called Gupso (vital target). Gupso is a vulnerable area of the body where exposed nerves are located just under the skin. These targets can be easily attacked and cause severe pain with even minimal impact. There are approximately 280 Gupsos on the human body. There are 34 common targets in Taekwondo practice, including the philtrum (just below the nose), the solar plexus and the Danjun (lower abdomen).

When you practice Poomsae, you should assume that your opponent is the same height and body size as yourself, and block and strike to these targets accordingly. However, when you face an actual opponent, you must precisely attack to the vital targets on his or her body and defend accurately based on his or her body size.

Examples of Gupso

CHIN

SOLAR PLEXUS

TEMPLE

THROAT

SPINE

GROIN

THEORY

What is Gupso? The place to which impact is delivered by a strike.

Where are Gupso located? Gupso are located at the joints, connective tissue and exposed nerves.

What makes Gupso good targets? There is no way to toughen the vital points; they are innate vulnerabilities in the human body which result in severe pain when struck.

Examples of Bodily Weapons

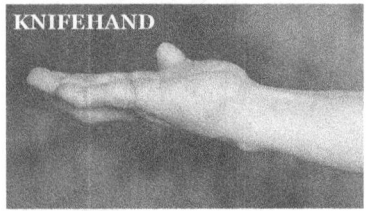
KNIFEHAND

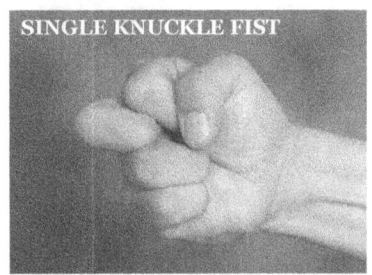
SINGLE KNUCKLE FIST

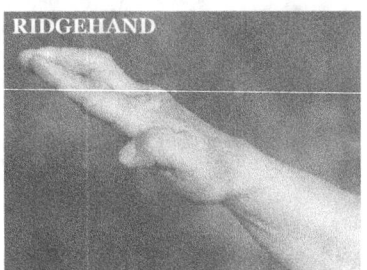
RIDGEHAND

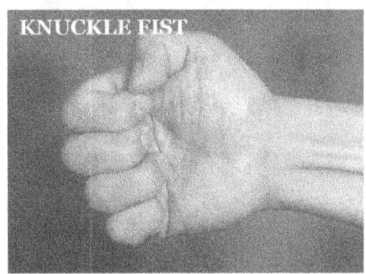
KNUCKLE FIST

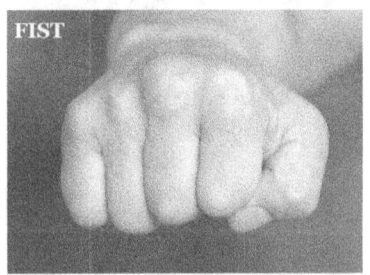
FIST

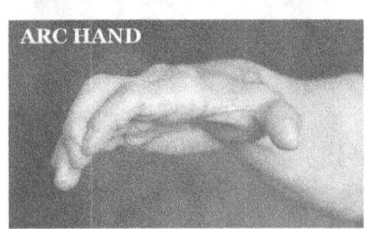
ARC HAND

Bodily Weapons

Taekwondo does not use weapons. Instead, it utilizes the strongest parts of the body as weapons. The joints and bones of the arms, hands, legs and feet are used for attacking because they can generate power by moving quickly. Using these firm, sharp parts of the body, you can execute a wide variety of attacking techniques including striking, kicking and punching.

Taekwondo's offensive techniques for the arms include striking with your fists, knifehands and elbows. The strong point of these arm and hand techniques is that they can strike the opponent's face and trunk using speed to create a powerful impact.

The specialty of Taekwondo is kicking, which uses the legs and feet for effective attacks. Many parts of the foot can be used to strike the target including the top of the foot, the blade of the foot, the bottom and back of the heels and the sole of the foot. Knee kicking is also used, particularly for women's self-defense since it is effective at attacking the opponent's groin and lower stomach at a close distance.

To increase the effectiveness and power of your techniques you must toughen your bodily weapons including your fists, knifehands and feet. There are two benefits to this type of training: you can increase the impact of your attacks by hardening your bodily weapons and you can decrease the risk of injury due to impact with the target. Some methods of training to toughen the body include striking a heavy bag, mitt, tire or Makiwara under the supervision of a knowledgeable instructor as part of a long-term training program. For Kyorugi training, hogu (chest protector) drills are also popular for strengthening the fists and feet through repeated impact with your training partner.

MASTER'S TIP

Toughening your bodily weapons can reduce the risk of injury when striking an opponent and increase the impact of your techniques. To effectively and safely toughen your hands, feet, elbows and shins, you should progressively increase your training intensity under the guidance of a qualified instructor.

Poomsae Fundamentals 63

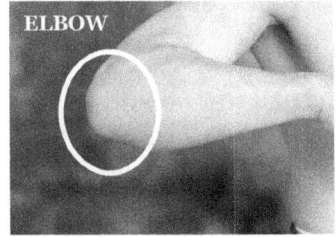
ELBOW

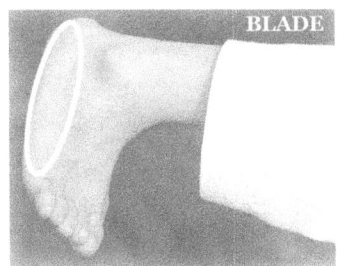
BLADE

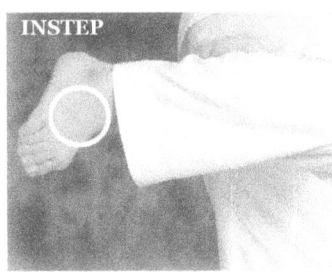
INSTEP

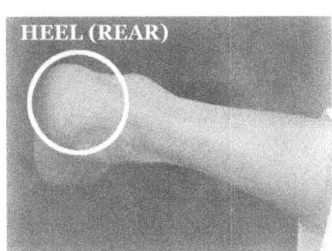
HEEL (REAR)

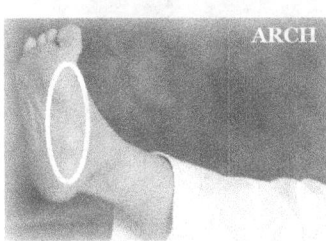
ARCH

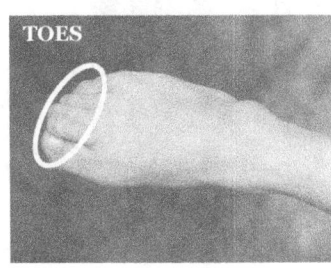
TOES

KNEE

BALL

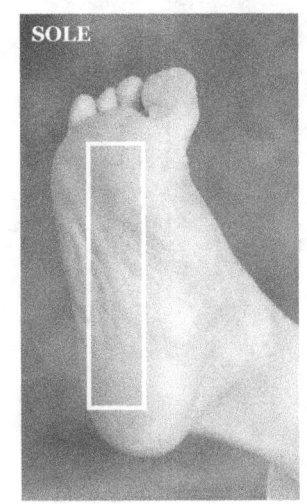
SOLE

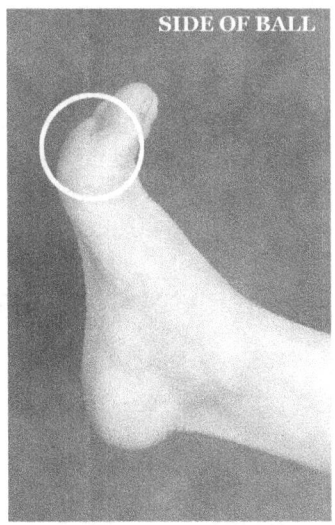
SIDE OF BALL

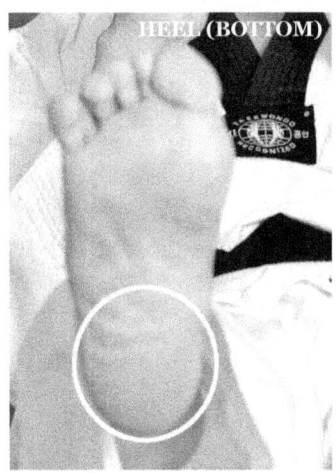
HEEL (BOTTOM)

Attacking Techniques

Attacking techniques are intended to defeat an opponent by using vital strikes such as punching, kicking, striking and whipping techniques. Which technique you use depends on what target you are attacking and what your objective is. Your attacking technique will also vary depending where your opponent is standing in relation to you and at what angle his body is positioned.

Even though there are numerous attacking techniques, arm techniques can be generally categorized as:

- Punching
- Thrusting
- Striking
- Pecking
- Slapping

Leg techniques can generally be categorized as:

- Kicking
- Whipping

Kicking and Whipping

Kicking is a typical attacking method using the legs in Taekwondo. Basic Taekwondo kicks include front kick, side kick, roundhouse kick, back kick, whip kick, axe kick, and knee kick. Advanced kicking techniques are applications of these basic kicks in combination with footwork. Examples of advanced kicking techniques are jumping kicks and double kicks.

Timing and distance are the keys to successful kicking techniques.

Poomsae Fundamentals 65

Punching

Punching is an attacking technique using the front part of the fist. According to your stance, a punch can be either a Barojireugi (straight punch) or a Bandaejireugi (reverse punch). When you are in left front stance and punch with your right arm, this is a Barojireugi. When you are in left front stance and punch with your left arm, this is a Bandaejireugi. The targets for punching include the trunk, face and low section. Finally, punches can be classified by your posture and the direction of punch, including side punch, vertical punch, and uppercut.

Striking

Striking refers any attacking techniques performed with your hands and elbows, excluding punches. Parts of the hand that are used for striking include the backfist, hammerfist and knifehand. Common striking techniques are: backfist strike to the face, downward hammerfist, single knifehand neck strike, swallow form neck strike and inward elbow strike.

Thrusting

Thrusting is an attacking technique using the fingertips. Types of thrusting techniques include fingertip thrust, scissors fingers and blunt fingertip thrust. Another method of classifying thrusting is by the position of your hand, including vertical thrusting, horizontal thrusting and upward thrusting. Thrusting techniques are not practical for actual combat. However, thrusting techniques are excellent for surprise attacks, through long-term and specialized training.

Pecking

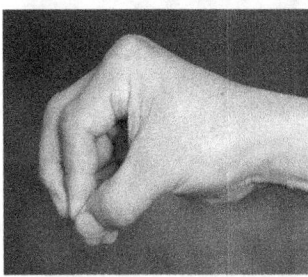

Pecking is a specialized attacking technique in which the tips of the fingers are held tightly together. It originated from the idea of a bird attacking an enemy with its beak. It is used to attack the eyes with the tips of the five fingers.

The Structural Principles and Types of Poomsae

Types of Taekwondo Poomsae

1. Official Poomsae

Official Poomsaes are those that have been mandated by an official organization.

2. Creative Poomsae

Creative Poomsaes are intended to go beyond the limited movements of the official Poomsae in order to express the beauty and extensiveness of Taekwondo in a unique and innovative way.

3. Taekwon-mu

Taekwon-mu is artistic martial dance routine, characterized by dance elements, rhythmic movements and Taekwondo techniques set to music. It combines artistic elements with basic Taekwondo techniques.

Creative Poomsae is an opportunity to incorporate a wider variety of movements in your Poomsae practice.

Cautions

Since Poomsae is system of offensive and defensive techniques, there are many variations. The linkage between techniques is also diverse, requiring attention to detail when learning and practicing each Poomsae. Pay special attention to the following points when practicing:

1) Understand the **significance and structural principle** of Poomsae practice.
2) Understand the **movement lines** and **performance** of each individual Poomsae.
3) When performing, maintain the **individual characteristics** of each Poomsae.
4) At the beginning and end of each Poomsae, **bow to show respect**.

Poomsae Fundamentals

Principles of Poomsae Creation

There are certain principles that must be followed when creating Poomsae. Poomsae has practical combat applications and yet it should be suitable for solo practice in a limited space. It should follow a certain movement line and both hands and feet must be utilized for offensive and defensive techniques.

The general principles of creating a Poomsae are:

1. The line of the movements should follow a fixed **Poomsae diagram**.
2. The movements should be **symmetrical** to the right and left and front and back so that both sides of the body are equally developed.
3. Always begin with a **defensive technique** and end with an **offensive technique**.
4. The **starting and ending place** should be the same.
5. One Poomsae has about **20 to 40 movements** (generally each technique takes about one second to perform).
6. Each Poomsae contains at least one **Kihap**.
7. Most Poomsae include a Kihap as part of the **last movement**. (Among the Taegeuk Poomsae, Taegeuk Yuk Jang and Taegeuk Pal Jang do not follow this rule.)

Taegeuk and Palgwae Poomsae Diagram

Koryo Poomsae Diagram

Chunkwon Poomsae Diagram

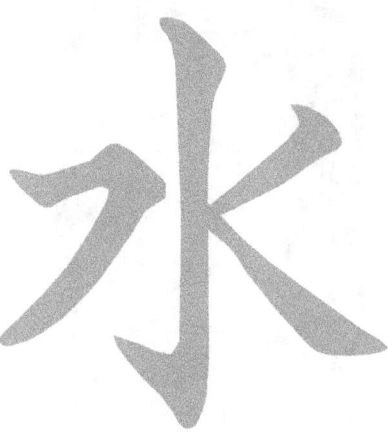

Hansoo Poomsae Diagram

Movement Principles of Poomsae

The movement order of each Poomsae is predetermined so you must practice accordingly. The predetermined movement line is called the Poomsae Seon. Every form begins and ends in the same place. Poomsae also begins and ends with etiquette, as manifested in the bow. There are three principles:

1. Poomsae must have beauty and power.
2. Rhythm is derived from softness and strength of force.
3. Technique is made of the slowness and rapidness of movement and the contraction and expansion of the body.

The detailed movement principles of Poomsae are as follows:

1. Each Poomsae movement is divided into **preparation for the movement** and the **main movement**. In preparation for a movement, you rotate your trunk, move your feet and prepare to block or strike. During this stage, relax your entire body and move your feet into a transitional stance while simultaneously chambering your arms or leg. Next, perform the main movement, the block, punch, strike or kick. At the moment of impact, focus your force on the target and snap your hand or foot to maximize the power of your movement.

2. For each movement, maximize the **rotational force** of your waist and the **snapping motion** of your strike. In Poomsae, you can increase your power by rotating your waist slightly when blocking, striking or punching. Avoid bending your trunk forward or sideways, as this reduces the power of your technique.

Using your waist as the axis, rotate your upper body to increase the power in your block or strike.

To maximize the power in your techniques, keep your trunk erect, avoiding bending to the side or front.

Poomsae Fundamentals 71

3. **Power and Rhythm**: When performing the preparation phase of a movement, relax your shoulders and coil your trunk to the side. When performing the main technique, focus all of your force into the target at the moment of impact.

4. **Rhythm and Speed** of movements: The preparation movement and main movement should be rhythmically and seamlessly linked. Avoid pausing in the middle of a technique.

5. When blocking, kicking and punching, always **use both arms**. In the preparation for the movement, one arm stretches toward the target direction while the other arm prepares to block or punch.

During the preparation phase of low section block, stretch your other arm toward the target, using both arms to perform the block.

During the preparation phase of knifehand neck strike, stretch your other arm toward the front, using both arms to perform the strike.

6. Always **look at the target** and **align your body** properly.

7. Accurately perform each stance. Adjust the **width and length of your stance** according to your height. When forming your stance, one step generally means the distance of one walking step forward. Pay attention to the degree of bend in your knees.

8. When kicking, **bend your knee** and kick as high as you can then quickly **recover your balance**.

THEORY

Essential components of Poomsae practice:

1. Eyesight
2. Accuracy of stance and posture
3. Precision of defensive and offensive movements
4. Center of gravity
5. Speed
6. Flexibility
7. Power
8. Breathing

Tips for Effective Poomsae Practice

1. Visualize your Poomsae practice as actual combat.

2. Be precise in your movements and follow the designated Poomsae line. Pay special attention to your:
   - Body direction
   - Hand position
   - Stance

3. Control the amount of power in your arm movements.
   - Relax your shoulders and apply snapping force at impact.
   - In every movement, use both arms equally and use your waist as the axis for your movements.

4. In transition, keep your knees bent and glide your feet just above the ground.

5. Perform with a constant speed and regular rhythm throughout the Poomsae.

6. Maintain your equilibrium in transition.

7. Look at the imaginary target for each technique.

8. Breathe silently with a regular rhythm.

9. Avoid unnecessary actions, such as turning your head before performing a technique.

10. Kihap loudly from your Danjun.

11. Master one Poomsae before you begin learning the next one.

When moving between stances, keep your knees bent and glide your feet just above the ground.

Visualize an imaginary opponent when performing each Poomsae movement.

Emphasis in Poomsae Training

For the most effective results of Poomsae training, the three elements of spirit, strength and technique are required. The integration of these three elements are possible when you master the spiritual, mental, physical and technical elements of Poomsae. In other words, the precise Poomsae performance originates in the harmony of the performer's defensive and offensive movements, body shifting, precision, speed, timing, breathing, focus of force and concentration. To master Poomsae, you must master the following elements:

1) Junbiseogi (ready stance)

1. Prior to performing the Poomsae, concentrate your mind and be alert to your surroundings and your physical condition.

2. Imagine there is an opponent in front of you and be prepared to respond to your opponent's actions.

3. When you finish your Poomsae performance, return to Jungri Jase (Ending Stance). Refocus your mind. Jungri Jase is the same as Junbiseogi, implying that every ending is a new beginning.

Poomsae training essentials:

1. Spirit
2. Strength
3. Technique

2) Stance

There are many variations in stances according to where your center of gravity is placed and where the centerline of your body is positioned as well as the position and movement of your feet. When your feet are closer together, the centerline of your body is more stable. When your knees are bent and your body is lowered, your center of gravity is lowered, creating a very strong and firm posture. However, when your stance is lower, the centerline of your body is much harder to maneuver, making it difficult to move quickly and reducing the explosiveness of your movements. Just as the distance between your feet affects the stability of your stance, it also impacts your ability to maintain your balance.

3) Eyesight

Eyesight means the direction where you are looking during each movement. Look directly at the target while using your peripheral vision to remain aware of your surroundings. Throughout each movement, keep your eyes focused on the target and be aware of your environment as well.

4) Force

Most Taekwondo movements begin from soft force and increase in force as they approach the target. In other words, the technique begins from a relaxed state and strikes the target powerfully. However, there are certain strength movements that require constant force from the beginning and throughout the movement. In order to maximize your force, you need to consider three elements: the direction of the force, leverage and the amount of power applied. More important, however, than creating the maximum amount of power in your techniques is how you apply that power.

Generating power:
1. The power to move the body comes from the muscles.
2. The body moves by the contraction and relaxation of muscles that are connected to joints.
3. Muscles function as leverage for power points while the bones function as levers and the joints as the fulcrum.
4. Power in Poomsae practice comes from variations in the methods of force application.

The application of power in a technique varies according to which body part is being used to strike with. **Generally preliminary or transitional movements require minimum application of force and main movements require maximum application of force.**

Movements requiring maximum force

- thrusting
- kicking
- striking
- colliding
- breaking
- pushing
- demolishing
- stomping
- penetrating
- twisting
- blocking

Movements requiring minimum force

- spinning
- chambering
- transitional footwork

SPINNING

CHAMBERING

TRANSITIONING

5) Breathing

Oxygen is essential to the human body to supply energy for exercise and nutrition to the muscles, therefore proper breathing during Poomsae performance is critical. Most importantly, in Taekwondo practice, you should momentarily hold your breath at the moment of impact.

Exhaling reduces internal resistance in your body and relaxes your muscles. Abruptly stopping your exhalation at the moment of impact maximizes the power of your technique. Using Kihap (yelling) when striking also helps to increase your mental focus. Your kihap should be short, sharp, and well timed. Making a long Kihap reduces its effectiveness in focusing the mind and body.

Without mental focus and breath control, you cannot perfect your offensive and defensive Taekwondo skills. This commonly happens in Kyorugi, when a competitor gets tired and loses his focus, which reduces his ability to effectively execute the necessary techniques to win. Through long-term practice and an understanding of the principles of force, as well as a wise application of your knowledge, mastery of Taekwondo will enable you to fully exploit your limited physical capacity.

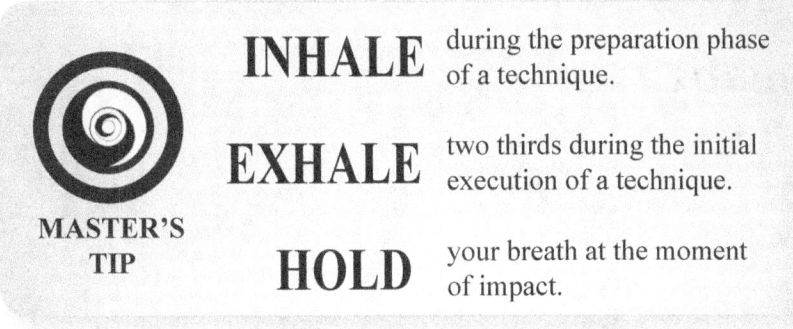

MASTER'S TIP

INHALE during the preparation phase of a technique.

EXHALE two thirds during the initial execution of a technique.

HOLD your breath at the moment of impact.

6) Kihap

Kihap is essential to Taekwondo practice. It is an external manifestation of your fighting spirit. It helps you focus your mind. The power of your Kihap shows your inner strength and Taekwondo spirit.

7) Accuracy

All Poomsae techniques, including stance, blocking, punching and striking, should be performed accurately according to the characteristics of each movement.

8) Visualization of the Target

Since Poomsae is a solo training practice, you should always have an imaginary target in mind when blocking, striking, kicking and changing stance.

Examples of **accurate target placement**:
1) Low section target: when blocking the low section, place your blocking hand one fist's distance from your thigh.
2) Trunk target: punch to the solar plexus.
3) Face target: strike to the bridge of the nose.
4) Flank target: strike to the rib cage.

Visualize the Target

9) Protection of Vital Targets

When you perform a block or attacking technique, always be sure to protect your vital targets. For example, when performing low section block, do not expose your solar plexus or lower abdomen by raising your hands too high.

10) Synchronization of the Body Parts

Synchronize the speed of movement of your eyes (spotting the target) with your offensive and defensive movements. For example, when performing Poomsae, you look at the target first, then move your feet then block or strike. However, while this looks organized and strong, in an actual combat situation, it is dangerous to move this way because it telegraphs your movement to your opponent.

11) Speed

Every technique has a different required speed, therefore you should adjust the speed of your movements according to the characteristics of the technique, particularly in the advanced Poomsae.

12) Elasticity

Coiling and uncoiling the body is used extensively in Poomsae practice. When you coil your trunk in one direction, it has a natural tendency to return to the place it came from, which creates elastic power in the movement.

13) Concentration

Focus your power at the moment of impact when executing a defensive or offensive technique. One target, one mind. Practicing oneness with the target enables you to attain oneness in your mind.

14) Action and Reaction

Every force has its own counter force in an opposing direction. The active force is the action and the counter force is the reaction. For example, when performing Juchumseo Momtongjireugi (horseriding stance middle punch), the punching arm is the action force and the arm that is pulled to the belt is the reaction force. Action and reaction are equally important in Taekwondo practice to maximize the power of each technique.

15) Balance and Stability

Generally, when two forces are moving in opposite directions with equal amounts of force, they are in equilibrium. This condition is called stability. There are five elements that promote stability in Poomsae practice:
1. The wider the base of your stance, the more stable it is.
2. The lower your center of gravity, the more stable your stance is.
3. The heavier a body is, the more stable it is.
4. When your body leans into an opposing force, your stance is more stable.
5. The closer your center gravity is to your centerline, the more stable your stance.

Additionally, to promote stability and balance in your Poomsae practice, your posture should maintain a constant height during all transitional movements, with the exception of certain special techniques.

To enhance your balance, maintain the height of your body when moving between stances.

16) Composure

Remain calm throughout the performance of each Poomsae.

17) Self-Confidence

Project confidence in your movements.

18) Types of Movement

There are three types of movements in Poomsae:

1. **Oppositional movements:** When two body parts are moving in opposite directions.

   Example: Waesanteulmakki (single mountain block).

2. **Augmenting movements:** When two body parts simultaneously move in the same direction.

   Example: Sonnalmakki (double knifehand block)

Types of movements:

1. Oppositional movements
2. Augmenting movements
3. Sequential movements

3. Sequential movements: When the entire body flows in one direction or when parts of the body sequentially move like a wave in one direction.

Example: Koaseogi, Deungjumeok Apchigi (cross stance, backfist strike)

19) Center of Gravity

The center of gravity of an object or body is the point where the weight of the object is concentrated. In Taekwondo Poomsae and Kyorugi, the center of gravity plays a particularly important part in evasion, defensive and offensive techniques. For example, spinning whip kick is most effective when you are able to precisely rotate around your center of gravity, anchoring the axis of your body and using your leg like a whip.

20) Spiritual Action

Poomsae training requires **concentration, composure and self-confidence**. Concentration is the ability to consciously bring your mental awareness to one focus point. Composure is the ability to maintain a calm mind regardless of your environmental and emotional circumstances. Self-confidence is the ability to resolutely cope with external threats and internal insecurity, which leads to inner freedom.

21) Etiquette

Etiquette means respecting others to promote mutual harmony and order as members of one community. Every Taekwondo practitioner should uphold the virtues of the society or community he or she belongs to.

Bow to show respect.

Mastery of Poomsae

There are five steps to master each Poomsae:

1) Form

The first step in learning each Poomsae is to learn the form. The emphasis in this training stage is on Kihap, eye direction and the structure and angle of the movements. The goal is to develop precision in your movements.

2) Meaning

Once you've learned the form and shape of the Poomsae, you should practice to gain an understanding of the function of your center of gravity, power control, speed and breathing as they relate to the techniques of the Poomsae. As you progress, the meaning of each technique, the relationship between the techniques and, finally, the significance of the form as a whole will become clear.

3) Application

Through practice, you will discover how to apply the techniques of the Poomsae to actual combat situations.

4) Personal Style

When you thoroughly understand a Poomsae, you must personalize the techniques in order to make them effective based on your body size and shape and your physical strengths and weaknesses.

5) Mastery

Beyond personalizing the techniques, you should endeavor to understand the true spirit of Taekwondo, which will bring you to the ultimate stage of mastery.

MASTER'S TIP

8 Poomsae Essentials

1. Harmony of offense & defense
2. Body shifting
3. Precision
4. Speed
5. Timing
6. Breathing
7. Focus of force
8. Concentration

POOMSAE
TERMINOLOGY

Poomsae Terminology

A

Agwison Khaljaebi	Arc hand strike
Anmakki	Inward block
Anpalmok Momtong Bitureomakki	Inner forearm twisting middle section block
Anpalmok Momtong Hechomakki	Middle section inner forearm opening block
Ap	Front
Apchagi	Front kick
Apkoaseogi	Front cross stance
Apkubi	Front stance
Apseogi	Walking stance
Arae	Low section
Arae Hechomakki	Low section opening block
Arae Yopmakki	Low section side block
Araemakki	Low section block

B

Bal	Foot
Bakkatmakki	Outward block
Bandaejireugi	Reverse punch
Barojireugi	Straight punch
Batangson	Palm heel
Batangson Kodureo Momtong Anmakki	Augmented palm heel inward middle section block
Batangson Momtong Nullomakki	Palm heel middle section pressing block
Batangson Nullomakki	Palm heel pressing block
Batangson Teokchigi	Palm heel jaw strike
Bawimilgi	Boulder pushing
Beomseogi	Tiger stance
Bojumeok	Covered fist

C

Chagi	Kick
Chetdarijireugi	Simultaneous punch
Chigi	Strike
Chil	Seven

D

Dangkyo Teokjireugi	Pulling high section uppercut
Deungjumeok Apchigi	Backfist strike
Deungjumeok Bakkatchigi	Outward backfist strike
Deungjumeok Dangkyo Teokchigi	Pulling backfist jaw strike
Deungjumeok Olgul Apchigi	Augmented high section backfist strike
Dollyochagi	Roundhouse kick

Doltzeogi	Hinge block
Dubeonjireugi	Double punch
Dujumeok Heoriseogi	Two hands at waist in close stance
Dujumeok Jecheojireugi	Double uppercut
Dumejumeok Yopkurichigi	Double hammerfist side strike
Dwi Koaseogi	Rear cross stance
Dwit	Back
Dwitjireugi	Rear punch
Dwitkubi	Back stance

E

Ee	Two

G

Gahn	Mountain
Gam	Water

H

Hakdariseogi	Crane stance
Hansonnal Araemakki	Single low section knifehand block
Hansonnal Bakkatchigi	Outward single knifehand strike
Hansonnal Bitureomakki	Single knifehand twist block
Hansonnal Mokchigi	Single knifehand neck strike
Hansonnal Momtong Anmakki	Single knifehand middle section inward block
Hansonnal Momtong Bakkatmakki	Single knifehand middle section outward block
Hansonnal Momtong Yopmakki	Single knifehand middle section side block
Hansonnal Olgulmakki	Single knifehand high section block
Hecho Santeulmakki	Opening mountain block
Hechomakki	Opening block
Hwangsomakki	Bull block

I

Il	One

J

Jageun Doltzeogi	Small hinge block
Jebipoom Mokchigi	Swallow form knifehand strike
Jebipoom Teokchigi	Swallow form palm heel strike to the chin
Jecheojireugi	Uppercut
Jin	Thunder

Juchumseo	Horseriding stance (adjective form)
Juchumseogi	Horseriding stance
Jumeok Pyojeok Jireugi	Target punch
Junbiseogi	Ready stance
Jungri Jase	Ending stance

K

Kawimakki	Scissors block
Keodup Yopchagi	Double side kick
Keon	Sky, heaven
Keumgang Apjireugi	Diamond front punch
Keumgang Momtong Makki	Diamond middle section block
Keumgang Yopjireugi	Diamond side punch
Keumgangmakki	Diamond block
Kheun Dolzteogi	Large hinge block
Kihap	Shout
Kodureo	Augmented
Kodureo Arraemakki	Augmented low section block
Kodureo Momtong Bakkatmakki	Augmented outward middle section block
Kodureo Momtongmakki	Augmented middle block
Kodureo Olgul Yopmakki	Augmented high section side block
Kohn	Earth
Kureo Olligi	Pulling up
Kubi	Bent knee stance
Kyopson Junbiseogi	Overlapping hands ready stance
Kyotdariseogi	Assisting stance

M

Makki	Block
Mejumeok	Hammerfist strike
Mejumeok Arae Pyojeokchigi	Low section hammerfist target strike
Mejumeok Bakkatchigi	Outward hammerfist strike
Mejumeok Naeryochigi	Downward hammerfist strike
Mejumeok Pyojeokchigi	Hammerfist target strike
Meongechigi	Double elbow strike
Meongeppaegi	Escape posture
Moaseogi	Close stance
Modeumbal Moaseogi	Feet together close stance
Momdollyo Yopchagi	Turning side kick
Momtong	Middle section (torso)
Momtong Anmakki	Inward middle block
Momtong Bakkatmakki	Outward middle block
Momtong Bandaejireugi	Reverse middle punch
Momtong Barojireugi	Straight middle punch
Momtong Hechomakki	Middle section opening block
Momtong Makki	Middle block

Momtong Yopjireugi	Middle section side punch
Momtong Yopmakki	Middle section lateral block
Mureupchigi	Knee strike
Mureupkukki	Knee break

N

Naeryochigi	Hammer strike
Nalgaepyogi	Wingspreading posture
Naranhiseogi	Parallel stance
Nolpke Bollyoseogi	Wide stance
Nullomakki	Pressing block

O

Ogeumseogi	Crane back stance
Oh	Five
Olgul	High section (face)
Olgul Bakkatmakki	High section outward block
Olgul Bandaejireugi	High section reverse punch
Olgul Dollyochagi	High section roundhouse kick
Olgulmakki	High section block
Oreun	Right
Oreunbal	Right foot
Oreunseogi	Right stance
Otkoreo Arraemakki	Low section cross block
Otkoreo Olgulmakki	High section cross block

P

Pal	Eight
Palkup	Elbow
Palkup Dollyochigi	Inward elbow strike
Palkup Dwitchigi	Rear elbow strike
Palkup Ollyochigi	Elbow uppercut
Palkup Pyojeokchigi	Elbow target strike
Palkup Yopchigi	Lateral elbow strike
Pyojeok Araemakki	Target low section block
Pyojeokchagi	Target kick
Pyonsonkkeut Arae Jeochotzireugi	Low section fingertip thrust
Pyonsonkkeut Sewotzireugi	Vertical fingertip thrust
Pyonsonkkeut Upeo Tzireugi	Horizontal (palm down) fingertip thrust

R

Ri	Fire

S

Sah	Four
Sam	Three
Santeulmakki	Mountain block
Seogi	Upright stance
Seon	Line
Sohn	Wind
Sonbadak Kodureo Momtong Bakkatmakki	Palm augmented outward middle section block
Sonnal Araemakki	Double knifehand low section block
Sonnal Arae Hechomakki	Double knifehand low section opening block
Sonnal Bakkatchigi	Outward knifehand strike
Sonnal Keumgangmakki	Knifehand diamond block
Sonnal Mokchigi	Inside knifehand strike, knifehand neck strike
Sonnal Momtongmakki	Double knifehand block
Sonnal Otkoreo Araemakki	Knifehand low section cross block
Sonnal Waesanteulmakki	Single knifehand mountain block
Sonnal Yopchigi	Knifehand side strike
Sonnaldeung Momtongmakki	Ridgehand middle section block
Sonnaldeung Momtong Hechomakki	Ridgehand middle section opening block
Sosumjireugi	Double knuckle uppercut

T

Tae	River
Taegeuk	Supreme ultimate
Taesanmilgi	Mountain pushing posture
Tongmilgi Junbiseogi	Pushing hands ready stance
Twio Yopchagi	Jump side kick

W

Wesanteul Makki	Single mountain block
Wen	Left
Wenbal	Left foot
Wenseogi	Left stance

Y

Yop	Side
Yopchagi	Side kick
Yopjireugi	Side punch
Yuk	Six

POOMSAE
WARM-UP

Poomsae Warm-up

Here is a simple warm-up routine you can use before beginning your Poomsae practice.

Knee Rotation

Place your hands on your knees and rotate them gently ten times in each direction.

Hip Rotation

Place your hands on your hips and rotate them gently ten times in each direction.

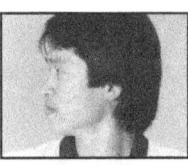

Neck Rotation

Turn your head slowly from side to side ten times.

Arm Swings

Cross your arms in front of you, then open them to the sides ten times.

Arm Raises

Swing your arms up above your head then down behind your waist ten times.

Arm Scissors

Alternately raise one arm while lowering the other in a scissors motion. Repeat twenty times.

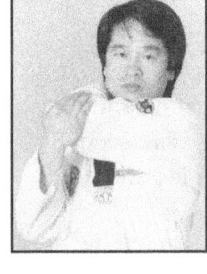

Elbow Press

Wrap your arm over your opposite shoulder and press your elbow gently with your other hand. Hold for five seconds. Repeat three times on each side.

Arm Pull

Raise your arm behind your head, reaching for your opposite shoulder. Pull your wrist gently outward with your other hand. Hold for five seconds. Repeat three times on each side.

Side Bend

Raise your right arm above your head then bend to the left. Count to two then bend slightly more. Repeat ten times on each side.

Forward Bend

Raise your arms above your head then bend forward and try to touch your toes or the floor. Repeat ten times.

Leg Cross Forward Bend

Cross your right leg in front of your left leg and bend forward to touch your toes or the floor. Hold for five seconds then cross your left leg in front of your right leg and hold. Repeat three times.

Reach Through

Place your feet a little wider than your shoulders. Bend forward and reach through your legs, trying to touch the floor behind you. Stand up, place your hands on your hips and lean backward, opening your chest. Repeat ten times.

Windmills

Cross your feet. Bend forward and touch your right hand to the floor on the left side of your feet while raising your left arm, then touch your left hand to the floor on your right side. Alternate ten times.

Knee Raises 1

Alternately raise each knee to the opposite elbow without pausing. Repeat twenty times.

Knee Raises 2

Alternately raise each knee outward without pausing. Repeat twenty times.

Partner Stretch

If you have a partner, have him or her raise your leg and hold for ten seconds. Repeat three times on each side.

Butterfly Stretch

Sit with your knees bent and the soles of your feet touching. Lean forward from the waist and hold for five seconds. Repeat three times.

Leg Extension

Place your hand on your instep and extend your leg to front as straight as you can. Hold for five seconds. Repeat three times on each side.

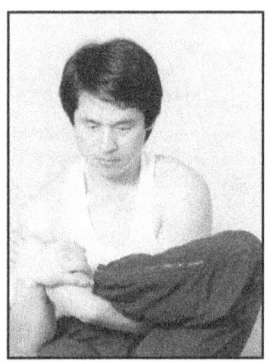

Leg Pull

Place your hands on your ankle and pull your lower leg toward your chest. Hold for five seconds. Repeat three times on each side.

Seated Trunk Twist

Extend one leg and cross the other leg over it. Place your opposite hand on your knee and turn toward the rear. Hold for five seconds. Repeat three times on each side.

Crunch

Lie on your back with your knees bent. Bring your head, shoulders and knees up toward each other. Hold for five seconds. Repeat ten times.

Plough

With your legs held straight, lower your toes toward the floor behind your head. Hold for five seconds. Repeat three times.

Prone Trunk Twist

Lying on your back, raise one leg and slowly lower it to your outstretched hand on the opposite side. Hold for five seconds. Repeat three times on each side.

Modified Bridge

Lie on your back with your knees bent and feet flat on the ground. Raise your hips and hold for five seconds. Repeat three times.

Back Stretch

Kneel and bend forward from the waist. Stretch your arms as far forward as you can and hold for five seconds. Repeat three times.

Squat and Stretch

Squat on one leg while stretching your other leg out to the side. Hold for five seconds. Repeat three times on each side.

Side Split

Stretch one leg out to the front and the other to the rear. If you can, bend your body forward from the waist toward your front leg. Hold for five seconds. Repeat three times on each side.

Front Split

Stretch your legs out to the side and bend your body forward from the waist. Hold for five seconds. Repeat three times.

TAEGEUK
POOMSAE

Principles of Taegeuk

What is Taegeuk?

The Taegeuk Poomsaes are the official forms required for all color belt students of World Taekwondo Federation affiliated schools or members. Taegeuk is a system of patterns comprised of defensive and offensive techniques used in traditional martial arts. The word "Tae" means "bigness" such as that of the universe and "Geuk" means "infinity" or "ultimate". Thus, "Taegeuk" symbolizes the "Supreme Ultimate" which has no beginning or end but is the origin of everything in the universe.

Taegeuk, or supreme ultimate, refers to the origin from which all life forms arise and to which they return when their lifecycles end. Similarly Taekwondo practice encompasses a complete martial art system, from the most basic elements of fighting skills to advanced levels of philosophical understanding of the relationships between you and your opponent, you and your surroundings, your body and mind, your mind and the universe, winning and losing, fear and joy, and ultimately life and death. All of these components arise from the Taegeuk and occur throughout your life. Thus, Taegeuk is an important concept worthy of further study.

Origin of Taegeuk

The origin of Taegeuk comes from ancient Eastern metaphysics, where two primal opposing yet complementary forces found in all things in the universe. Um, the darker element is passive, feminine, cold and downward seeking; Yang, the brighter element, is active, masculine, warm and upward seeking. If Um represents night, Yang is day.

Nature of Um and Yang

Um and Yang (also known as Yin and Yang) are complementary opposites rather than absolutes: Although Um and Yang are opposing forces, they need and consume each other and work in unity. They each contain a seed of the opposite transforming into the other. Nothing in the universe is totally Um or Yang in nature. Part of Um is in Yang and vice versa.

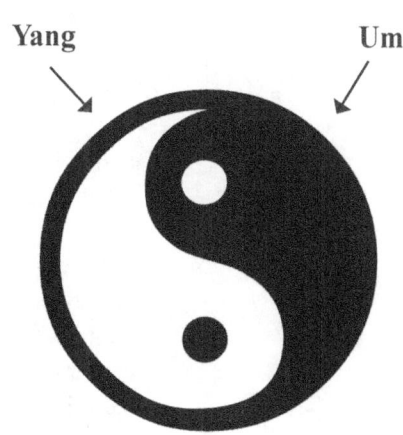

The qualities of each are not absolute; the opposition is relative and temporary. Um constantly becomes Yang while Yang changes to Um. They are dependent elements with an interdependent nature. Um cannot exist without Yang just as there cannot be night without day.

When Um is excessive, Yang becomes deficient; when Yang becomes dominant, Um weakens. The imbalance makes the energy level of the weaker more intensely focused, which helps it become stronger in turn. They regain their balance as a pair until one dominates the other again.

The state of balance and unbalance of the two forces constantly transforms themselves through expansion and condensation and fluctuates throughout life. The process of this transformation further divides into Um and Yang producing eight different phenomena called Palgwae.

Palgwae Trigrams from Taegeuk

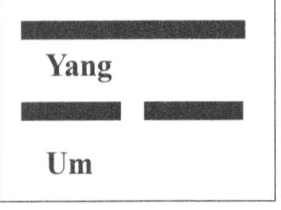

Palgwae is the by-product of the transformational cycle of the Taegeuk, which in the end returns to Taegeuk. The symbol for Um is a broken bar and for Yang a solid bar. The two divide into the four stages of Um and Yang and further divide into the eight trigrams. From the top of the diagram, the trigrams begin clockwise from Keon (heaven), Sohn (wind), Gam (water), Gahn (mountain), Gon (earth), Jin (thunder), Ri (fire), to Tae (river).

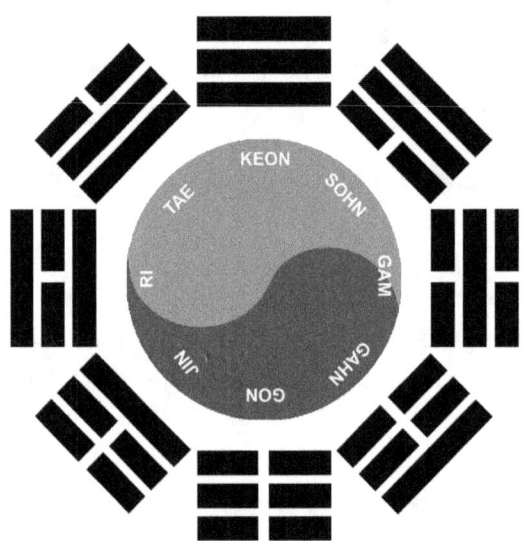

Um and Yang Applied to Poomsae

The opposing phenomena of nature are the main formula of the Taegeuk Poomsae: challenge and response, offense and defense, attack and retreat, fast and slow, hard and soft. An offensive technique must be able to instantly change into a defensive technique. A defensive technique must have offensive readiness.

The keys in practicing the Taegeuk Poomsaes, therefore, are in managing the internal and external energy properly and performing with adequate breath, speed, and power control. Special attention must be given to the transitional techniques, by shifting the center of gravity perpendicular to the ground, in order not to lose the balance. Each technique must be performed with complete focus and dynamic energy.

Symbols for Eight Taegeuk Poomsae

There are eight Taegeuk Poomsaes. Each Poomsae is built upon the previous one, adding more complicated movements, yet every form has unique characteristics and principles that students must adhere to and search for.

Taegeuk Il Jang: Keun meaning heaven: the spirit of solid foundation
Taegeuk Ee Jang: Tae meaning river: inner strength and external gentleness
Taegeuk Sam Jang: Ri meaning fire: the spirit of enthusiasm
Taegeuk Sah Jang: Jin meaning thunder: the spirit of undeniable power and dignity
Taegeuk Oh Jang: Sohn meaning wind: the spirit of gentle power
Taegeuk Yuk Jang: Gam meaning water: the spirit of flow and ultimate flexibility
Taegeuk Chil Jang: Gahn meaning mountain: the spirit of firmness and strength
Taegeuk Pal Jang: Gon meaning earth: the spirit of humbleness

TAEGEUK
IL JANG

KEON

Meaning of Taegeuk Il Jang

The symbol for Taegeuk Il Jang is Keon meaning the sky or heaven, which is the base for the cosmos. It is where everything originates. Thus Taegeuk Il Jang is the most basic form of Taekwondo. This form consists of fundamental movements such as walking stance, front stance, low block, high block, inside block, middle punch, and front kick. It helps a practitioner build a solid base for more complex techniques. This form is for the 8th Gup. There are 18 movements.

Poomsae Line of Taegeuk Il Jang

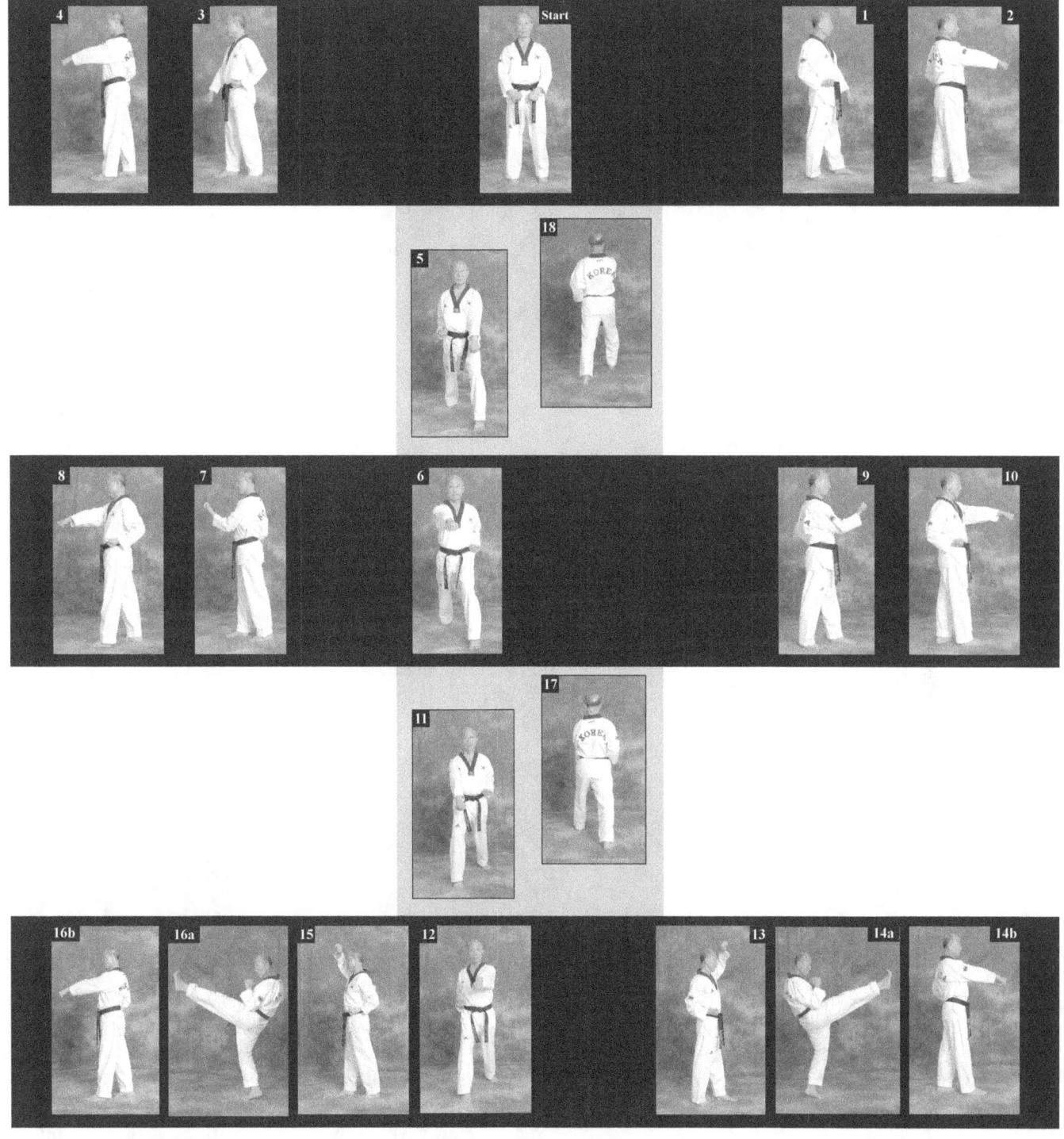

Taegeuk Il Jang

Begin from **ready stance** (junbiseogi), eyes looking forward and feet shoulder width apart.

1. Move the left foot to the left into **left walking stance** (wen apseogi) and execute a **left low section block** (araemakki).

2. Step forward with the right foot into **right walking stance** (oreun apseogi) and execute a **right reverse middle punch** (momtong bandaejireugi).

4. Step forward with the left foot into **left walking stance** (wen apseogi) and execute a **left reverse middle punch** (momtong bandaejireugi).

3. Moving the right foot, turn 180° clockwise to the rear into **right walking stance** (oreun apseogi) and execute a **right low section block** (araemakki).

Poomsae Taegeuk Il Jang (1)

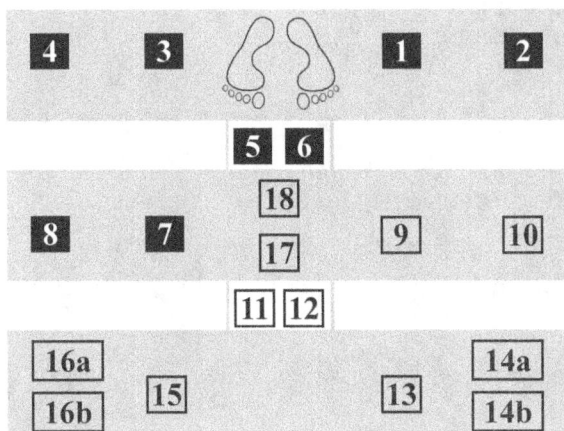

5. Moving the left foot, step 90° to the left into **left front stance** (wen apkubi) and execute a **left low section block** (araemakki).

8. Step forward with the left foot into **left walking stance** (wen apseogi) and execute a **right straight middle punch** (momtong barojireugi).

7. Moving the right foot, step 90° to the right into **right walking stance** (oreun apseogi) and execute a **left inward middle block** (momtong anmakki).

6. Without moving the feet, execute a **right straight middle punch** (momtong barojireugi).

9. Moving the left foot, turn 180° counterclockwise to the rear into **left walking stance** (wen apseogi) and execute a **right inward middle block** (momtong anmakki).

10. Step forward with the right foot into **right walking stance** (oreun apseogi) and execute a **left straight middle punch** (momtong barojireugi).

11. Moving the right foot, step 90° to the right into **right front stance** (oreun apkubi) and execute a **right low section block** (araemakki).

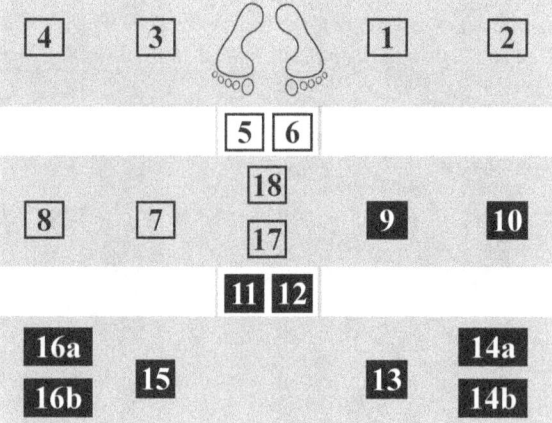

12. Without moving the feet, execute a **left straight middle punch** (momtong barojireugi).

Poomsae Taegeuk Il Jang (1) 113

13. Moving the left foot, step 90° to the left into **left walking stance** (wen apseogi) and execute a **left high section block** (olgulmakki).

14a. With the left foot fixed, execute a **right front kick** (oreunbal apchagi).

14b. Set the right foot down in **right walking stance** (oreun apseogi), execute a **right reverse middle punch** (momtong bandaejireugi).

16b. Set the left foot down in **left walking stance** (wen apseogi), execute a **left reverse middle punch** (momtong bandaejireugi).

16a. With the right foot fixed, execute a **left front kick** (wenbal apchagi).

15. Moving the right foot, turn 180° clockwise to the rear into **right walking stance** (oreun apseogi) and execute a **right high section block** (olgulmakki).

17. Moving the left foot, step 90° to the right into **left front stance** (wen apkubi) and execute a **left low section block** (araemakki).

18. Step forward into **right front stance** (oreun apkubi) and execute a **right reverse middle punch** (momtong bandaejireugi). **Kihap** when punching.

Moving the left foot, return to ready stance by turning 180° counterclockwise.

New Movements in Taegeuk Il Jang

Walking Stance
Apseogi
Walking stance looks like you've stopped walking midstride. The feet are about one stride apart, with their inner edges on one line. The legs are straight and the weight is evenly distributed. The rear foot may turn outward 30° if this is more comfortable.

Front Stance
Apkubi
The feet are about one and a half strides apart. The front foot points forward and the rear foot is turned outward 30°. Bend the front knee so that the shin is perpendicular to the floor. The weight is 2/3 on the front foot. The upper body is slightly angled away from the front.

Low Section Block
Araemakki
When making Araemakki, the fist of the blocking hand first comes up to shoulder level, with the inside of the fist toward the face. When completed, the distance between the blocking fist and the thigh is about 2 fist widths. The other fist rests on the side at belt level.

Inward Middle Block
Momtong Anmakki
When making momtong anmakki, the clenched palm faces forward then snaps toward the centerline. At completion, the elbow is bent slightly less than 90° and the clenched palm faces toward the body.

High Section Block
Olgulmakki
The wrist of the blocking arm passes directly in front of the face and finishes one fist's distance from the forehead. The other fist rests on the side at belt level.

Reverse Middle Punch / Straight Middle Punch
Momtong Bandaejireugi / Momtong Barojireugi
When punching, using the pulling force of the non-punching to generate power. Upon completion, the striking fist is aligned with the solar plexus and the other fist rests on the side at belt level. The target is the solar plexus.

Front Kick
Apchagi
Pull the toes back, striking the target with the ball of the foot. The standing foot may come slightly off the ground but should not fully lift up onto the toes.

TAEGEUK

EE JANG

118 Taegeuk Poomsae

Meaning of Taegeuk Ee Jang

The symbol of Taegeuk Ee Jang is Tae meaning river which implies internal strength and external gentleness. After diligent practice of Taegeuk Il Jang, now you have a stronger base to develop yourself further. There are more front kicks and block-kick-punch combinations in Taegeuk Ee Jang. Techniques must be performed gently but with dynamic inner power. This form is for the 7th Gup. There are 18 movements.

Poomsae Line of Taegeuk Ee Jang

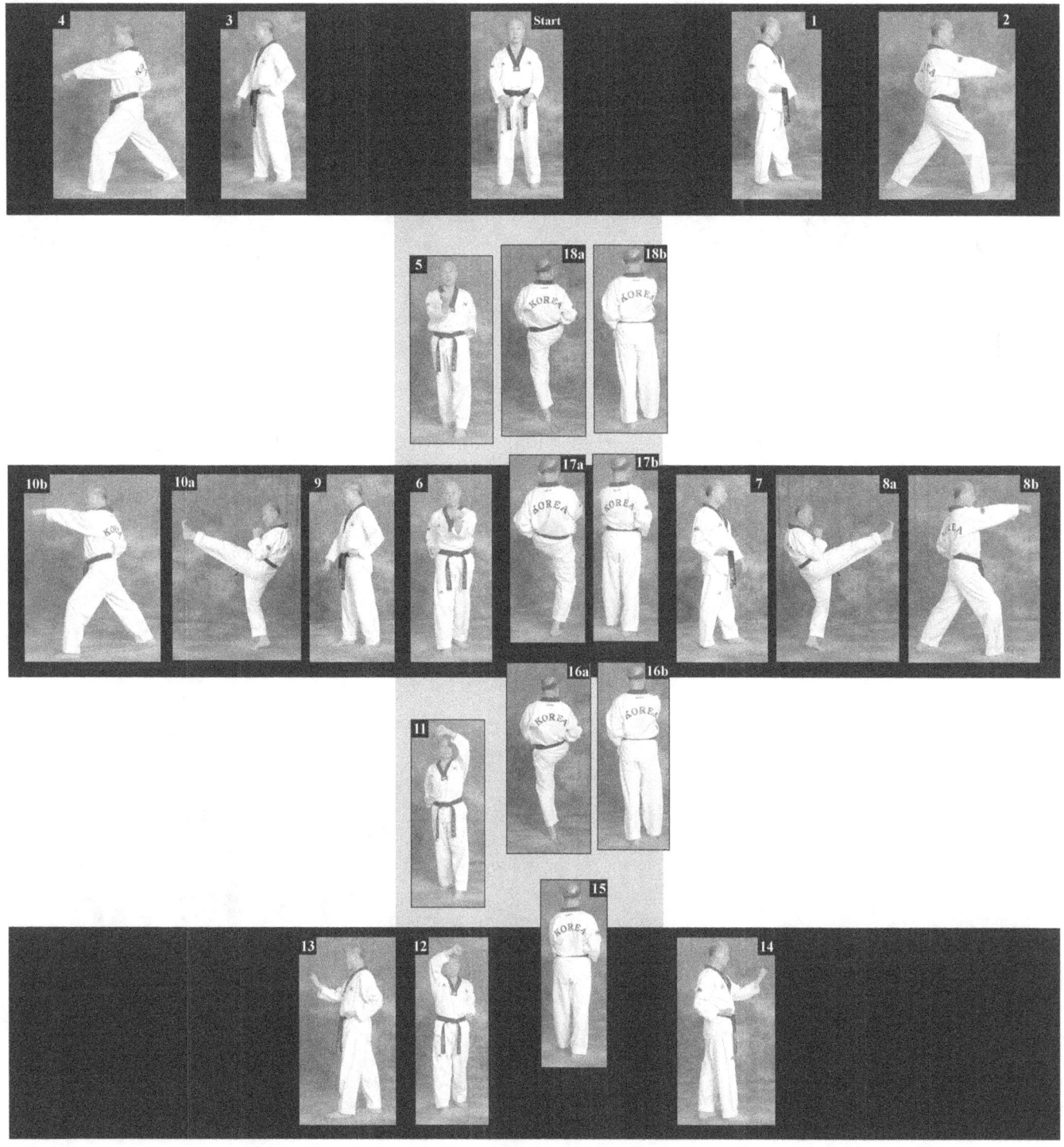

Taegeuk Ee Jang

Begin from **ready stance** (junbiseogi), eyes looking forward and feet shoulder width apart.

1. Move the left foot to the left into **left walking stance** (wen apseogi) and execute a **left low section block** (araemakki).

2. Step forward with the right foot into **right front stance** (oreun apkubi) and execute a **right reverse middle punch** (momtong bandaejireugi).

4. Step forward with the left foot into **left front stance** (wen apkubi) and execute a **left reverse middle punch** (momtong bandaejireugi).

3. Moving the right foot, turn 180° clockwise to the rear into **right walking stance** (oreun apseogi) and execute a **right low section block** (araemakki).

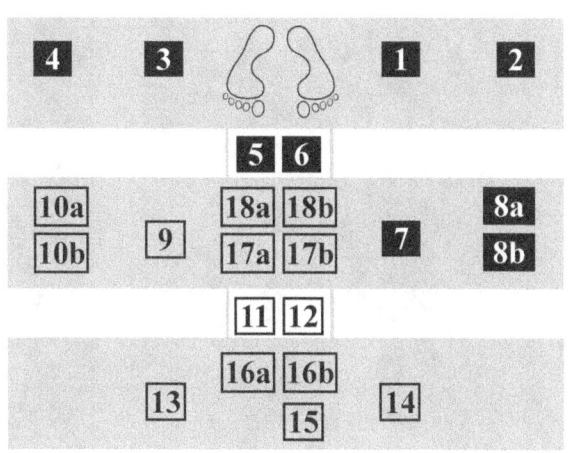

5. Moving the left foot, turn 90° into **left walking stance** (wen apseogi) and execute a **right inward middle block** (momtong anmakki).

6. Step forward with the right foot into **right walking stance** (oreun apseogi) and execute a **left inward middle block** (momtong anmakki).

7. Moving the left foot, turn 90° into **left walking stance** (wen apseogi) and execute a **left low section block** (araemakki).

8a. With the left foot fixed, execute a **right front kick** (oreunbal apchagi).

8b. Set the right foot down in **right front stance** (oreun apkubi), execute a **right high section reverse punch** (olgul bandaejireugi).

11. Moving the left foot, step 90° into **left walking stance** (wen apseogi) and execute a **left high section block** (olgulmakki).

10b. Set the left foot down in **left front stance** (wen apkubi), execute a **left high section reverse punch** (olgul bandaejireugi).

10a. With the right foot fixed, execute a **left front kick** (wenbal apchagi).

9. Moving the right foot, turn 180° clockwise to the rear into **right walking stance** (oreun apseogi) and execute a **right low section block** (araemakki).

12. Stepping forward into **right walking stance** (oreun apseogi) and execute a **right high section block** (olgulmakki).

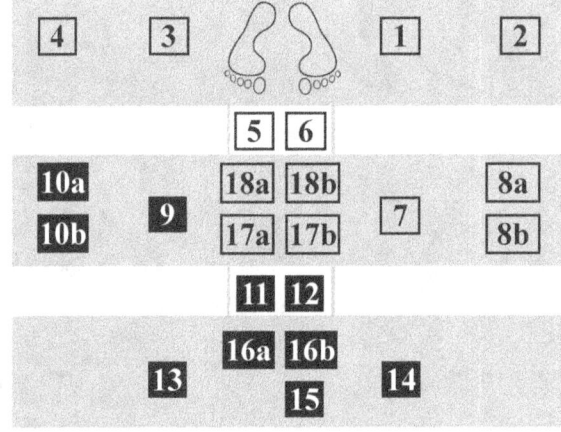

Poomsae Taegeuk Ee Jang (2)

13. Moving the left foot, turn 270° counterclockwise into **left walking stance** (wen apseogi) and execute a **right inward middle block** (momtong anmakki).

14. Sliding the right foot slightly to the right, pivot 180° into **right walking stance** (oreun apseogi) and execute a **left inward middle block** (momtong anmakki).

15. Moving the left foot, step 90° into **left walking stance** (wen apseogi) and execute a **left low section block** (araemakki).

16a. With the left foot fixed, execute a **right front kick** (oreunbal apchagi).

16b. Set the right foot down in **right walking stance** (oreun apseogi), execute a **right reverse middle punch** (momtong bandaejireugi).

124   Taegeuk Poomsae

17a. With the right foot fixed, execute a **left front kick** (wenbal apchagi).

17b. Set the right foot down in **left walking stance** (wen apseogi), execute a **left reverse middle punch** (momtong bandaejireugi).

18a. With the left foot fixed, execute a **right front kick** (oreunbal apchagi).

18b. Set the right foot down in **right walking stance** (oreun apseogi), execute a **right reverse middle punch** (momtong bandaejireugi) with **Kihap**P

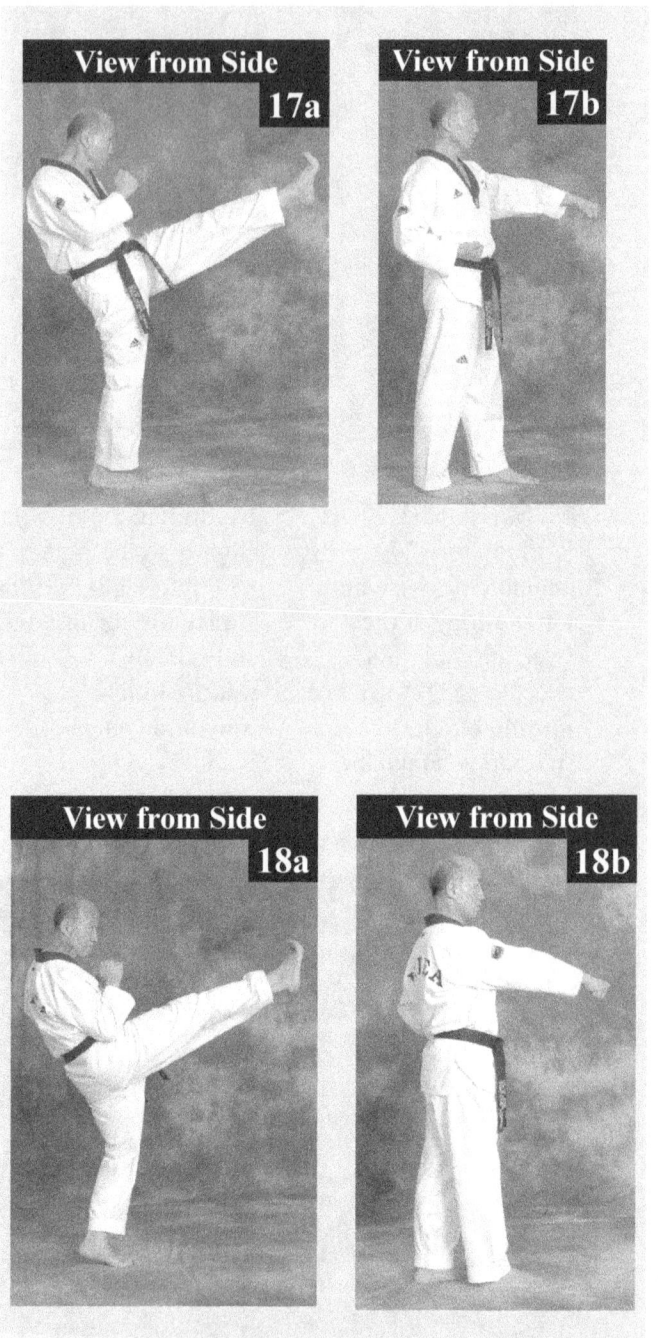

Moving the left foot, return to ready stance by turning 180° counterclockwise.

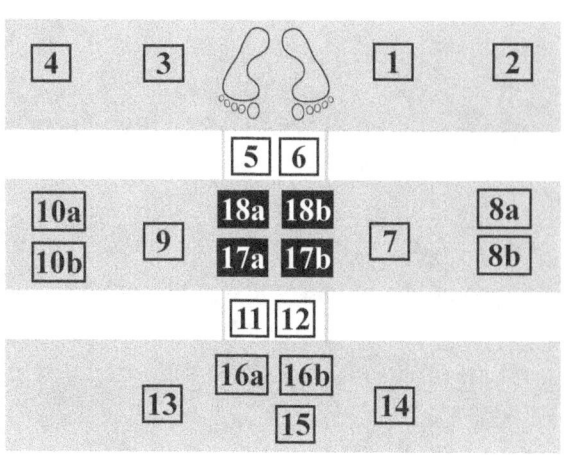

New Movements in Taegeuk Ee Jang

High Section Reverse Punch
Olgul Bandaejireugi
The high section punch is executed like the middle section punch except the target is just below the nose.

TAEGEUK
SAM JANG

Meaning of Taegeuk Sam Jang

The symbol of Taegeuk Sam Jang is Ri meaning fire. Through Taekwondo training, you have developed physical strength, and inner power. At this stage, the more effort you put out, the more your enthusiasm burns. New movements in Taegeuk Sam Jang are back stance, knifehand strike and knifehand block. The block-punch and block-kick combinations require quickness and the ability to coordinate your body to create integral forces. Use speed in defending and power in attacking. This form is for the 6th Gup. There are 20 movements.

Poomsae Line of Taegeuk Sam Jang

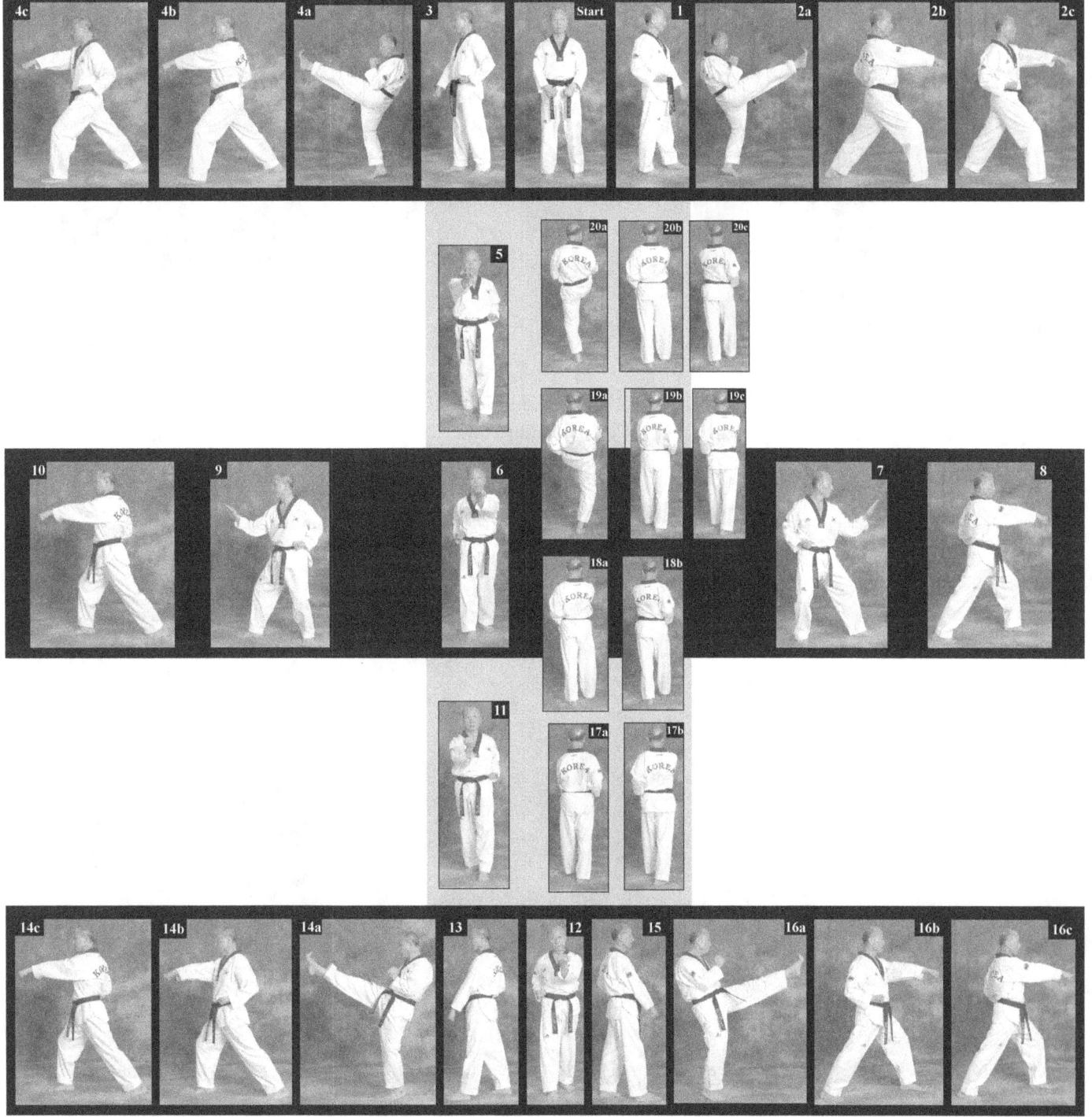

Taegeuk Sam Jang

Begin from **ready stance** (junbiseogi), eyes looking forward and feet shoulder width apart.

1. Move the left foot to the left into **left walking stance** (wen apseogi) and execute a **left low section block** (araemakki).

2. With the left foot fixed, execute a **right front kick** (oreunbal apchagi).

4b-c. Set the left foot down in **left front stance** (wen apkubi) and execute a **double punch** (dubeonjireugi), punching with the left hand first then the right.

2b-c. Set the right foot down in **right front stance** (oreun apkubi) and execute a **double punch** (dubeonjireugi), punching with the right hand first then the left.

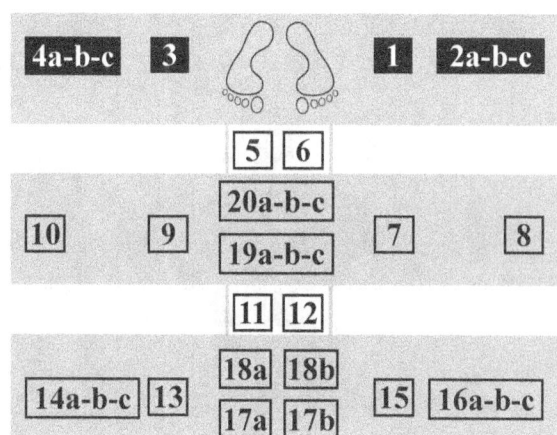

4a. With the right foot fixed, execute a **left front kick** (wenbal apchagi).

3. Moving the right foot, turn 180° clockwise to the rear into **right walking stance** (oreun apseogi) and execute a **right low section block** (araemakki).

132   Taegeuk Poomsae

5. Moving the left foot, step 90° into **left walking stance** (wen apseogi) and execute a right **inside knifehand strike** (sonnal mokchigi).

6. Stepping forward into **right walking stance** (oreun apseogi), execute a **left inside knifehand strike** (sonnal mokchigi).

7. Moving the left foot, step 90° into **right back stance** (oreun dwitkubi) and execute a **left single knifehand middle section outward block** (hansonnal momtong bakkatmakki).

8. Moving the left foot forward into **left front stance** (wen apkubi), execute a **right straight middle punch** (momtong barojireugi).

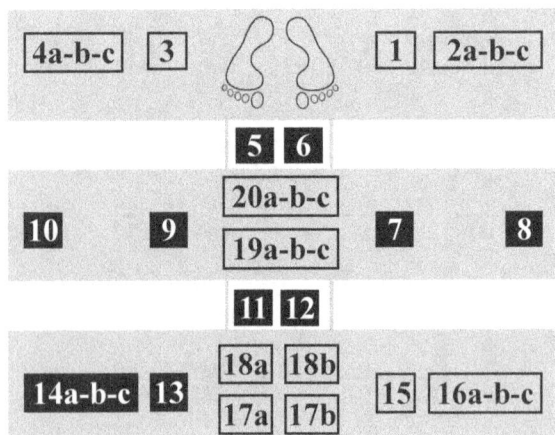

10. Moving the right foot forward into **right front stance** (oreun apkubi), execute a **left straight middle punch** (momtong barojireugi).

9. Sliding the right foot, turn the body 180° clockwise to the rear into **left back stance** (wen dwitkubi) and execute a **right single knifehand middle section outward block** (hansonnal momtong bakkatmakki).

Poomsae Taegeuk Sam Jang (3) 133

11. Moving the left foot, pivot 90° counterclockwise into **left walking stance** (wen apseogi) and execute a **right inward middle block** (momtong anmakki).

12. Step forward into **right walking stance** (oreun apseogi) and execute a **left inward middle block** (momtong anmakki).

14b-c. Set the right foot down in **right front stance** (oreun apkubi) and execute a **double punch** (dubeonjireugi), punching with the right hand first then the left.

14a. With the left foot fixed, execute a **right front kick** (oreunbal apchagi).

13. Moving the left foot, pivot 270° counterclockwise into **left walking stance** (wen apseogi) and execute a **left low section block** (araemakki).

15. Moving the right foot, turn 180° clockwise into **right walking stance** (oreun apseogi) and execute a **right low section block** (araemakki).

16a. With the right foot fixed, execute a **left front kick** (wenbal apchagi).

16b-c. Set the left foot down in **left front stance** (wen apkubi) and execute a **double punch** (dubeonjireugi), punching with the left hand first then the right.

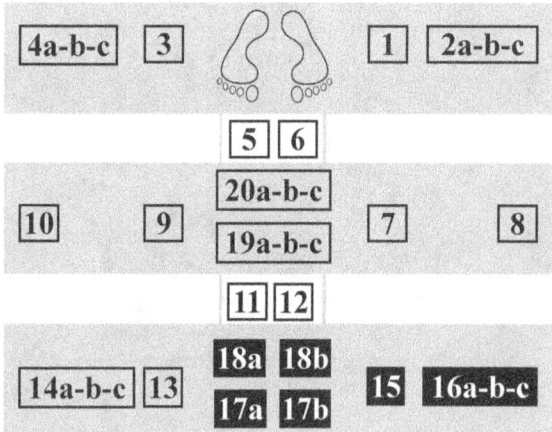

Poomsae Taegeuk Sam Jang (3) 135

17a. Moving the left foot, step 90° into **left walking stance** (wen apseogi) and execute a **left low section block** (araemakki).

17b. Without moving the feet, immediately execute a **right straight middle punch** (momtong barojireugi).

18a. Step forward into **right walking stance** (oreun apseogi) and execute a **right low section block** (araemakki).

18b. Without moving the feet, immediately execute a **left straight middle punch** (momtong barojireugi).

19a. With the right foot fixed, execute a **left front kick** (wenbal apchagi).

19b. Set the left foot down in **left walking stance** (wen apseogi) and execute a **left low section block** (araemakki).

19c. Without moving the feet, immediately execute a **right straight middle punch** (momtong barojireugi).

Poomsae Taegeuk Sam Jang (3) 137

20a. With the left foot fixed, execute a **right front kick** (oreunbal apchagi).

20b. Set the left foot down in **right walking stance** (oreun apseogi) and execute a **right low section block** (araemakki).

20c. Without moving the feet, immediately execute a **left straight middle punch** (momtong barojireugi) with **Kihap**.

Moving the left foot, return to ready stance by turning counterclockwise.

New Movements in Taegeuk Sam Jang

Double Punch
Dubeonjireugi
The double punch is performed by executing two punches in rapid succession, first punching with the front hand and then with the rear hand. The target for both punches is the solar plexus.

Single Knifehand Middle Section Outward Block
Hansonnal Momtong Bakkatmakki
The front hand forms a blade with the wrist straight. The rear hand forms a fist at belt level. Two thirds of the weight is on the rear leg and one third is on the front leg.

Straight Middle Punch
Momtong Barojireugi
Performed in the same way as a middle punch except the punch is executed with the rear hand. The target is the solar plexus.

Inside Knifehand Strike
Sonnal Mokchigi
The striking knife hand travels from out to in while twisting the forearm. The force is maximized by snapping at impact.

Back Stance
Dwitkubi
The rear foot points outward at a 90° angle and the front foot points straight forward. The front foot is about one stride from the rear foot and the heels are aligned. The knees are bent about 60 -70 degrees. The weight is about two thirds on the rear foot.

TAEGEUK
SAH JANG

Meaning of Taegeuk Sah Jang

The symbol of Taegeuk Sah Jang is Jin meaning thunder, undeniable power and dignity. As the power comes from the concentrated energy, the actions in the form must be dynamic and focused. There are more advanced movements in this Poomsae such as double knifehand block, fingertip thrust, swallow stance knifehand strike, consecutive side kicks, and cross stance back fist. To prepare for Kyorugi practice, there are more transitional movements to help you improve body shifting and coordination. This is for the 5th Gup. There are 20 movements.

Poomsae Line of Taegeuk Sah Jang

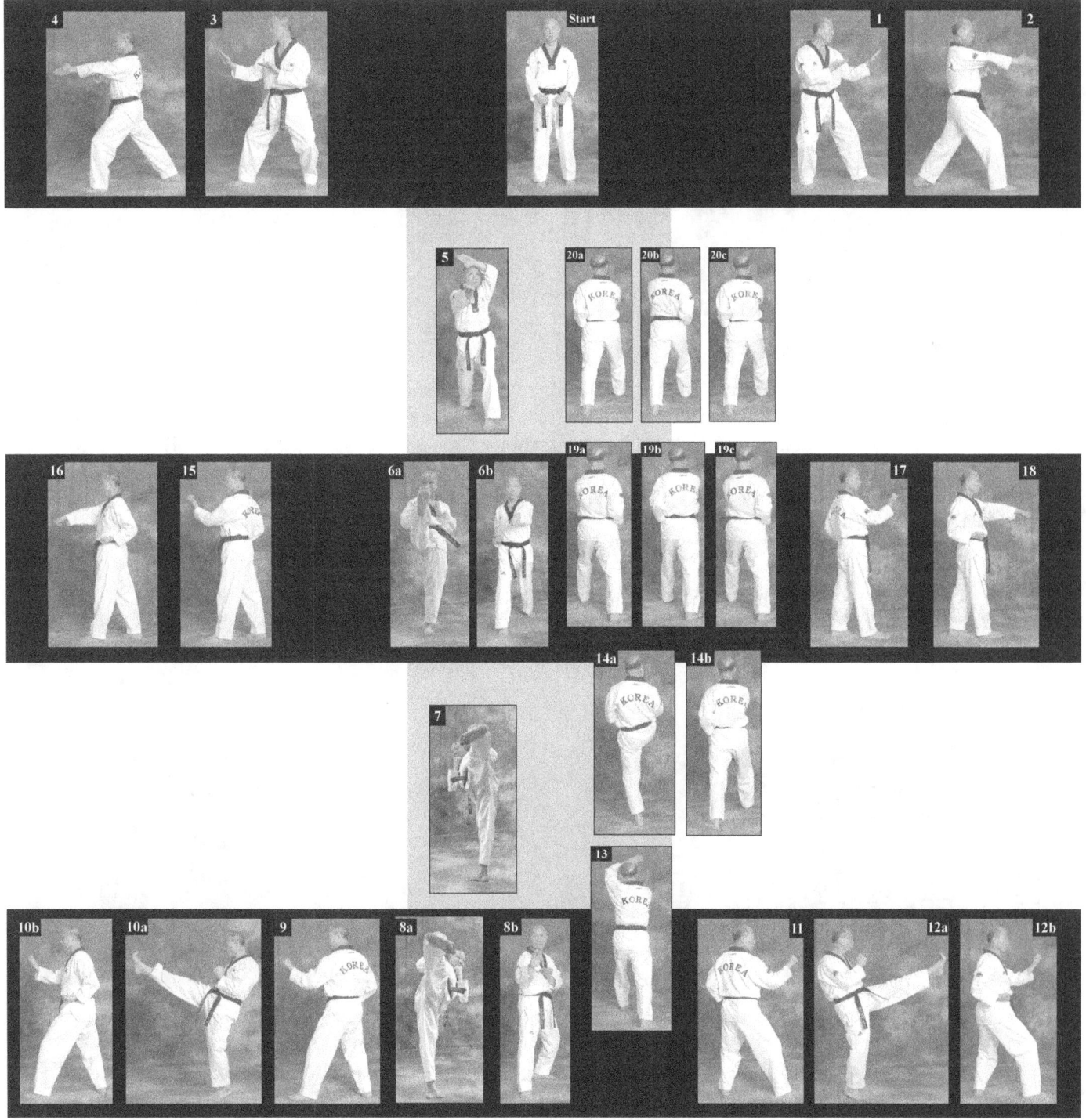

Taegeuk Sah Jang

Begin from **ready stance** (junbiseogi), eyes looking forward and feet shoulder width apart.

1. Move the left foot to the left into **right back stance** (oreun dwitkubi) and execute a **double knifehand block** (sonnal momtongmakki).

2. Step forward with the right foot into **right front stance** (oreun apkubi) and execute a **right vertical fingertip thrust** (pyonsonkkeut sewotzireugi).

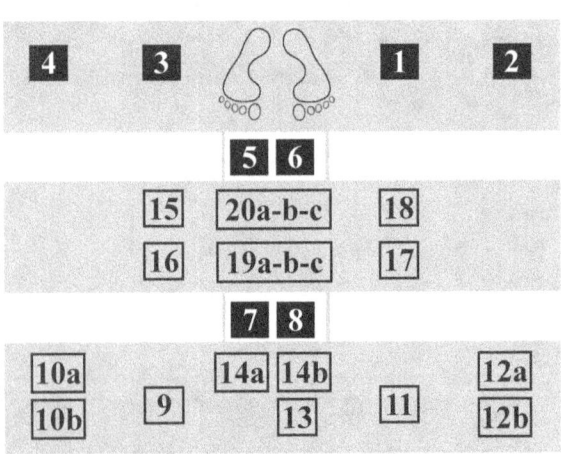

4. Step forward with the left foot into **left front stance** (wen apkubi) and execute a **left vertical fingertip thrust** (pyonsonkkeut sewotzireugi).

3. Moving the right foot, turn 180° clockwise to the rear into **left back stance** (wen dwitkubi) and execute a **double knifehand block** (sonnal momtongmakki).

Poomsae Taegeuk Sah Jang (4)

5. Moving the left foot, turn 90° into **left front stance** (wen apkubi) and execute a **swallow form knifehand strike** (jebipoom mokchigi).

6a. With the left foot fixed, execute a **right front kick** (oreunbal apchagi).

6b. Step down into **right front stance** (oreun apkubi) and execute a **left straight middle punch** (momtong barojireugi).

7. Pivoting on the right foot, execute a **left side kick** (wenbal yopchagi).

8a. Pivoting on the left foot, execute a **right side kick** (oreunbal yopchagi).

8b. Set the right foot down in **left back stance** (wen dwitkubi), execute a **double knifehand block** (sonnal momtongmakki).

10b. Return the right foot to its original position in **right back stance** (oreun dwitkubi) and execute a **right inward middle block** (momtong anmakki).

10a. With the left foot fixed, execute a **right front kick** (oreun apchagi).

9. Moving the right foot, turn 270° counterclockwise into **right back stance** (oreun dwitkubi) and execute a **left outward middle block** (momtong bakkatmakki).

11. Pivoting the body 180° clockwise into **left back stance** (wen dwitkubi), execute a **right outward middle block** (momtong bakkatmakki).

12a. With the right foot fixed, execute a **left front kick** (wen apchagi).

12b. Return the left foot to its original position in **left back stance** (wen dwitkubi) and execute a **left inward middle block** (momtong anmakki).

Poomsae Taegeuk Sah Jang (4)   145

14b. Step down into **right front stance** (oreun apkubi) and execute a **right backfist strike** (deungjumeok apchigi).

14a. With the left foot fixed, execute a **right front kick** (oreun apchagi).

13. Moving the left foot, turn 90° counterclockwise into **left front stance** (wen apkubi) and execute a **swallow form knifehand strike** (jebipoom mokchigi).

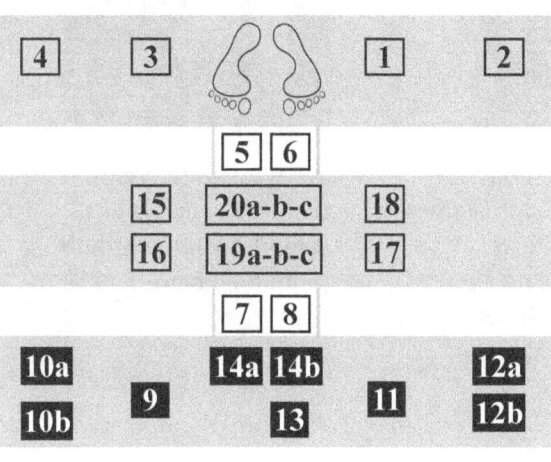

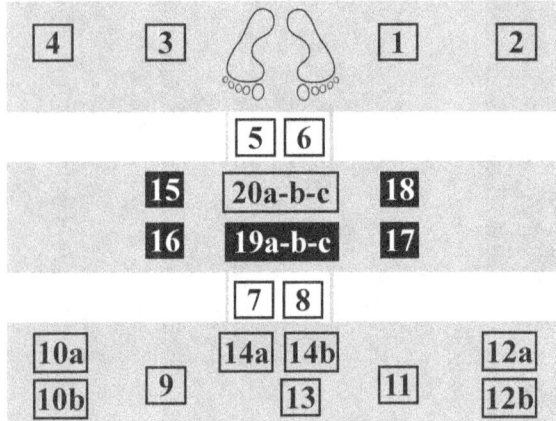

16. Without moving the feet execute a **right straight middle punch** (momtong barojireugi).

15. Moving the left foot, turn 90° counterclockwise into **left walking stance** (wen apseogi) and execute a **left inward middle block** (momtong anmakki).

17. Pivoting the body 180° clockwise into **right walking stance** (oreun apseogi), execute a **right inward middle block** (momtong anmakki).

18. Without moving the feet execute a **left straight middle punch** (momtong barojireugi).

19b-c. Without moving the feet, execute a **double punch** (dubeonjireugi), punching with the right hand first then the left.

19a. Moving the left foot, turn 90° counterclockwise into **left front stance** (wen apkubi) and execute a **left inward middle block** (momtong anmakki).

148 Taegeuk Poomsae

Moving the left foot, return to ready stance by turning counterclockwise.

20b-c. Without moving the feet, execute a **double punch** (dubeonjireugi), punching with the left hand first then the right.

20a. Step forward into **right front stance** (oreun apkubi) and execute a **right inward middle block** (momtong anmakki).

New Movements in Taegeuk Sah Jang

Double Knifehand Block
Sonnal Momtongmakki
The fingertips of the front hand are held at shoulder height, with the wrist straight and the palm facing front. The wrist of the supporting hand is aligned with the solar plexus, but not resting on the body.

Outward Middle Block
Momtong Bakkatmakki
The fist of the blocking arm should be held in line with the shoulder both vertically and horizontally. The other fist rests on the side at belt level.

Middle Block
Momtongmakki
The fist of the blocking arm is aligned with the center of the body, at shoulder height. The elbow is bent 90° to 120° and the wrist should not be bent. The other fist rests on the side at belt level.

Backfist Strike
Deungjumeok apchigi
The backfist strikes with the first and second knuckles. The target is the face, just below the nose. Turn the upper body about 45° away from the front. Pull the striking fist directly under the opposite armpit when performing the strike.

Vertical Fingertip Thrust
Pyonsonkkeut Sewotzireugi
The supporting hand performs a pressing block, with the hand open and the palm facing downward. The striking hand rests on the knuckles of the blocking hand. The target for the fingertip strike is the solar plexus. Keep the wrist and fingers of the striking hand straight and fold the thumb down onto the palm.

Swallow Form Knifehand Strike
Jebipoom Mokchigi
The front hand is held just above the forehead in a high section knifehand block. The rear hand executes a knifehand strike to the neck. Keep both wrists straight and fully extend the striking arm, twisting the upper body and hips into the strike.

Side Kick
Yopchagi
Begin the side kick by lifting the kicking leg, bending the knee then turning to the side. Once the body is facing sideways, pivot the supporting foot (on the ball of the foot) fully away from the direction of the target and extend the leg to kick. Strike the target with the foot blade and heel. The head and upper body should be raised so the body forms a Y shape at the pinnacle of the kick. The eyes should be on the target, which is the face or solar plexus.

TAEGEUK
OH JANG

Meaning of Taegeuk Oh Jang

The symbol of Taegeuk Oh Jang is Sohn meaning the wind. The wind is so gentle when it is a breeze and devastating when it becomes a hurricane. Human power can also be used either way. Taegeuk Oh Jang is designed to develop the inner energy and kinetic force of the body with the application of the two opposite phenomena of nature. New movements are hammer fist, elbow strike, sidekick with side punch, and jumping cross stance. Special attention should be paid to striking a specific target area with the elbow. This form is for the 4th Gup. There are 20 movements.

Poomsae Taegeuk Oh Jang (5)   153

Poomsae Line of Taegeuk Oh Jang

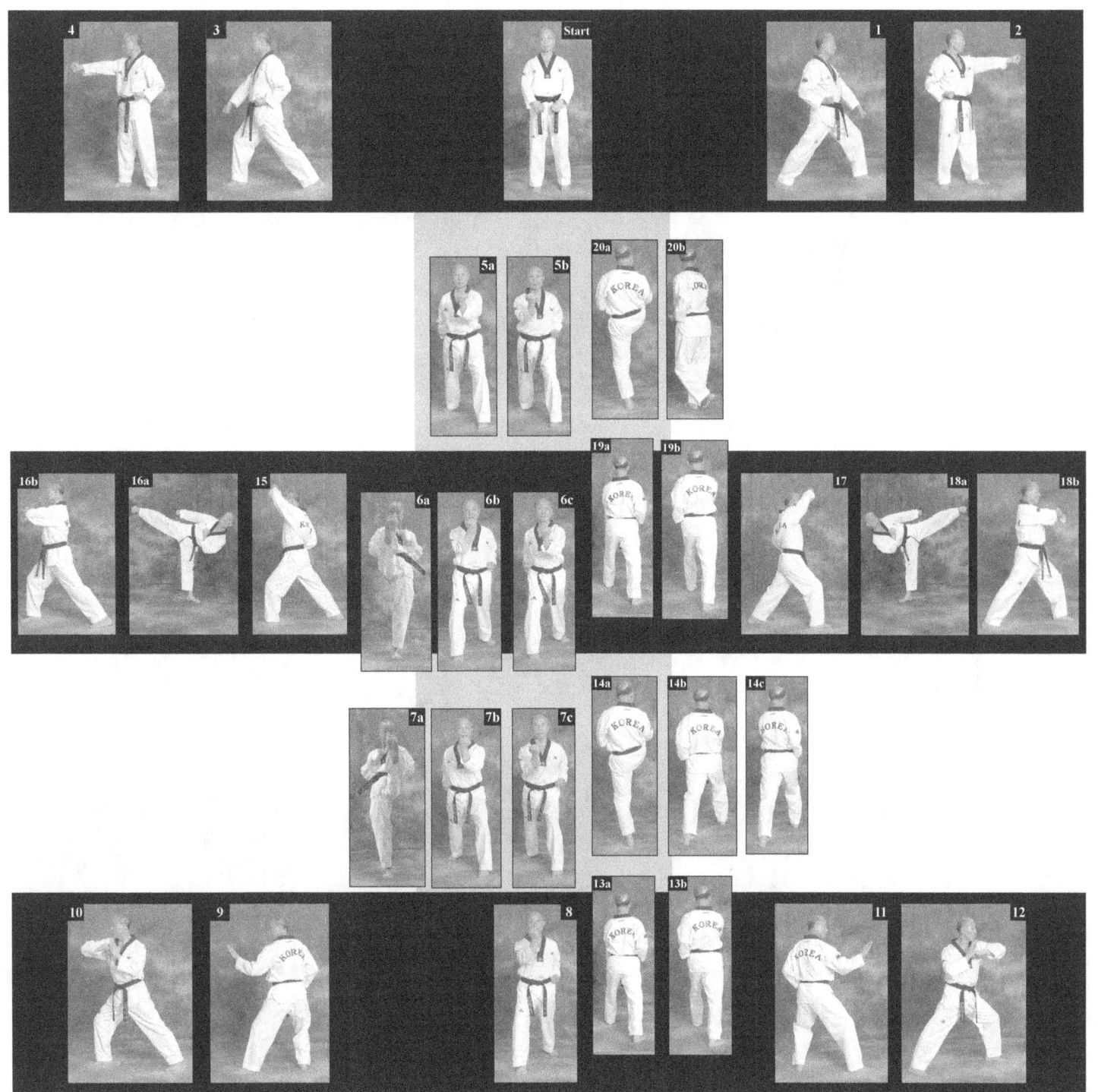

Taegeuk Oh Jang

Begin from **ready stance** (junbiseogi), eyes looking forward and feet shoulder width apart.

1. Move the left foot to the left into **left front stance** (wen apkubi) and execute a **left low section block** (araemakki).

2. Draw the left foot toward the right foot into **left stance** (wenseogi) and execute a **left downward hammerfist strike** (mejumeok naeryochigi).

3. Turn to the right into **right front stance** (oreun apkubi) and execute a **right low section block** (araemakki).

4. Draw the right foot toward the left foot into **right stance** (oreunseogi) and execute a **right downward hammerfist strike** (mejumeok naeryochigi).

Poomsae Taegeuk Oh Jang (5) 155

5a. Moving the left foot, turn 90° into **left front stance** (wen apkubi) and execute a **left inward middle block** (momtong anmakki).

5b. With the feet fixed, immediately execute a **right inward middle block** (momtong anmakki).

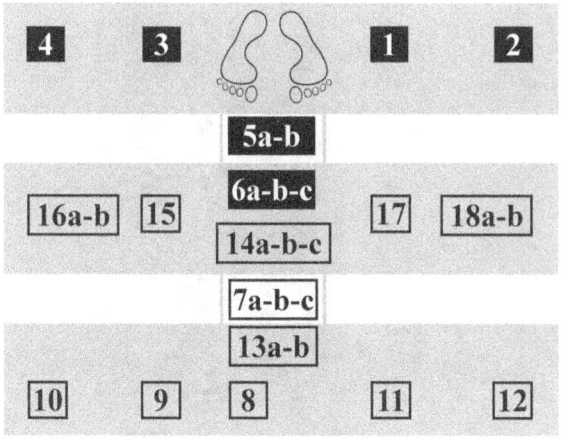

6a. With the left foot fixed, execute a **right front kick** (oreunbal apchagi).

6b. Set the right foot down in **right front stance** (oreun apkubi) and execute a **right backfist** (deungjumeok apchigi).

6c. With the feet fixed, immediately execute a **left inward middle block** (momtong anmakki).

7a. With the right foot fixed, execute a **left front kick** (wenbal apchagi).

7b. Set the left foot down in **left front stance** (wen apkubi) and execute a **left backfist** (deungjumeok apchigi).

7c. With the feet fixed, immediately execute a **right inward middle block** (momtong anmakki).

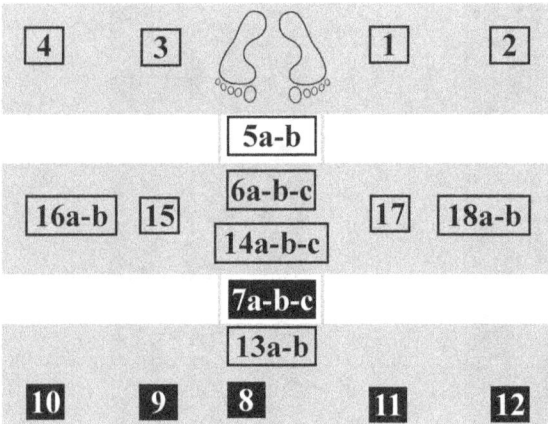

8. Step forward into **right front stance** (oreun apkubi) and execute a **right backfist** (deungjumeok apchigi).

Poomsae Taegeuk Oh Jang (5)

10. Step forward into **right front stance** (oreun abkubi) and execute a **right inward elbow strike** (palkup dollyochigi).

9. Moving the left foot, turn 270° counterclockwise into **right back stance** (oreun dwitkubi) and execute a **single knifehand middle section outward block** (hansonnal momtong bakkatmakki).

11. Moving the right foot, turn 180° into **left back stance** (wen dwitkubi) and execute a **single knifehand middle section outward block** (hansonnal momtong bakkatmakki).

12. Step forward into **left front stance** (wen abkubi) and execute a **left inward elbow strike** (palkup dollyochigi).

158   Taegeuk Poomsae

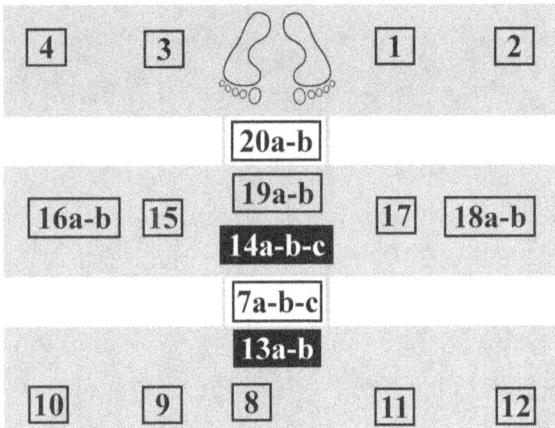

13b. Without moving the feet, execute a **right inward middle block** (momtong anmakki).

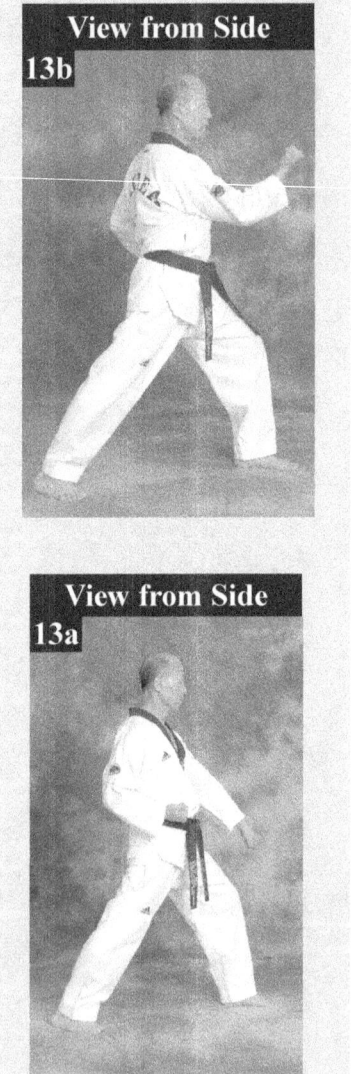

13a. Moving the left foot, turn 90° into **left front stance** (wen apkubi) and execute a **left low section block** (araemakki).

14c. Without moving the feet, execute a **left inward middle block** (momtong anmakki).

14b. Set the right foot down in **right front stance** (oreun apkubi) and execute a **right low section block** (araemakki).

14a. With the left foot fixed, execute a **right front kick** (oreunbal apchagi).

16b. Set the right foot down into **right front stance** (oreun apkubi) and execute a **left elbow target strike** (palkup pyojeokchigi).

16a. Pivoting on the left foot, execute a **right side kick** (oreunbal yopchagi).

15. Moving the left foot, turn 90° counterclockwise into **left front stance** (wen apkubi) and execute a **left high section block** (ogulmakki).

17. Moving the right foot, turn 180° clockwise into **right front stance** (oreun apkubi) and execute a **right high section block** (ogulmakki).

18a. Pivoting on the right foot, execute a **left side kick** (wenbal yopchagi).

18b. Set the left foot down into **left front stance** (wen apkubi) and execute a **right elbow target strike** (palkup pyojeokchigi).

Poomsae Taegeuk Oh Jang (5)

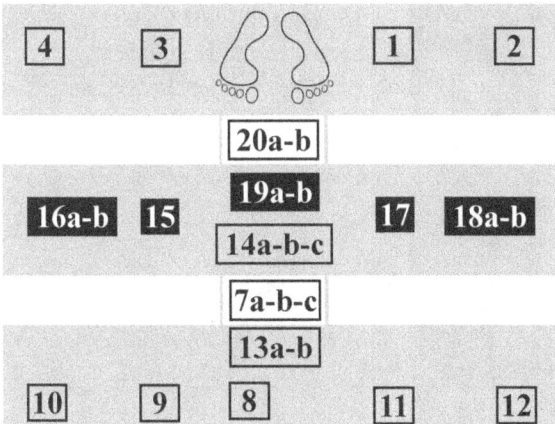

19b. Without moving the feet, execute a **right inward middle block** (momtong anmakki).

19a. Moving the left foot, turn 90° into **left front stance** (wen apkubi) and execute a **left low section block** (araemakki).

162   Taegeuk Poomsae

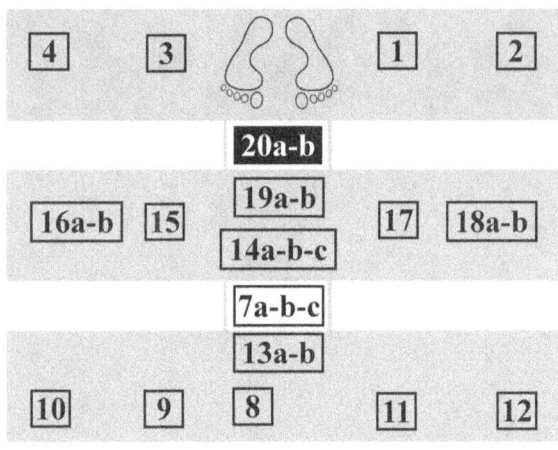

Moving the left foot, return to ready stance by turning counterclockwise.

20b. Before setting the right foot down, jump forward a step landing in **rear cross stance** (dwi koaseogi) and execute a **backfist strike** (deungjumeok apchigi) with **Kihap**.

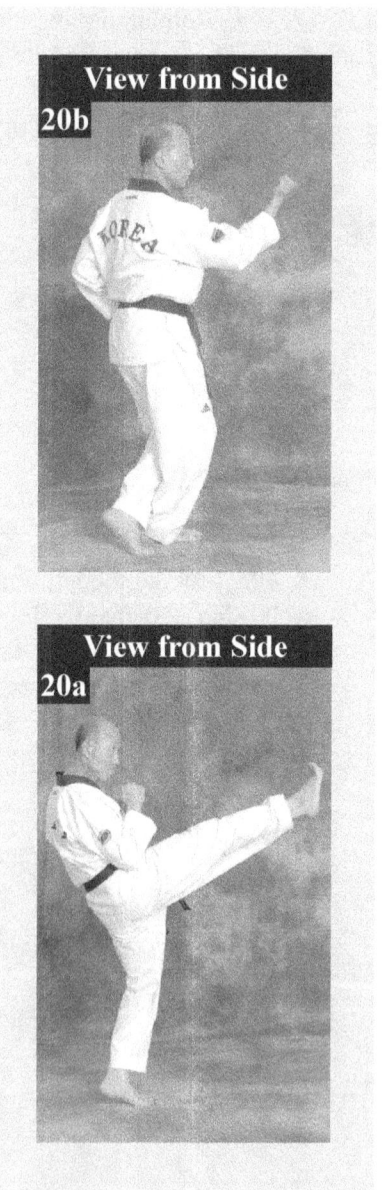

20a. With the left foot fixed, execute a **right front kick** (oreunbal apchagi).

New Movements in Taegeuk Oh Jang

Left or Right Stance
Wenseogi or Oreunseogi
From ready stance, turn the right foot outward 90° for right stance or the left foot outward 90° for left stance. This stance is used for hammerfist and backfist techniques in the Taegeuk Poomsae.

Rear Cross Stance
Dwi Koaseogi
When making cross stance, the front foot lands hard (pounding the ground), with the rear foot immediately following. The toes of the rear foot are placed beside the blade of the front foot and the right calf touches the left in an X formation. Both knees are bent.

Inward Elbow Strike
Palkup Dollyochigi
The elbow is held just above shoulder height and aligned with the front shoulder. The fist faces the floor and is held slightly away from the body. Turn the upper body into the strike.

Elbow Target Strike
Palkup Pyojeokchigi
To execute the elbow target strike, first stretch the target hand out, arm straight and hand open. Strike the elbow into the target hand, rather than slapping the target hand against the elbow. Keep the target hand open and do not place the thumb on the elbow.

Downward Hammerfist Strike
Mejumeok Naeryochigi

In an in-to-out circular motion, strike vertically downward with the soft side of the clenched fist. At completion, the arm should be parallel to the floor. In Taegeuk Oh Jang, the fist is aligned with the inside edge of the chest.

TAEGEUK
YUK JANG

Meaning of Taegeuk Yuk Jang

The symbol for Taegeuk Yuk Jang is Gam meaning water, the sustenance of life. Water symbolizes a constant flow and the ultimate flexibility. Not only must the techniques flow like water but the mind must be flexible as well. New techniques are single knifehand high section block, roundhouse kick, and palm heel pressing block. Special attention must be paid to the foot position right after executing the two roundhouse kicks. This form is for the 3rd Gup. There are 19 movements.

Poomsae Line of Taegeuk Yuk Jang

Taegeuk Yuk Jang

Begin from **ready stance** (junbiseogi), eyes looking forward and feet shoulder width apart.

1. Move the left foot to the left into **left front stance** (wen apkubi) and execute a **left low section block** (araemakki).

2a. With the left foot fixed, execute a **right front kick** (oreunbal apchagi).

2b. Set the right foot down in **right back stance** (oreun dwitkubi) and execute a **left outward middle block** (momtong bakkatmakki)

4b. Set the left foot down in **left back stance** (wen dwitkubi) and execute a **right outward middle block** (momtong bakkatmakki).

4a. With the right foot fixed, execute a **left front kick** (wenbal apchagi).

3. Turn to the right into **right front stance** (oreun apkubi) and execute a **right low section block** (araemakki).

Poomsae Taegeuk Yuk Jang (6)

5. Moving the left foot, turn 90° into **left front stance** (wen apkubi) and execute a **right single knifehand twist block** (hansonnal bitureomakki).

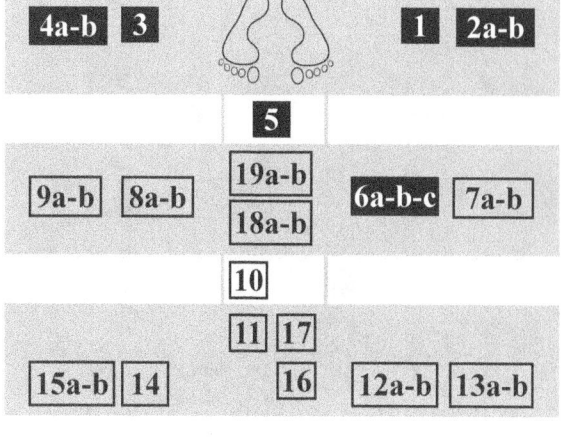

6a. Pivoting on the left foot, execute a **right high section roundhouse kick** (oreunbal olgul dollyochagi).

6b. Set the right foot down in front, then turn 90° to the left into **left front stance** (wen apkubi) and execute a **left high section outward block** (olgul bakkatmakki).

6c. With the feet fixed, immediately execute a **right straight middle punch** (momtong barojireugi).

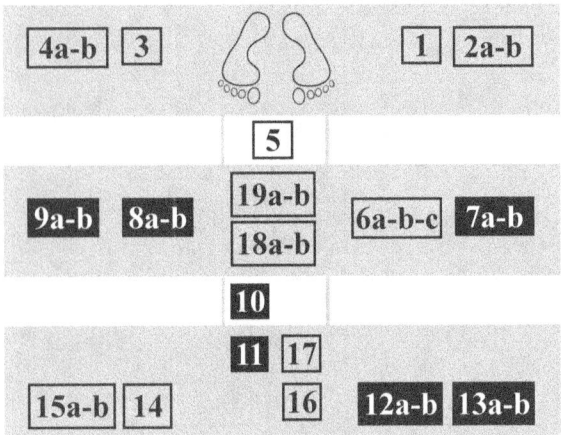

7a. With the left foot fixed, execute a **right front kick** (oreunbal apchagi).

7b. Set the right foot down in **right front stance** (oreun apkubi) and execute a **left straight middle punch** (momtong barojireugi).

9b. Set the left foot down in **left front stance** (wen apkubi) and execute a **right straight middle punch** (momtong barojireugi).

9a. With the right foot fixed, execute a **left front kick** (wenbal apchagi).

8b. With the feet fixed, immediately execute a **left straight middle punch** (momtong barojireugi).

8a. Moving the right foot, turn 180° counterclockwise into **right front stance** (oreun apkubi) and execute a **right high section outward block** (olgul bakkatmakki).

Poomsae Taegeuk Yuk Jang (6)

10. Moving the left foot, turn 90° counterclockwise into **parallel stance** (naranhiseogi) and execute a **low section opening block** (arae hechomakki).

11. Moving the right foot, step forward into **right front stance** (oreun apkubi) and execute a **left single knifehand twist block** (hansonnal bitureomakki).

12a. Pivoting on the right foot, execute a **left high section roundhouse kick** (wenbal olgul dollyochagi) with **kihap**.

12b. Set the left foot down in front, then turn 270° counterclockwise (moving the right foot) into **right front stance** (oreun apkubi) and execute a **right low section block** (araemakki).

13a. With the right foot fixed, execute a **left front kick** (wenbal apchagi).

13b. Set the left foot down in **left back stance** (wen dwitkubi) and execute a **right outward middle block** (momtong bakkatmakki).

15b. Set the right foot down in **right back stance** (oreun dwitkubi) and execute a **left outward middle block** (momtong bakkatmakki).

15a. With the left foot fixed, execute a **right front kick** (oreunbal apchagi).

14. Moving the left foot, turn 180° counterclockwise into **left front stance** (wen apkubi) and execute a **left low section block** (araemakki).

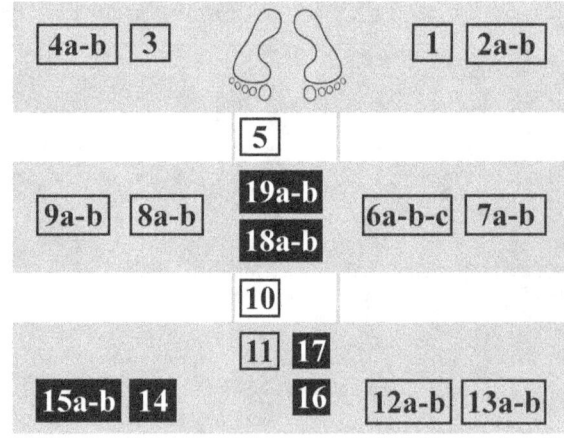

16. Moving the right foot, turn 90° counterclockwise into **right back stance** (oreun dwitkubi) and execute a **double knifehand block** (sonnal momtongmakki).

17. Moving the left foot, step backward into **left back stance** (wen dwitkubi) and execute a **double knifehand block** (sonnal momtongmakki).

19a. Moving the left foot, step backward into **right front stance** (oreun apkubi) and execute a **right palm heel middle section block** (oreun batangson momtongmakki).

19b. With the feet fixed, immediately execute a **left straight middle punch** (momtong barojireugi).

Moving the left foot, return to ready stance by stepping forward.

18a. Moving the right foot, step backward into **left front stance** (wen apkubi) and execute a **left palm heel middle section block** (wen batangson momtongmakki).

18b. With the feet fixed, immediately execute a **right straight middle punch** (momtong barojireugi).

New Movements in Taegeuk Yuk Jang

Parallel Stance
Naranhiseogi
The feet are one foot's width apart and parallel to each other. The legs are straight and the weight is evenly distributed.

Single Knifehand Twist Block
Hansonnal Bitureomakki
The rear hand forms a blade with the wrist straight. The front hand forms a fist at belt level. Two thirds of the weight is on the front leg and one third is on the rear leg. The upper body twists against the block to add power.

High Section Outward Block
Olgul Bakkatmakki
The wrist of the blocking arm passes directly in front of the face and finishes just outside the body. The other fist rests on the side at belt level.

Palm Heel Middle Section Block
Batangson Momtongmakki
The palm is turned parallel to the chest with the fingertips pointing upward. The other fist rests on the side at belt level.

Poomsae Taegeuk Yuk Jang (6) 175

Low Section Opening Block
Arae Hechomakki
When making low section opening block, use a slow controlled movement, exhaling forcefully for the duration of the execution. Look straight ahead throughout the movement.

High Section Roundhouse Kick
Olgul Dollyochagi
Transfer the weight to the pivot foot and immediately chamber the kicking leg and pivot on the ball of the foot. Strike the target with the ball of the foot or the instep. Stop the foot at the target and retract along the same path; do not follow through the target.

TAEGEUK
CHIL JANG

178   Taegeuk Poomsae

Meaning of Taegeuk Chil Jang

The symbol of Taegeuk Chil Jang is Gahn meaning mountain. A mountain is the spirit of firmness and strength. At this level the practitioner's dedication to training starts firmly rooting in the heart. The meaning of self-improvement through Taekwondo becomes deeper daily. Therefore, it is recommended that you reexamine all of the learned skills so that the foundatoin of skills is strongly secured. You may experience some difficulties and obstacles mentally and physically. Effort is required to get through this stage. New techniques are double knifehand low section block, scissors block, knee strike, middle section opening block, cross block, side punch, tiger stance and horseriding stance. Powerful and articulate execution is required in single movements and smooth transitions are necesary in combination techniques. This form is for the 2nd Gup. There are 25 movements.

Poomsae Line of Taegeuk Chil Jang

Taegeuk Chil Jang

Begin from **ready stance** (junbiseogi), eyes looking forward and feet shoulder width apart.

1. Move the left foot to the left into **left tiger stance** (wen beomseogi) and execute a **right palm heel middle section block** (batangson momtongmakki).

2a. With the left foot fixed, execute a **right front kick** (oreunbal apchagi).

2b. Set the right foot down in **left tiger stance** (wen beomseogi) and execute a **left inward middle block** (momtong anmakki).

4b. Set the left foot down in **right tiger stance** (oreun beomseogi) and execute a **right inward middle block** (momtong anmakki).

4a. With the right foot fixed, execute a **left front kick** (wenbal apchagi).

3. Turn to the right into **right tiger stance** (oreun beomseogi) and execute a **left palm heel middle section block** (batangson momtongmakki).

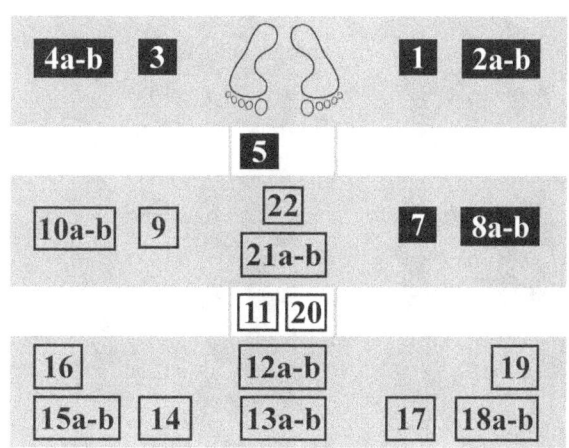

5. Moving the left foot, turn 90° into **right back stance** (oreun dwitkubi) and execute a **left double knifehand low section block** (sonnal arraemakki).

6. Moving the right foot, step forward into **left back stance** (wen dwitkubi) and execute a **right double knifehand low section block** (sonnal arraemakki).

7. Moving the left foot, turn 90° clockwise into **left tiger stance** (wen beomseogi) and execute an **augmented palm heel inward middle section block** (batangson kodureo momtong anmakki).

8a-b. With the feet fixed, twist the upper body to execute a **right backfist strike** (deungjumeok apchigi).

8a-b. With the feet fixed, twist the upper body to execute a **left backfist strike** (deungjumeok apchigi).

9. Pivot 180° clockwise into **right tiger stance** (orcun beomseogi) and execute an **augmented palm heel inward middle section block** (batangson kodureo momtong anmakki).

  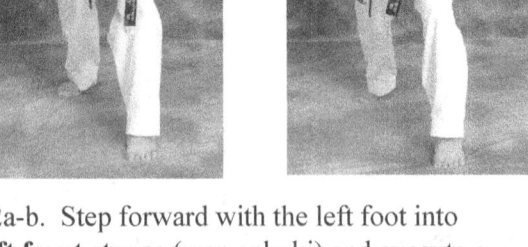

11. Turning 90° counterclockwise, draw the left foot to the right foot, making **close stance** (moaseogi). Execute a **covered fist** (bojumeok).

12a-b. Step forward with the left foot into **left front stance** (wen apkubi) and execute a **scissors block** (kawimakki).

Poomsae Taegeuk Chil Jang (7)

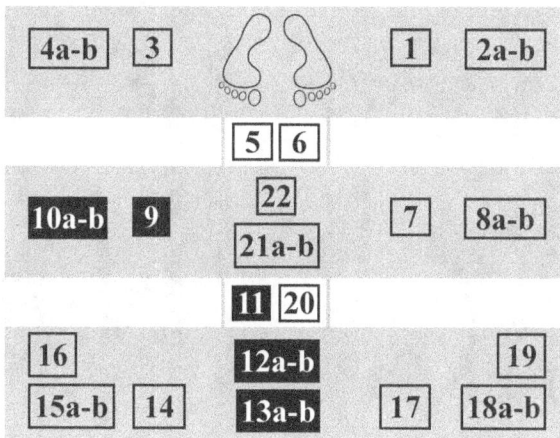

13a-b. Step forward with the right foot into **right front stance** (oreun apkubi) and execute a **scissors block** (kawimakki).

15a. With the left foot fixed, open the hands then execute a **right knee strike** (oreunbal mureupchigi). As you pull downward into the strike, clench the fists.

15b. Jump forward into **left rear cross stance** (wenbal dwi koaseogi) and execute a **double uppercut** (dujumeok jecheojireugi).

16. With the right foot fixed, step the left foot back into **right front stance** (oreun apkubi) and execute a **low section cross block** (otkoreo araemakki).

17. Moving the right foot, turn 180° clockwise into **right front stance** (oreun apkubi) and execute a **middle section opening block** (momtong hechomakki).

18a. With the right foot fixed, open the hands then execute a **left knee strike** (wenbal mureupchigi). As you pull downward into the strike, clench the fists.

17b. Jump forward into **right rear cross stance** (oreunbal dwi koaseogi) and execute a **double uppercut** (dujumeok jecheojireugi).

Poomsae Taegeuk Chil Jang (7) 185

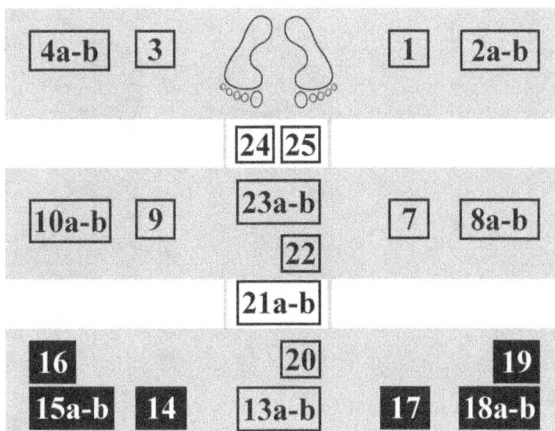

14. Moving the left foot, turn 270° counterclockwise into **left front stance** (wen apkubi) and execute a **middle section opening block** (momtong hechomakki).

19. With the left foot fixed, step the right foot back into **left front stance** (wen apkubi) and execute a **low section cross block** (otkoreo araemakki).

186   Taegeuk Poomsae

21b. Stepping down into **horseriding stance** (juchumseogi), execute a **right elbow target strike** (oreunpalkup pyojeokchigi).

21a. Without moving the left foot, execute a **right target kick** (pyojeokchagi).

20. Moving the left foot, turn 90° counterclockwise into **left walking stance** (wen apseogi) and execute a **left outward backfist strike** (deungjumeok bakkatchigi).

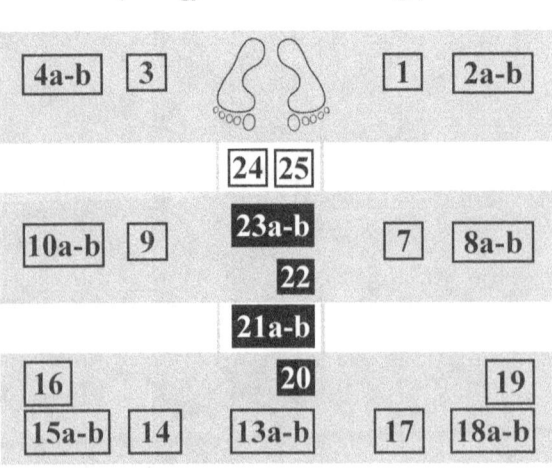

Poomsae Taegeuk Chil Jang (7)   187

23b. Stepping down into **horseriding stance** (juchumseogi), execute a **left elbow target strike** (wenpalkup pyojeokchigi).

23a. Without moving the right foot, execute a **left target kick** (pyojeokchagi).

22. With the right foot fixed, draw the left foot slightly forward into **right walking stance** (oreun apseogi) and execute a **right outward backfist strike** (deungjumeok bakkatchigi).

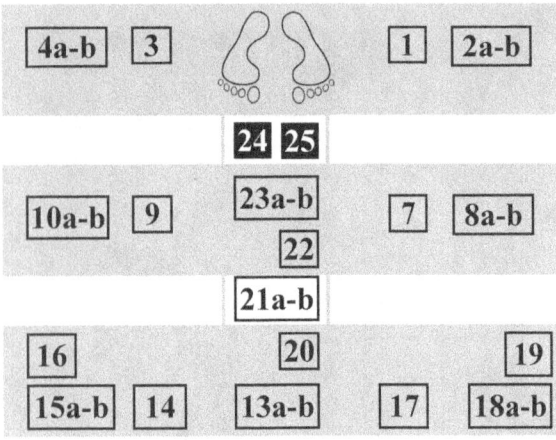

Moving the left foot, return to ready stance.

25. Pulling the opponent with the left hand, step forward with the right foot into **horseriding stance** (juchumseogi) and execute a **right middle section side punch** (momtong yopjireugi) with **kihap**.

24. With the feet fixed, execute a **left single knifehand middle section side block** (wen hansonnal momtong yopmakki).

New Movements in Taegeuk Chil Jang

Tiger stance
Beomseogi
From close stance, move one foot about a foot's length forward and turn the other foot outward 30°. The weight is entirely on the rear foot and the muscles of the abdomen are tensed. The knees should be aligned with the toes when looking down at the feet.

Close Stance
Moaseogi
Stand upright with the feet touching and the knees straight. Tighten your Danjun and relax your shoulders. Tuck in your chin.

Horseriding Stance
Juchumseogi
The feet are approximately two feet apart with the soles parallel to each other. Bend the knees to about 120° and pull them inward. Spread the weight evenly between both feet and focus it inward, tensing the muscles of the abdomen.

Double Knifehand Low Section Block
Sonnal Arraemakki
The front hand is held about 2 fists' distance from the front thigh, parallel to the surface of the thigh. The supporting hand is held in front of the solar plexus but does not touch the body. The wrists should be straight.

Augmented Palm Heel Inward Middle Section Block

Batangson Kodureo Momtong Anmakki

Bring the augmented fist under the elbow of the blocking arm with the blocking palm facing inward. Keep the thumb of the blocking hand bent.

Middle Section Opening Block

Momtong Hechomakki

Middle section opening block is two simultaneous outward middle blocks. The wrists should be positioned no wider than the shoulders.

Scissors Block

Kawimakki

One hand makes low block and the other makes outward middle block. While making scissors block, the arms should cross in front of the chest and the hands should arrive at the stopping points simultaneously.

Low Section Cross Block

Otkoreo Arraemakki

The wrists are crossed and the palms face outward. When executing low section cross block, both fists are raised to the side of the rear foot and the block is delivered from the centerline of the body. The arm on the same side as the front leg is always on the bottom.

Single Knifehand Middle Section Side Block
Hansonnal Momtong Yopmakki
Align the tip of the knifehand with the line of the shoulders. Keep the back of the hand wrist and forearm straight with the arm bent approximately 90°. Position the other hand at belt level.

Covered Fist
Bojumeok
Cover the right fist with the left hand. Position the hands just below chin-height, with the elbows tucked within the vertical line of the shoulders.

Outward Backfist Strike
Deungjumeok Bakkatchigi
Strike outward using the two major knuckles. Align the fist with the height of the shoulder. Position the other hand at belt level.

Middle Section Side Punch
Momtong Yopjireugi
From the waist, execute the punch to the side, with the fist ending at shoulder height. The eyes are looking in the same direction as the punch and the body is turned sideways.

Double Uppercut
Dujumeok Jecheojireugi
From the waist, snap both fists upward. At completion, the fists should be aligned with each other, just below shoulder height. Tuck the elbows in close to the trunk.

Knee Strike
Mureupchigi
Bring the knee upward, with the toes pointed and the ankle drawn toward the thigh. Simultaneously bring the hands downward to offset the reaction force of the knee strike.

Target Kick
Pyojeokchagi
Place the target hand at the intended position and slap the palm with the instep. The position of the target hand should remain fixed; do not move the hand to meet the foot.

TAEGEUK
PAL JANG

KOHN

Meaning of Taegeuk Pal Jang

The symbol of Taegeuk Pal Jang is Kohn meaning earth, which is the foundation of growth for all life and the place to which all life returns. Taegeuk Pal Jang is the last Poomsae before becoming a black belt. This end is a new beginning. Perfection of all basic Taekwondo skills and maturity of character are the goals at this stage. If pride, confidence, and dignity are the results of training, honesty and humbleness are prerequisites for the black belt stage. Students must perfect Taegeuk Il Jang through Taegeuk Pal Jang to be eligible to apply for First Dan black belt. New techniques are jump front kick, single mountain block, and uppercut. Accurate footwork is necessary for the combinations in Taegeuk Pal Jang. This form is required for the 1st Gup. There are 27 movements.

Poomsae Line of Taegeuk Pal Jang

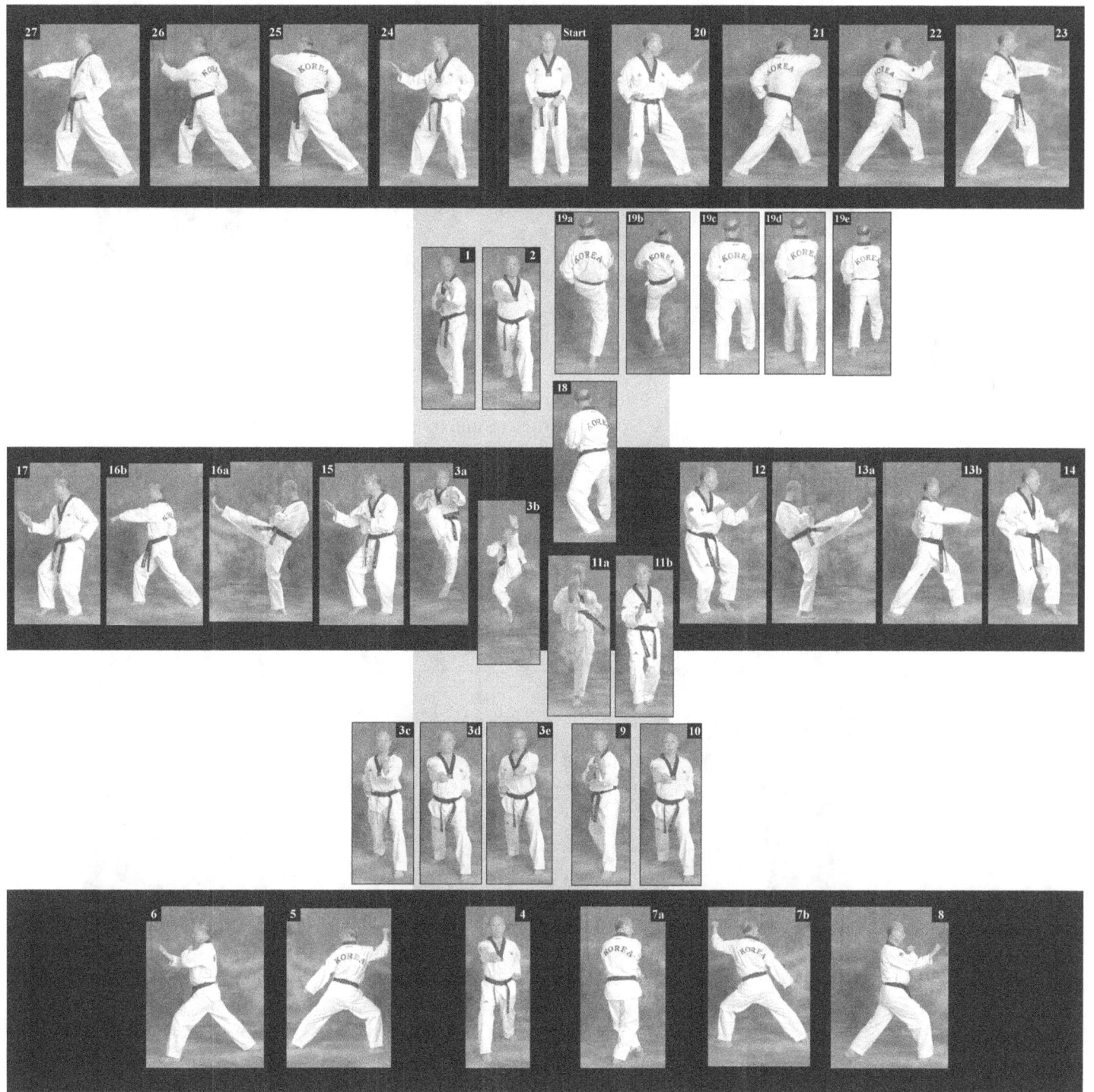

Taegeuk Pal Jang

Begin from **ready stance** (junbiseogi), eyes looking forward and feet shoulder width apart.

1. Moving the left foot, step forward into **right back stance** (oreun dwitkubi) and execute an **augmented outward middle section block** (kodureo momtong bakkatmakki).

2. Sliding the left foot forward into **left front stance** (wen apkubi), execute a **right straight middle punch** (momtong barojireugi).

3a. Begin executing a **double front kick** (dubal dangseong apchagi) by jumping with a **right front kick** (oreunbal apchagi).

3b. Follow immediately with a higher jumping **left front kick** (wenbal apchagi) with **kihap** to complete the double kick.

3c. Land two steps forward in **left front stance** (wen apkubi) and execute a **left inward middle block** (momtong anmakki).

Poomsae Taegeuk Pal Jang (8)

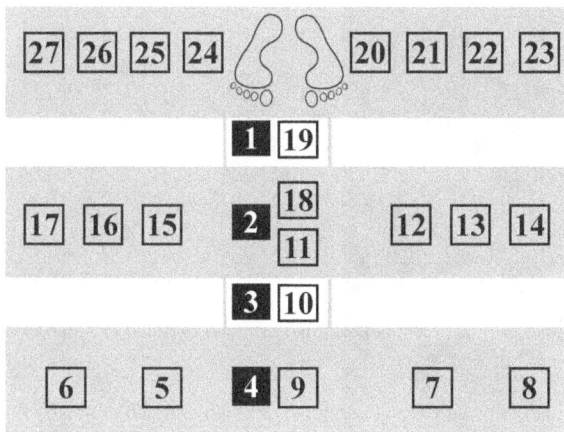

3d-e. With the feet fixed, execute a **double punch** (momtong dubeonjireugi), punching first with the right hand and then with the left.

4. Step forward with the right foot into **right front stance** (oreun apkubi) and execute a **right reverse middle punch** (momtong bandaejireugi).

6. Without stepping, slowly pivot into **left front stance** (wen apkubi) and execute a **pulling high section uppercut** (dangkyo teokjireugi) with slow concentrated force.

5. Moving the left foot, turn 270° counterclockwise into **right front stance** (oreun apkubi) and execute a **single mountain block** (wesanteul makki). Look toward the left side of the body.

7a. Step the left foot in front of the right into **front cross stance** (apkoaseogi).

7b. Moving the right foot, step into **left front stance** (wen apkubi) execute a **single mountain block** (wesanteul makki). Look toward the right side of the body.

8. Without stepping, slowly pivot into **right front stance** (oreun apkubi) and execute a **pulling high section uppercut** (dangkyo teokjireugi) with slow concentrated force.

Poomsae Taegeuk Pal Jang (8)   199

9. Moving the right foot, turn 90° counterclockwise into **right back stance** (oreun dwitkubi), executing a **double knife hand block** (sonnal momtongmakki).

10. Slide the left forward into **left front stance** (wen apkubi) and execute a **right straight middle punch** (momtong barojireugi).

11a. With the left foot fixed, execute a **right front kick** (oreunbal apchagi) then set the right foot down in its original position.

11b. Draw the left foot back into **right tiger stance** (oreun beomseogi) and execute a **right palm heel middle section block** (batangson momtongmakki).

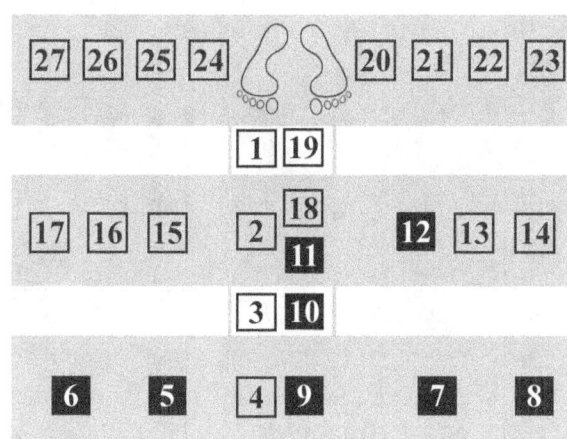

12. Moving the left foot, turn 90° counterclockwise into **left tiger stance** (wen beomseogi), and execute a **double knife hand block** (sonnal momtongmakki).

200 Taegeuk Poomsae

13a. With the right foot fixed, execute a **left front kick** (wenbal apchagi).

13b. Set the left foot down into **left front stance** (wen apkubi) and execute a **right straight middle punch** (momtong barojireugi).

14. Move the left foot toward the right into **left tiger stance** (wen beomseogi) and execute a **left palm heel block** (batangsonmakki).

17. Move the right foot toward the left into **right tiger stance** (oreun beomseogi) and execute a **right palm heel block** (batangsonmakki).

16b. Set the right foot down into **right front stance** (oreun apkubi) and execute a **left straight middle punch** (momtong barojireugi).

16a. With the left foot fixed, execute a **right front kick** (oreunbal apchagi).

15. Moving the left foot, turn 270° counterclockwise into **right tiger stance** (oreun beomseogi) and execute a **double knifehand block** (sonnal momtongmakki).

Poomsae Taegeuk Pal Jang (8)

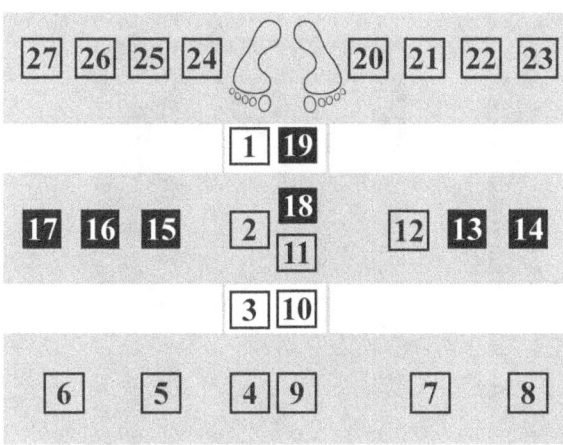

19a-b. Execute a **left front kick** (wenbal apchagi) followed immediately by a **right jump front kick** (oreunbal twio apchagi) with **kihap**.

18. Moving the left foot, turn 90° clockwise into **left back stance** (wen dwitkubi) and execute a **right augmented low section block** (kodureo arraemakki).

202 Taegeuk Poomse

19d-e. With the feet fixed, execute a **double punch** (dubeon jireugi), punching first with the left hand and then with the right.

19c. After kicking, land in **right front stance** (oreun apkubi) and execute a **right inward middle block** (momtong anmakki).

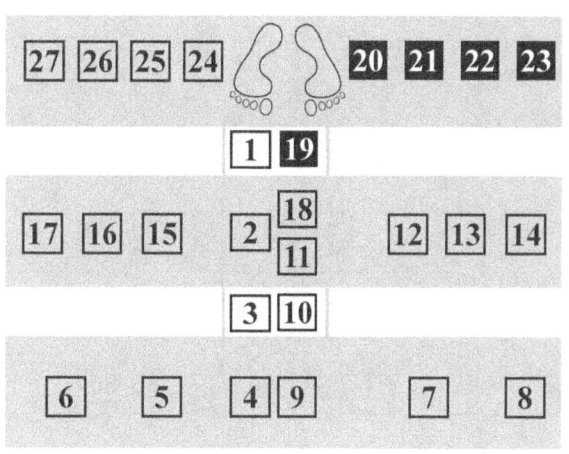

20. Moving the left foot, turn 270° into **right back stance** (oreun dwitkubi) and execute a **single knifehand middle section outward block** (hansonnal momtong bakkatmakki).

21. Slide the left foot forward into **left front stance** (wen apkubi) and execute a **right elbow strike** (oreun palkup dollyochigi).

22. With the feet fixed, execute a **right backfist strike** (oreun deungjumeok apchigi).

23. With the feet fixed, execute a **left reverse middle punch** (momtong bandaejireugi).

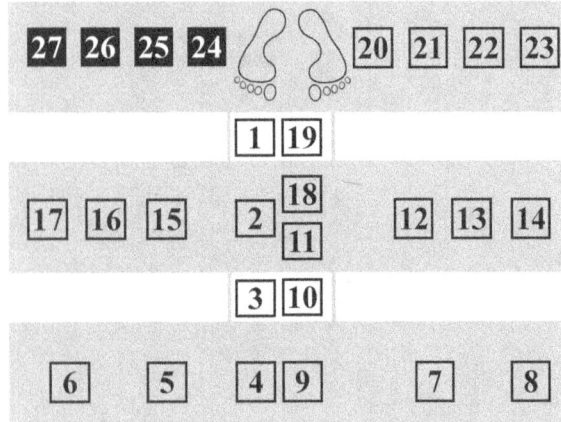

25. Slide the right forward into **right front stance** (oreun apkubi) and execute a **left elbow strike** (wen palkup dollyochigi).

24. Pivoting, turn 180° clockwise into **left back stance** (wen dwitkubi) and execute a **single knifehand middle section outward block** (hansonnal momtong bakkatmakki).

Moving the left foot, return to ready stance.

27. With the feet fixed, execute a **right reverse middle punch** (momtong bandaejireugi).

26. With the feet fixed, execute a **left backfist strike** (wen deungjumeok apchigi).

New Movements in Taegeuk Pal Jang

Front Cross Stance
Apkoaseogi
This is a transitional stance that allows you to move sideways between front stances or horseriding stances. One foot crosses in front of the other, with its small toe placed beside the sole of the fixed foot. The knees are bent and the shins form an X. Keep the feet as close together as possible.

Augmented Outward Middle Section Block
Kodureo Momtong Bakkatmakki
The palm of the blocking fist faces away from the body and the palm of the augmenting fist faces upward. The augmenting fist should be aligned on the same plane as the elbow of the blocking arm.

Single Mountain Block
Wesanteul Makki
The fist of the arm blocking the lower part of the body is held two fists' width from the thigh and the fist of the arm blocking the upper part of the body is aligned with the temple.

Augmented Low Section Block
Kodureo Arraemakki
The front hand is held about two fists' distance from the front thigh. The supporting hand is held in front of the solar plexus but does not touch the body. The wrists should be straight.

Pulling High Section Uppercut
Dangkyo Teokjireugi
Pulling the opponent's jaw with one hand, the other hand delivers an uppercut to the jaw. When completed the punching fist is at jaw height and the pulling fist is laid against the opposite shoulder. The pulling and punching motions should be simultaneous.

PALGWAE
POOMSAE

Principles of Palgwae

What is Palgwae Poomsae?

The Palgwae Poomsaes are a system of patterns comprised of defensive and offensive techniques used in Korean martial arts. The Palgwae Poomsaes are the traditional forms of the World Taekwondo Federation. The word "Pal" means "Eight" and "Gwae" means "Trigrams". Thus, "Palgwae" symbolizes the "Eight Trigrams" that govern cosmic phenomena.

Palgwae Trigrams

Palgwae is the by-product of the transformational cycle of the Taegeuk. The symbol for Um is a broken bar and for Yang a solid bar. Each Gwae has three bars. The trigrams are formed by one of the following combinations:

- one Um and two Yangs
- two Ums and one Yang
- three Ums
- three Yangs

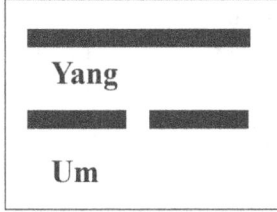

Palgwae Diagram

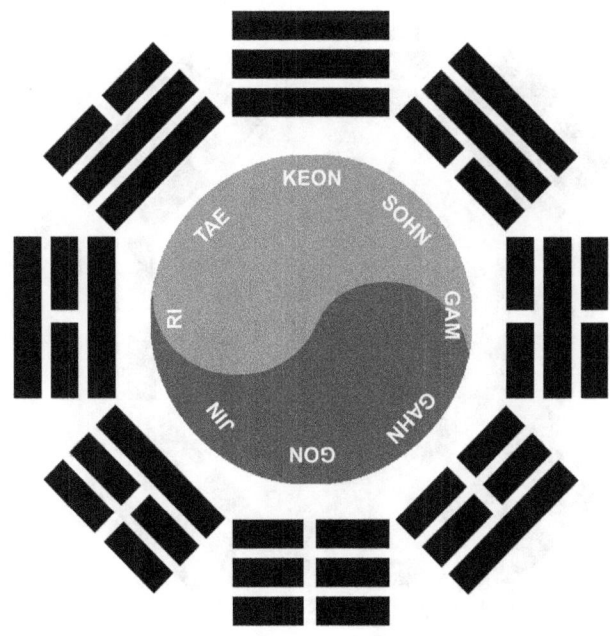

Eight combinations of Um and Yang bars make up the eight Palgwae trigrams. The eight trigrams encircle the symbol of Um and Yang with opposing pairs positioned across from one another. The opposing trigrams are in fact not in confrontational relationships, but rather they are interdependent and mutually supporting elements.

With the exception of Keon (heaven) and Gon (earth), each Gwae is composed of two dominant forces and one submissive one. From the top of the symbol, the trigrams are clockwise: Keon (heaven), Sohn (wind), Gam (water), Gahn (mountain), Gon (earth), Jin (thunder), Ri (fire), to Tae (river).

Symbols for Eight Palgwae Poomsae

There are eight Palgwae Poomsaes. Each Poomsae is built upon the previous one, progressively adding more complicated movements. Every form has unique characteristics and principles:

Palgwae Il Jang: Keon meaning heaven: the spirit of solid foundation
Palgwae Ee Jang: Tae meaning river: inner strength and external gentleness
Palgwae Sam Jang: Ri meaning fire: the spirit of enthusiasm
Palgwae Sah Jang: Jin meaning thunder: the spirit of undeniable power and dignity
Palgwae Oh Jang: Sohn meaning wind: the spirit of gentle power
Palgwae Yuk Jang: Gam meaning water: the spirit of flow and ultimate flexibility
Palgwae Chil Jang: Gahn meaning mountain: the spirit of firmness and strength
Palgwae Pal Jang: Gon meaning earth: the spirit of humbleness

PALGWAE
IL JANG

Meaning of Palgwae Il Jang

The symbol of Palgwae Il Jang is Keon meaning the sky or heaven, which symbolizes the beginning of the universe. This form consists of fundamental movements, which will establish a firm base for beginners. This form is for the 8th Gup. There are 20 movements.

Poomsae Line of Palgwae Il Jang

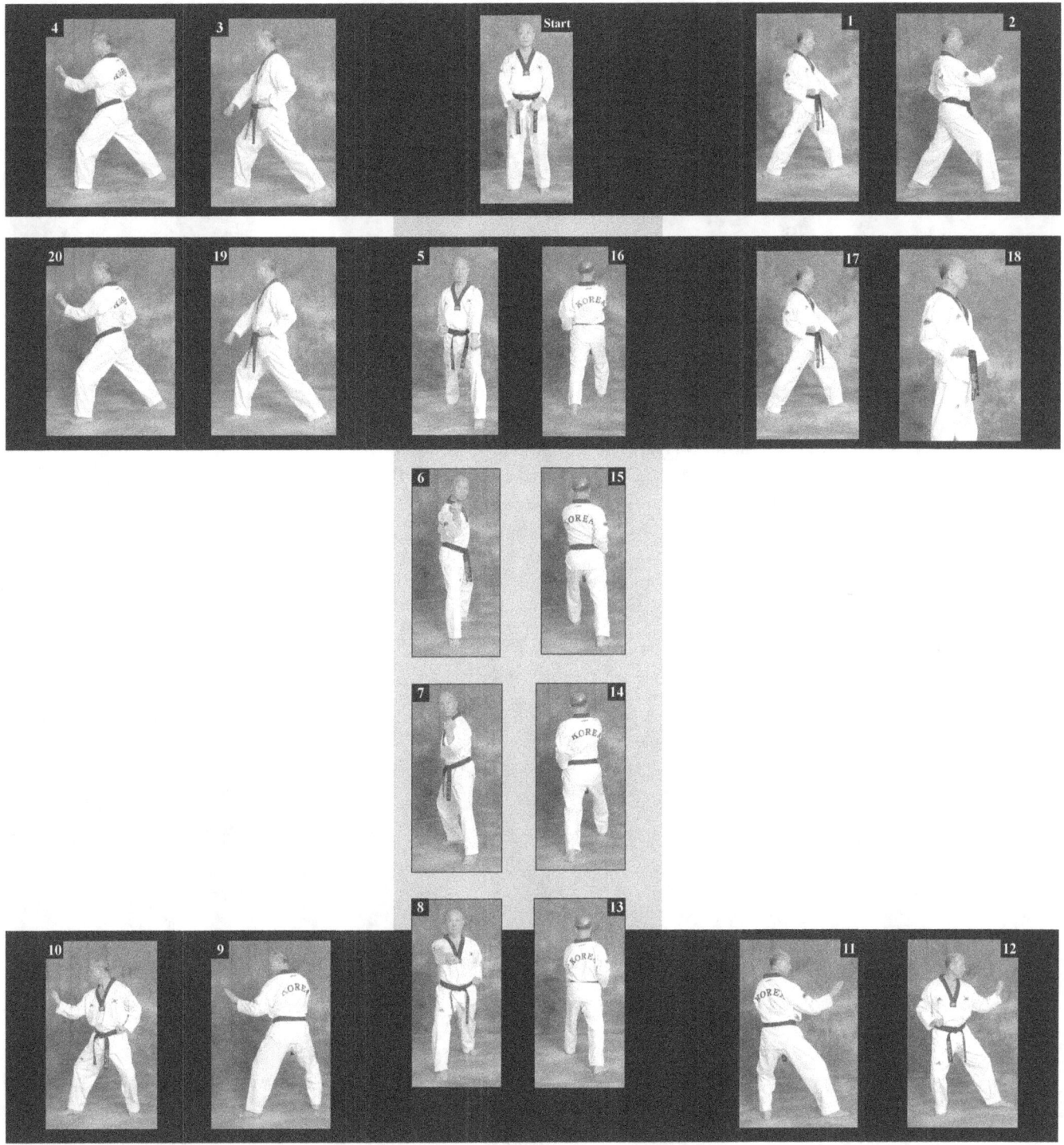

Palgwae Il Jang

Begin from **ready stance** (junbiseogi), eyes looking forward and feet shoulder width apart.

1. Move the left foot to the left into **left front stance** (wen apkubi) and execute a **left low section block** (araemakki).

2. Step forward with the right foot into **right front stance** (oreun apkubi) and execute a **right middle block** (momtong makki).

4. Step forward with the left foot into **left front stance** (wen apkubi) and execute a **left middle block** (momtong makki).

3. Moving the right foot, turn 180° clockwise to the rear into **right front stance** (oreun apkubi) and execute a **right low section block** (araemakki).

5. Moving the left foot, step 90° to the left into **left front stance** (wen apkubi) and execute a **left low section block** (araemakki).

6. Moving the right foot, step forward into **left back stance** (wen dwitkubi) and execute a **right outward middle section lateral block** (momtong yopmakki).

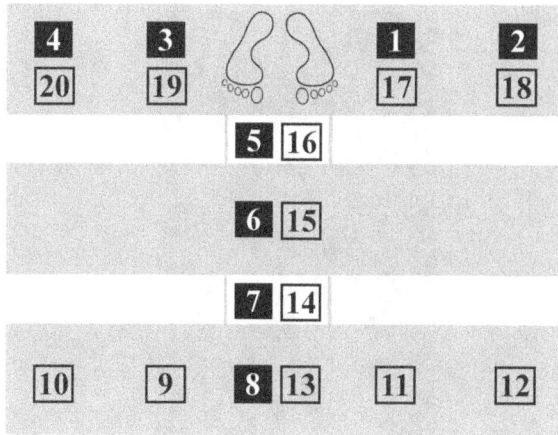

7. Moving the left foot, step forward into **right back stance** (oreun dwitkubi) and execute a **left outward middle section lateral block** (momtong yopmakki).

8. Step forward with the right foot into **right front stance** (oreun apkubi) and execute a **right reverse middle punch** (momtong bandaejireugi). **Kihap**.

10. Stepping forward with the right foot into **left back stance** (wen dwitkubi), execute a **right middle block** (momtong yopmakki).

9. Moving the left foot, turn 270° counterclockwise into **right back stance** (oreun dwitkubi) and execute a **double knifehand block** (sonnal momtongmakki).

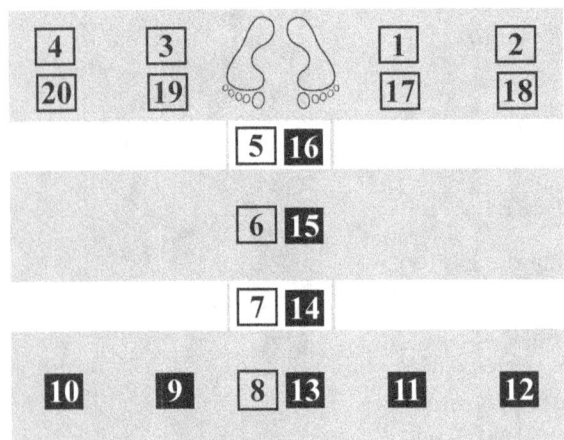

11. Moving the right foot, turn 180° clockwise into **left back stance** (wen dwitkubi) and execute a **double knifehand block** (sonnal momtongmakki).

12. Stepping forward with the left foot into **right back stance** (oreun dwitkubi), execute a **left middle block** (momtong yopmakki).

Poomsae Palgwae Il Jang (1) 219

14. Step forward into **right front stance** (oreun apkubi) and execute a **right knifehand neck strike** (sonnal mokchigi).

13. Moving the left foot, turn 90° counterclockwise into **left front stance** (wen apkubi). Execute a **left low section block** (araemakki).

16. Step forward into **right front stance** (oreun apkubi) and execute a **right reverse middle punch** (momtong bandaejireugi). **Kihap**.

15. Step forward into **left front stance** (wen apkubi) and execute a **left knife hand neck strike** (sonnal mokchigi).

220 Palgwae Poomsae

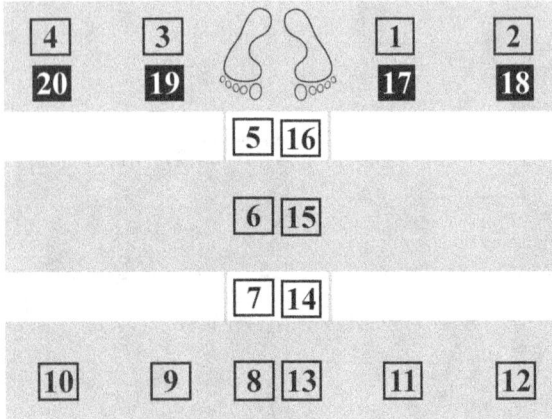

17. Moving the left foot, turn 270° counterclockwise into **left front stance** (wen apkubi) and execute a **left low section block** (araemakki).

18. Step forward with the right foot into **right front stance** (oreun apkubi) and execute a **right middle block** (momtong makki).

Moving the left foot, return to ready stance.

20. Step forward with the left foot into **left front stance** (wen apkubi) and execute a **left middle block** (momtong makki).

19. Moving the right foot, turn 180° clockwise to the rear into **right front stance** (oreun apkubi) and execute a **right low section block** (araemakki).

New Movements in Palgwae Il Jang

Front Stance
Apkubi
The feet are about one and a half strides apart. The front foot points forward and the rear foot is turned outward 30°. Bend the front knee so that the shin is perpendicular to the floor. The weight is 2/3 on the front foot. The upper body is slightly angled away from the front.

Back Stance
Dwitkubi
The rear foot points outward at a 90° angle and the front foot points straight forward. The front foot is about one stride from the rear foot and the heels are aligned. The knees are bent about 60 to 70°. The weight is about 2/3 on the rear foot.

Low Section Block
Araemakki
When making Araemakki, the fist of the blocking hand first comes up to shoulder level, with the inside of the fist toward the face. When completed, the distance between the blocking fist and the thigh is about two fist widths. The other fist rests on the side at belt level.

Outward Middle Section Lateral Block
Momtong Yopmakki
The blocking fist is held at shoulder height with the elbow covering the upper rib cage. The wrist should be straight and the back of the fist faces outward. The rear fist rests at belt level.

Double Knife Hand Block
Sonnal Momtongmakki
The fingertips of the front hand are held at shoulder height, with the wrist straight and the palm facing front. The wrist of the supporting hand is aligned with the solar plexus, but not resting on the body.

Middle Block
Momtongmakki
The fist of the blocking arm is aligned with the center of the body, at shoulder height. The elbow is bent 90° to 120° and the wrist should not be bent. The other fist rests on the side at belt level.

Knife Hand Neck Strike
Sonnal Mokchigi
The blade of the hand strikes at neck height, with the thumb bent and the four fingers held firmly together. The other fist rests on the side at belt level.

Reverse Middle Punch / Straight Middle Punch
Momtong Bandaejireugi / Momtong Barojireugi
When punching, using the pulling force of the non-punching to generate power. Upon completion, the striking fist is aligned with the solar plexus and the other fist rests on the side at belt level. The target for this punch is the solar plexus.

PALGWAE
EE JANG

Meaning of Palgwae Ee Jang

The symbol of Palgwae Ee Jang is Tae meaning river, which symbolizes a gentle and strong mind. This form should be done with smooth yet dynamic inner force. This form is for the 7th Gup. There are 20 movements.

Poomsae Line of Palgwae Ee Jang

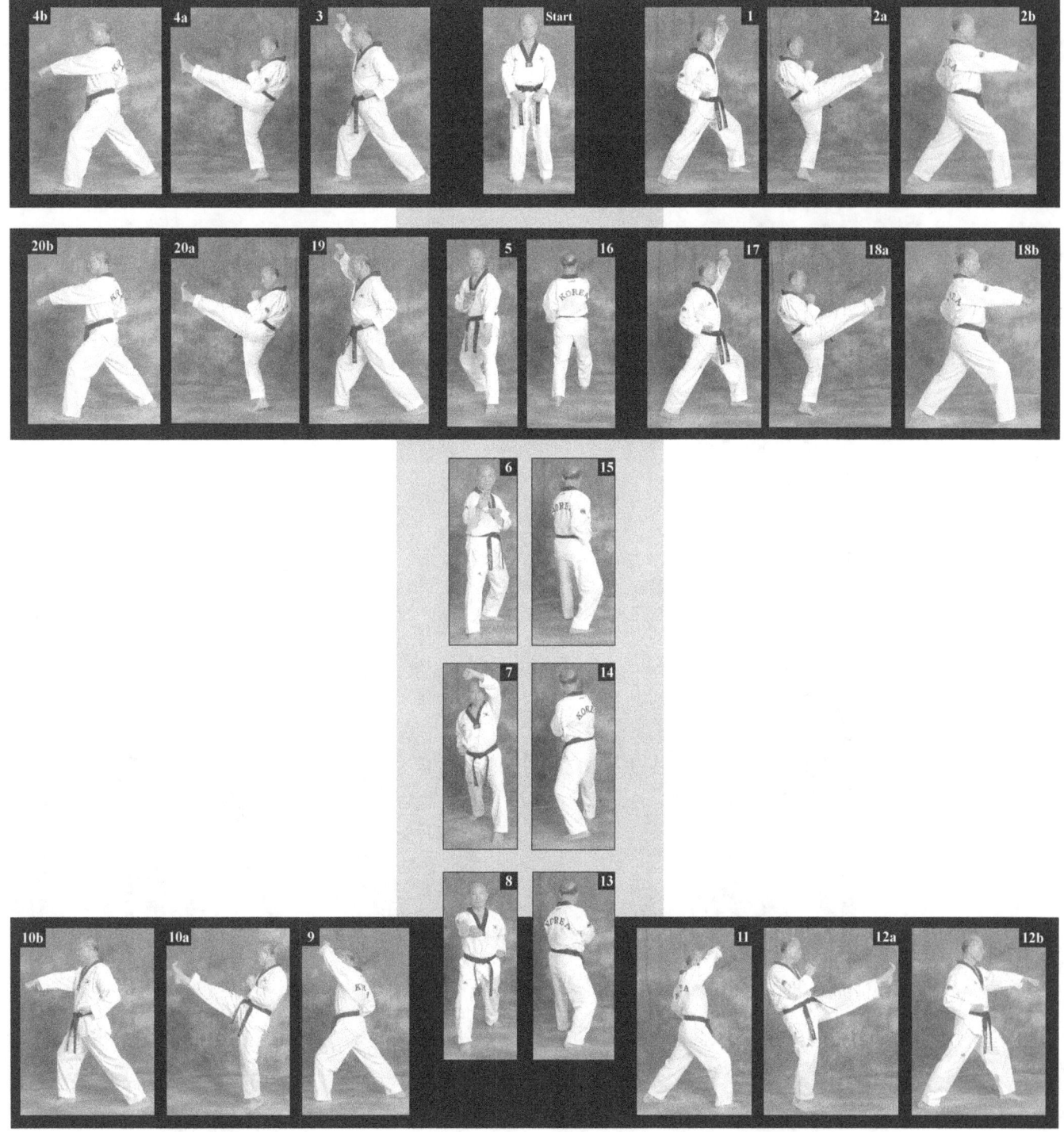

Palgwae Ee Jang

Begin from **ready stance** (junbiseogi), eyes looking forward and feet shoulder width apart.

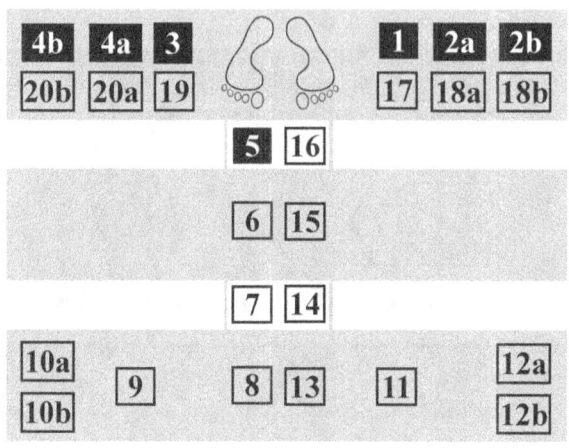

1. Move the left foot to the left into **left front stance** (wen apkubi) and execute a **left high section block** (olgulmakki).

2a. With the left foot fixed, execute a **right front kick** (oreunbal apchagi).

2b. Set the right foot down in **right front stance** (oreun apkubi) and execute a **right reverse middle punch** (momtong bandaejireugi).

4b. Set the left foot down in **left front stance** (wen apkubi), execute a **left reverse middle punch** (momtong bandaejireugi).

4a. With the right foot fixed, execute a **left front kick** (wenbal apchagi).

3. Moving the right foot, turn 180° clockwise into **right front stance** (oreun apkubi) and execute a **right high section block** (olgulmakki).

5. Moving the left foot, turn 90° into **right back stance** (oreun dwitkubi) and execute a **double knifehand low section block** (sonnal arraemakki).

228   Palgwae Poomsae

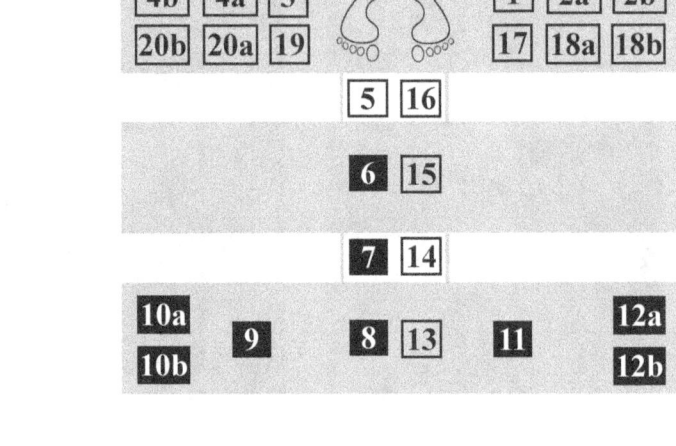

6. Moving the right foot, step forward into **left back stance** (wen dwitkubi) and execute a **double knifehand block** (sonnal momtongmakki).

7. Moving the left foot, step forward into **left front stance** (wen apkubi) and execute a **left high section block** (olgulmakki).

8. Moving the right foot, step forward into **right front stance** (oreun apkubi) and execute a **right reverse middle punch** (momtong bandaejireugi). **Kihap**.

9. Moving the left foot, turn 270° counterclockwise to the rear into **left front stance** (wen apkubi) and execute a **left high section block** (olgulmakki).

10a. With the left foot fixed, execute a **right front kick** (oreunbal apchagi).

10b. Set the right foot down in **right front stance** (oreun apkubi), execute a **right reverse middle punch** (momtong bandaejireugi).

11. Moving the right foot, turn 180° clockwise to the rear into **right front stance** (oreun apkubi) and execute a **right high section block** (olgulmakki).

12a. With the right foot fixed, execute a **left front kick** (wenbal apchagi).

12b. Set the left foot down in **left front stance** (wen apkubi), execute a **left reverse middle punch** (momtong bandaejireugi).

230 Palgwae Poomsae

14. Step forward into **left back stance** (wen dwitkubi). and execute an **augmented outward middle section block** (kudureo momtongmakki).

16. Step forward into **right front stance** (oreun apkubi) and execute a **right reverse middle punch** (momtong bandaejireugi). **Kihap**.

13. Moving the left foot, turn 90° counterclockwise into **right back stance** (oreun dwitkubi) and execute an **augmented low section block** (kudureo araemakki).

15. Step forward into **right back stance** (oreun dwitkubi) and execute a **left middle section block** (momtongmakki).

17. Moving the left foot, turn 270° counterclockwise into **left front stance** (wen apkubi) and execute a **left high section block** (olgulmakki).

18a. With the left foot fixed, execute a **right front kick** (oreunbal apchagi).

18b. Set the right foot down in **right front stance** (oreun apkubi), execute a **right reverse middle punch** (momtong bandaejireugi).

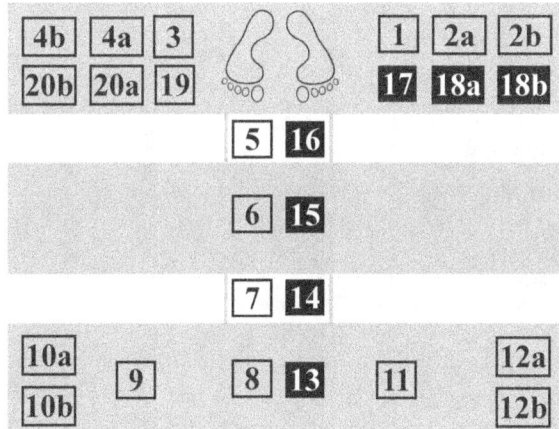

232   Palgwae Poomsae

20b. Set the left foot down in **left front stance** (wen apkubi), execute a **left reverse middle punch** (momtong bandaejireugi).

20a. With the right foot fixed, execute a **left front kick** (wenbal apchagi).

19. Moving the right foot, turn 180° clockwise into **right front stance** (oreun apkubi) and execute a **right high section block** (olgulmakki).

Moving the left foot, return to ready stance.

New Movements in Palgwae Ee Jang

High Section Block
Olgulmakki
The wrist of the blocking arm passes directly in front of the face and finishes one fist's distance from the forehead. The other fist rests on the side at belt level.

Double Knifehand Low Section Block
Sonnal Arraemakki
The front hand is held about 2 fists' distance from the front thigh, parallel to the surface of the thigh. The supporting hand is held in front of the solar plexus but does not touch the body. The wrists should be straight.

Augmented Low Section Block
Kodureo Arraemakki
The front hand is held about 2 fists' distance from the front thigh. The supporting hand is held in front of the solar plexus but does not touch the body. The wrists should be straight.

Augmented Outward Middle Section Block
Kodureo Momtongmakki
The palm of the front fist faces the body. The elbow of the blocking arm should not touch the supporting fist. The supporting hand is held in front of the solar plexus but does not touch the body. The wrists should be straight.

Front Kick
Apchagi

Pull the toes back, striking the target with the ball of the foot. The standing foot may come slightly off the ground but should not fully lift up onto the toes.

PALGWAE
SAM JANG

Meaning of Palgwae Sam Jang

The symbol of Palgwae Sam Jang is Ri meaning fire. Upon the foundation that has been developed through Palgwae Il Jang and Ee Jang, the practitioner can add more power and speed in his or her performance. As the physical strength and commitment grows, the passion for the art increases. Multiple techniques must be done in a quick and precise manner. This form should be performed with external force and inner enthusiasm. This form is for the 6th Gup There are 20 movements.

Poomsae Line of Palgwae Sam Jang

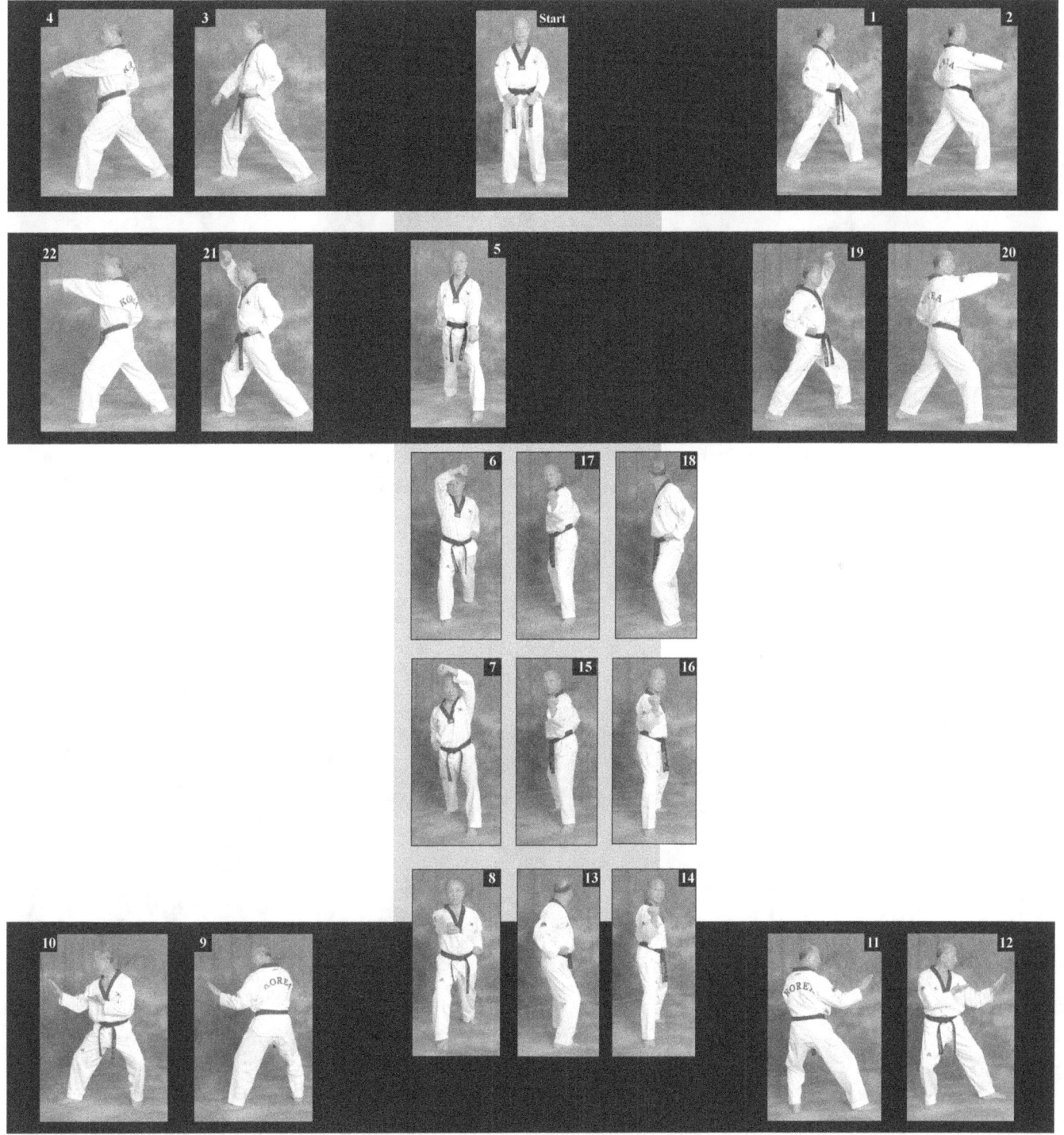

Palgwae Sam Jang

Begin from **ready stance** (junbiseogi), eyes looking forward and feet shoulder width apart.

1. Move the left foot to the left into **left front stance** (wen apkubi) and execute a **left low section block** (araemakki).

2. Step forward with the right foot into **right front stance** (oreun apkubi) and execute a **right reverse middle punch** (momtong bandaejireugi).

4. Step forward with the left foot into **left front stance** (wen apkubi) and execute a **left reverse middle punch** (momtong bandaejireugi).

3. Moving the right foot, turn 180° clockwise into **right front stance** (oreun apkubi) and execute a **right low section block** (arraemakki).

5. Moving the left foot, turn 90° into **left front stance** (wen apkubi) and execute a **low section block** (arraemakki).

6. Step forward with the right foot into **right front stance** (oreun apkubi) and execute a **right high section block** (olgulmakki).

7. Step forward with the left foot into **left front stance** (wen apkubi) and execute a **left high section block** (olgulmakki).

8. Step forward with the right foot into **right front stance** (oreun apkubi) and execute a **right reverse high section punch** (olgul bandaejireugi). **Kihap**.

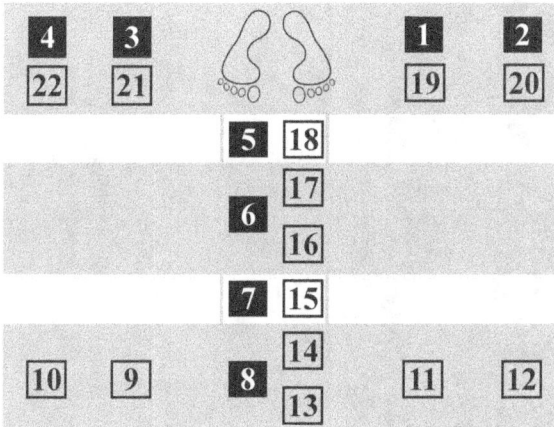

240   Palgwae Poomsae

10. Step forward with the right foot into **left back stance** (wen dwitkubi) and execute a **double knifehand middle section block** (sonnal momtong makki).

9. Moving the left foot, turn the body 270° counterclockwise into **right back stance** (oreun dwitkubi) and execute a **double knifehand middle section block** (sonnal momtong makki).

11. Moving the right foot, turn 180° clockwise into **left back stance** (wen dwitkubi) and execute a **double knifehand middle section block** (sonnal momtong makki).

12. Step forward with the left foot into **right back stance** (oreun dwitkubi) and execute a **double knifehand middle section block** (sonnal momtong makki).

Poomsae Palgwae Sam Jang (3) 241

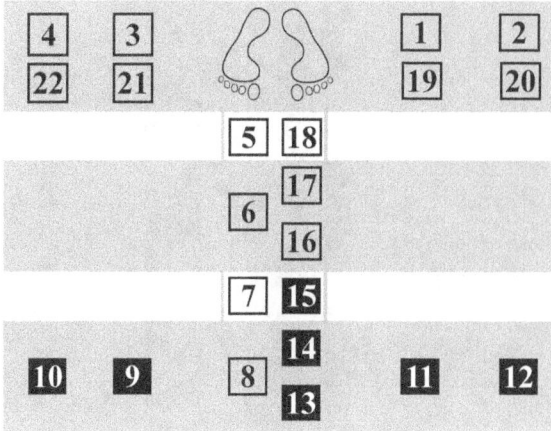

13. Moving the left foot, turn 90° counterclockwise into **right back stance** (oreun dwitkubi) and execute a **left outward middle section lateral block** (momtong yopmakki).

14. Turn the body 180° clockwise into **left back stance** (wen dwitkubi) and execute a **right outward middle section lateral block** (momtong yopmakki).

15. Moving the right foot, step backwards into **right back stance** (oreun dwitkubi) and execute a **left inward middle block** (momtong anmakki).

17. Moving the right foot, step backwards into **right back stance** (oreun dwitkubi) and execute a **left inward middle block** (momtong anmakki).

18. Turn the body 180° clockwise into **left back stance** (wen dwitkubi) and execute a **right outward middle section lateral block** (momtong yopmakki).

16. Moving the left foot, step backwards into **left back stance** (wen dwitkubi) and execute a **right inward middle block** (momtong anmakki).

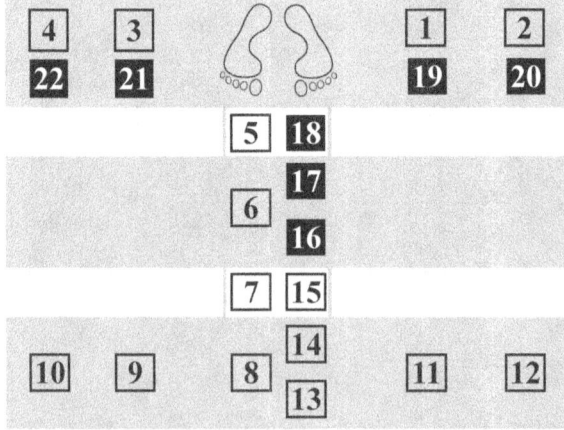

Poomsae Palgwae Sam Jang (3) 243

19. Moving the left foot, turn 270° counterclockwise into **left front stance** (wen apkubi) and execute a **left high section block** (olgulmakki).

20. Step forward with the right foot into **right front stance** (oreun apkubi) and execute a **right high section reverse punch** (olgul bandaejireugi).

Moving the left foot, return to ready stance.

22. Step forward with the left foot into **left front stance** (wen apkubi) and execute a **left high section reverse punch** (olgul bandaejireugi).

21. Moving the right foot, turn 180° clockwise to the rear into **right front stance** (oreun apkubi) and execute a **right high section block** (olgulmakki).

New Movements in Palgwae Sam Jang

Inward Middle Block
Momtong Anmakki
The palm of the front fist faces the body at shoulder height. It is aligned with the body's vertical centerline. The rear hand rests on the side at belt level.

High Section Reverse Punch
Olgul Bandaejireugi
The high section punch is executed like the middle section punch except the target is just below the nose.

PALGWAE
SAH JANG

Meaning of Palgwae Sah Jang

The symbol of Palgwae Sah Jang is Jin meaning thunder, undeniable power and dignity. This form consists of powerful strikes and blocks that should be performed in a seamlessly successive manner just as thunder follows lightning. Through this form, the practitioner must develop a calm mind that can stand strong in the face of danger. This is for the 5th Gup. There are 24 movements.

Poomsae Line of Palgwae Sah Jang

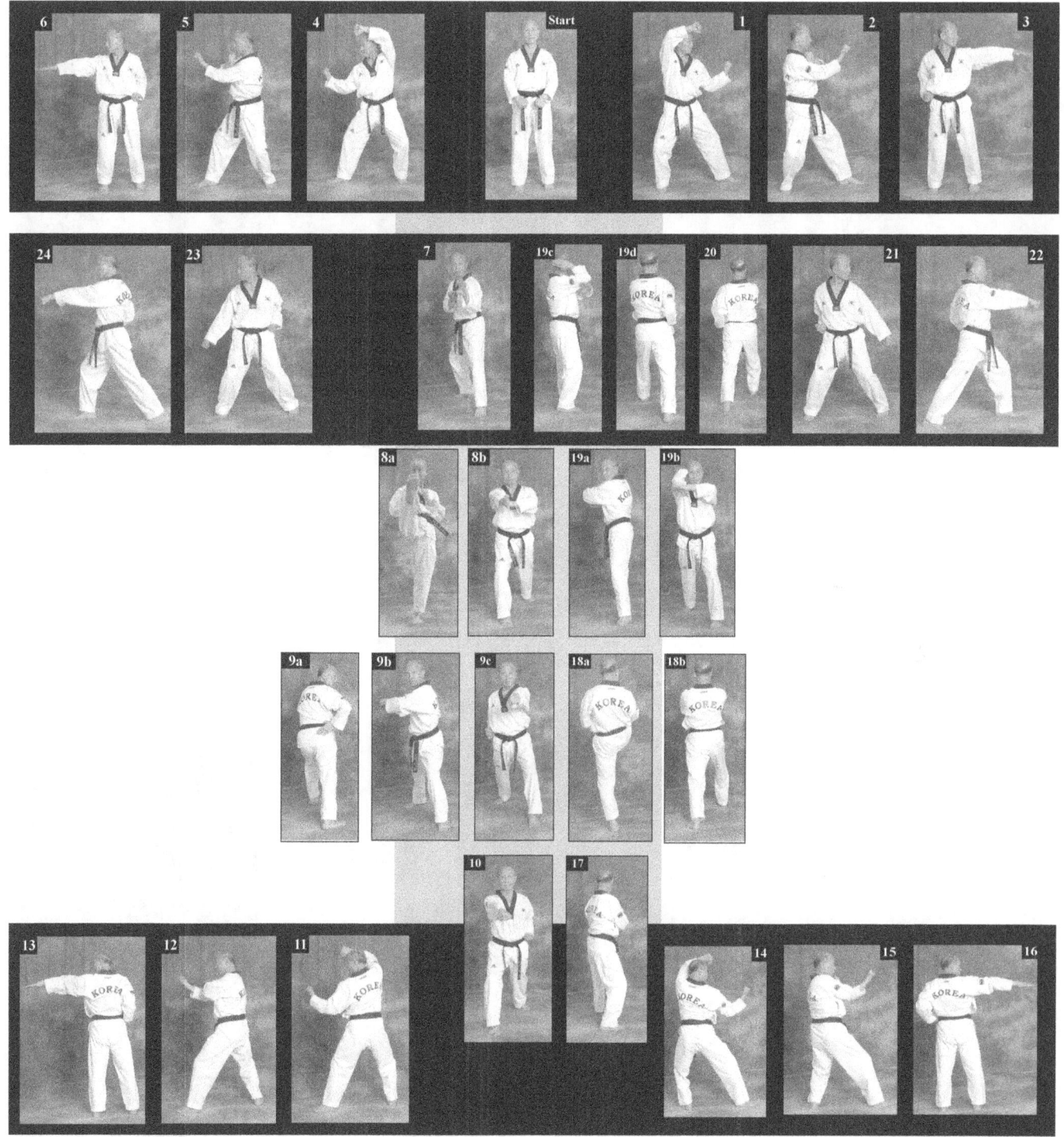

Palgwae Sah Jang

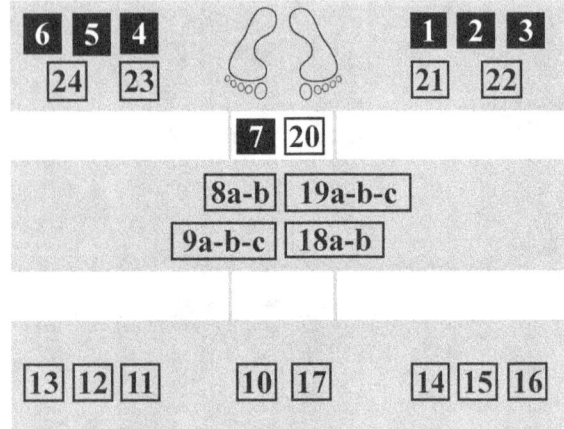

Begin from **ready stance** (junbiseogi), eyes looking forward and feet shoulder width apart.

1. Move the left foot to the left into **right back stance** (oreun dwitkubi) and execute a **diamond middle section block** (keumgang momtong makki).

7. Slide the right foot to the left foot then move the left foot into **right back stance** (oreun dwitkubi) and execute a **double knifehand block** (sonnalmaki).

6. Pull the right foot toward the left foot making **parallel stance** (naranhiseogi) and execute a **right palm down outward knifehand strike** (sonnal bakkatchigi).

Poomsae Palgwae Sah Jang (4) 249

2. With the feet fixed, pivot slightly to the front and execute a **pulling high section uppercut** (dangkyo teokjireugi).

3. Pull the left foot toward the right foot making **parallel stance** (naranhiseogi) and execute a **left palm down outward knifehand strike** (sonnal bakkatchigi).

5. With the feet fixed, pivot slightly to the front and execute a **pulling high section uppercut** (dangkyo teokjireugi).

4. Slide the left foot to the right foot then move the right foot into **left back stance** (wen dwitkubi) and execute a **diamond middle section block** (keumgang momtong makki).

250   Palgwae Poomsae

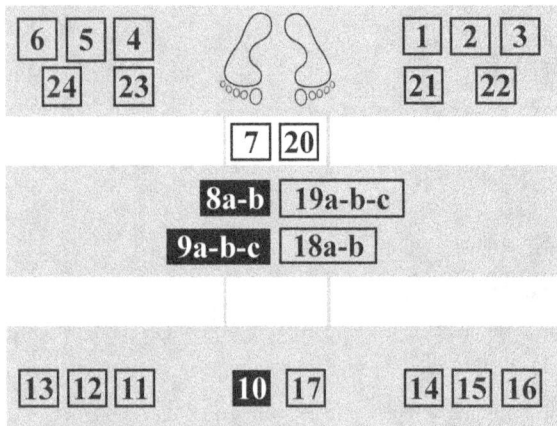

8a. With the left foot fixed, execute a **right front kick** (oreunbal apchagi).

8b. Set the right foot down in **right front stance** (oreun apkubi), execute a **right vertical fingertip thrust** (pyonsonkkuet sewotzireugi).

9a. Pivot counterclockwise to the rear while bringing the right hand to the belt, palm facing outward.

9b. Turn and step 180° counterclockwise into **left front stance** (wen apkubi).

9c. In **left front stance** (wen apkubi) and execute a left **outward hammerfist strike** (mejumeok bakkatchigi).

10. Stepping forward with the right foot into **right front stance** (oreun apkubi), execute a **right reverse middle punch** (momtong bandaejireugi). **Kihap**.

13. Pull the left foot toward the right foot making **parallel stance** (naranhiseogi) and execute a **left palm down outward knifehand strike** (sonnal bakkatchigi).

12. With the feet fixed, pivot slightly to the front and execute a **pulling high section uppercut** (dangkyo teokjireugi).

11. Turn 270° counterclockwise into **right back stance** (oreun dwitkubi) and execute a **diamond middle section block** (keumgang momtong makki).

14. Slide the left foot to the right foot then slide the right foot into **left back stance** (wen dwitkubi) and execute a **diamond middle section block** (keumgang momtong makki).

15. With the feet fixed, pivot slightly to the front and execute a **pulling high section uppercut** (dangkyo teokjireugi).

16. Pull the right foot toward the left foot making **parallel stance** (naranhiseogi) and execute a **right palm down outward knifehand strike** (sonnal bakkatchigi).

18b. Set the right foot down in **right front stance** (oreun apkubi), execute a **right vertical fingertip thrust** (pyonsonkkuet sewotzireugi).

18a. With the left foot fixed, execute a **right front kick** (oreunbal apchagi).

17. Slide the right foot to the left foot then move the left foot forward into **right back stance** (oreun dwitkubi) and execute a **double knifehand block** (sonnal momtongmakki).

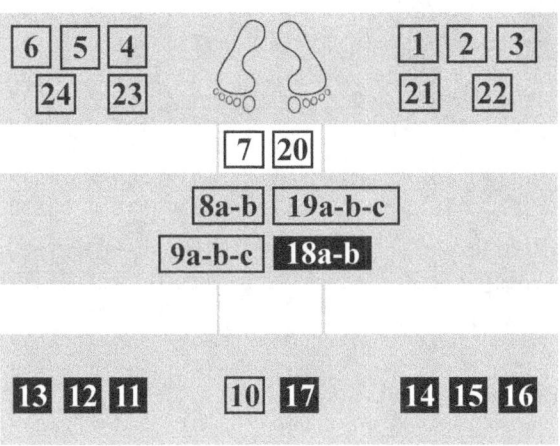

254 Palgwae Poomsae

20. Moving the right foot, step forward into **right front stance** (oreun apkubi) and execute a **right middle section reverse punch** (momtong bandaejireugi). **Kihap**.

19d. Step into **left front stance** (wen apkubi) and execute a **left outward hammerfist strike** (mejumeok bakkatchigi).

19a. Pivot counterclockwise to the rear while twisting the right arm clockwise.

19b. Complete your pivot, shifting your weight into **left front stance** (wen apkubi) and bringing your left hand to support your right elbow.

19c. Step forward with the right foot, keeping your arms in place.

Poomsae Palgwae Sah Jang (4)

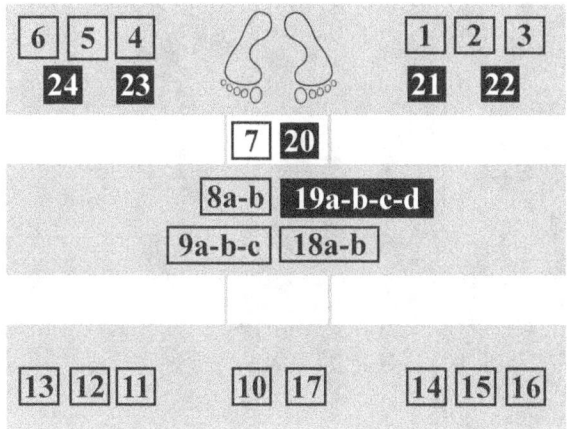

21. Turn 270° counter-clockwise into **horseriding stance** (juchumseogi) and execute a **left low section side block** (arae yopmakki).

22. Pivot the feet and shift the weight into **left front stance** (wen apkubi) and execute **a right straight middle punch** (momtong barojireugi).

Moving the left foot, return to ready stance.

24. Pivot the feet and shift the weight into **right front stance** (oreun apkubi) and execute a **left straight middle punch** (momtong barojireugi).

23. Slide the left foot to ready stance then move the right foot into **horseriding stance** (juchumseogi) and execute a **right low section side block** (arae yopmakki).

New Movements in Palgwae Sah Jang

Horseriding Stance
Juchumseogi
The feet are approximately two feet apart with the soles parallel to each other. Bend the knees to about 120° and pull them inward. Spread the weight evenly between both feet and focus it inward, tensing the muscles of the abdomen.

Low Section Side Block
Arae Yopmakki
The blocking fist is aligned with the side of the thigh. The eyes look in the blocking direction. The blocking motion is the same as in low block except the movement finishes on the side of the body.

Parallel Stance
Naranhiseogi
The feet are one foot apart and parallel to each other. The legs are straight and the weight is evenly distributed.

Diamond Middle Section Block
Keumgang Momtong Makki
This block is made up of a high section block and a middle section block executed simultaneously.

Reverse Middle Punch
Momtong Barojireugi
Performed in the same way as a middle punch except the punch is executed with the rear hand. The target is the solar plexus.

Vertical Fingertip Thrust
Pyonsonkkeut Sewotzireugi
The supporting hand performs a pressing block, with the hand open and the palm facing downward. The striking hand rests on the knuckles of the blocking hand. The target for the fingertip strike is the solar plexus. Keep the wrist and fingers of the striking hand straight and fold the thumb down onto the palm.

Pulling High Section Uppercut
Dangkyo Teokjireugi
Pulling the opponent's jaw with one hand, the other hand delivers an uppercut to the jaw. When completed the punching fist is at jaw height and the pulling fist is laid against the opposite shoulder. The pulling and punching motions should be simultaneous.

Outward Knifehand Strike
Sonnal Bakkatchigi
The palm faces downward and the knifehand is formed with a slightly curved palm. Hold the hand at shoulder level with the arm parallel to the floor.

Outward Hammerfist Strike
Mejumeok Bakkatchigi
The soft part of the clenched fist strikes the target in an outward motion. The targets are the rib cage or solar plexus. The rear fist rests on the side at belt level.

PALGWAE
OH JANG

SOHN

Meaning of Palgwae Oh Jang

The symbol of Palgwae Oh Jang is Sohn meaning wind. As the wind is gentle when it is a breeze and devastating when it becomes a hurricane, human power can also be used either way. Palgwae Oh Jang is designed to develop the kinetic force of the body that can penetrate an object in a single blow. Yet, this form is also good for developing the humbleness that encompasses the violent nature of the physical prowess. This form is for the 4th Gup. There are 35 movements.

Poomsae Line of Palgwae Oh Jang

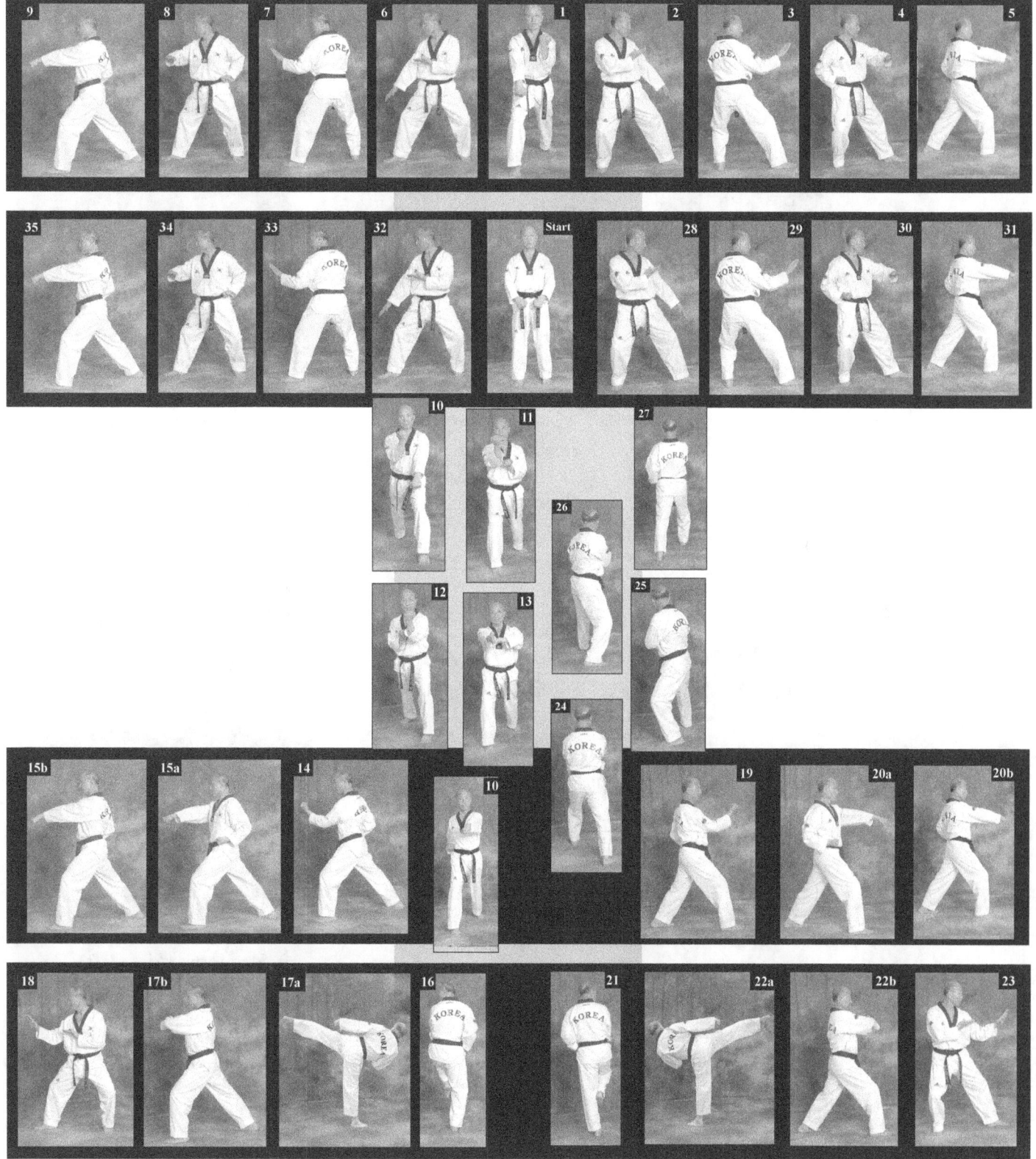

Palgwae Oh Jang

Begin from **ready stance** (junbiseogi), eyes looking forward and feet shoulder width apart.

1. Move the left foot one step backward into **right front stance** (oreun apkubi) and execute a **scissors block** (kawimakki).

2. Moving the left foot, turn 90° into **right back stance** (oreun dwitkubi) and execute a **double knifehand low section block** (sonnal araemakki).

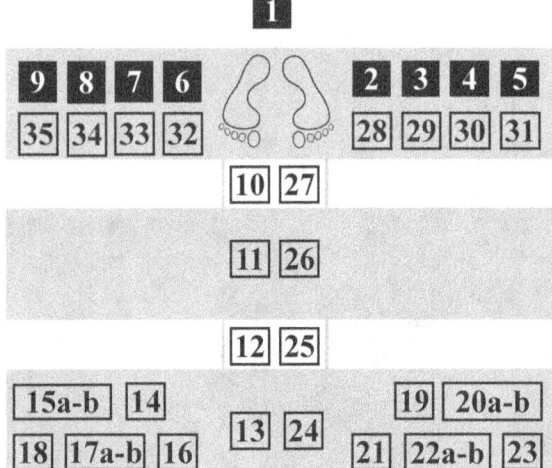

9. Step forward into **left front stance** (wen apkubi) and execute a **left reverse middle punch** (momtong bandaejireugi).

Poomsae Palgwae Oh Jang (5)

3. Step forward into **left back stance** (wen dwitkubi) and execute a **double knifehand block** (sonnal momtongmakki).

4. Slide the right foot back one step into **right back stance** (oreun dwitkubi) and execute a **palm heel middle section pressing block** (batangson momtong nullomakki).

5. Step forward into **right front stance** (oreun apkubi) and execute a **right reverse middle punch** (momtong bandaejireugi).

8. Slide the left foot back one step into **left back stance** (wen dwitkubi) and execute a **palm heel middle section pressing block** (batangson momtong nullomakki).

7. Step forward into **right back stance** (oreun dwitkubi) and execute a **double knifehand block** (sonnal momtongmakki).

6. Moving the right foot, turn 180° into **left back stance** (wen dwitkubi) and execute a **double knifehand low section block** (sonnal araemakki).

264   **Palgwae Poomsae**

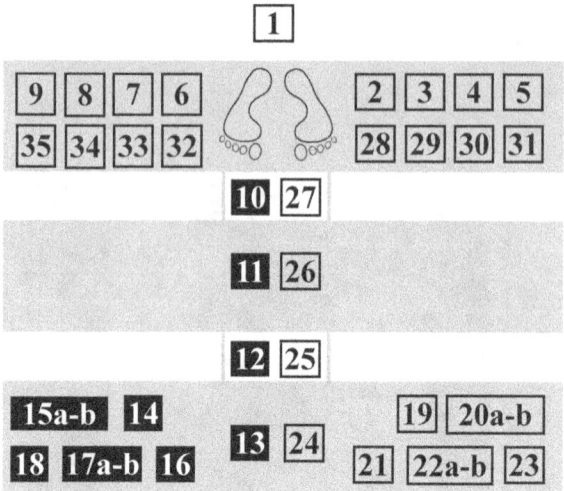

10. Moving the left foot, turn 90° into **left front stance** (wen apkubi) and execute a **scissors block** (kawimakki).

11. Step forward into **right front stance** (oreun apkubi) and execute a **right augmented middle block** (kodureo momtongmakki).

12. Step forward into **left front stance** (wen apkubi) and execute a **left augmented middle block** (kodureo momtongmakki).

13. Step forward into **right front stance** (oreun apkubi) and execute a **vertical fingertip thrust** (pyonsonkkeut sewotzireugi).

15a-b. With the feet fixed, execute a **double punch** (dubeonjireugi), punching first with the right hand and then with the left.

14. Moving the left foot, turn 270° counterclockwise into **left front stance** (wen apkubi) and execute a **left outward middle block** (momtong bakkatmakki).

18. Step forward into **left back stance** (wen dwitkubi) and execute a **double knifehand block** (sonnal momtongmakki).

17b. Place the left foot down in **left front stance** (wen abkubi) and execute a **right elbow target strike** (palkup pyojeokchigi).

17a. Simultaneously execute a **left side kick** (yopchagi) and a **left punch** (jireugi).

16. With the right foot fixed, raise the left foot to the right knee making **crane stance** (hakdariseogi).

Palgwae Poomsae

19. Moving the right foot, turn 180° clockwise into **right front stance** (oreun apkubi) and execute a **right outward middle block** (momtong bakkatmakki).

20a-b. With the feet fixed, execute a **double punch** (dubeonjireugi), punching first with the left hand and then with the right.

21. With the left foot fixed, raise the right foot to the left knee making **crane stance** (hakdariseogi).

22a. Simultaneously execute a **right side kick** (yopchagi) and a **right punch** (jireugi).

22b. Place the right foot down in **right front stance** (oreun abkubi) and execute a **left elbow target strike** (palkup pyojeokchigi).

23. Step forward into **right back stance** (oreun dwitkubi) and execute a **double knifehand block** (sonnal momtongmakki).

Poomsae Palgwae Oh Jang (5)   267

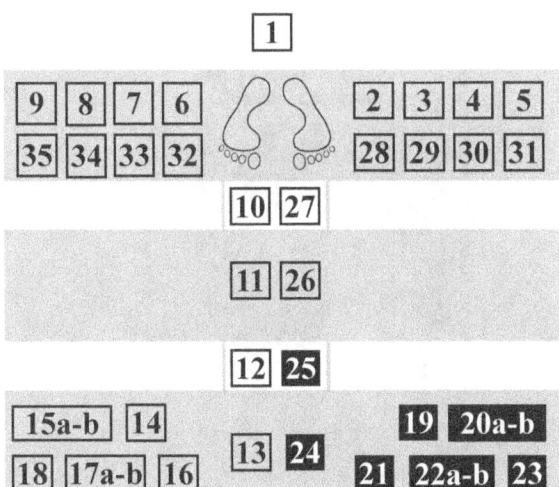

25. Step forward into **left back stance** (wen dwitkubi) and execute a **right augmented low section block** (kodureo araemakki).

24. Moving the left foot, turn 90° counterclockwise into **left front stance** (wen apkubi) and execute a **scissors block** (kawimakki).

268 Palgwae Poomsae

27. Step forward into **right front stance** (oreun apkubi) and execute a **right reverse middle punch** (momtong bandaejireugi). **Kihap**.

26. Step forward into **right back stance** (oreun dwitkubi) and execute a **left augmented low section block** (kodureo araemakki).

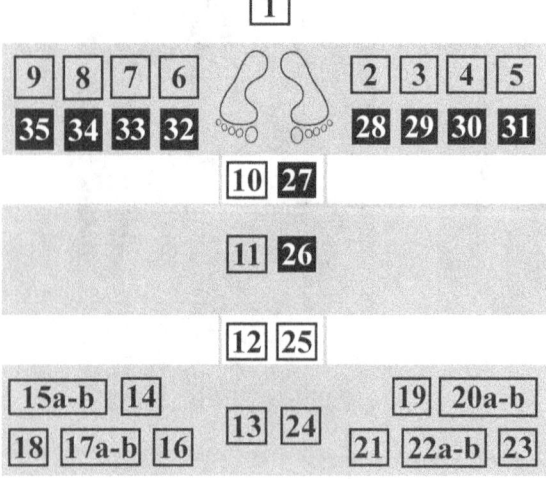

Moving the left foot, return to ready stance by turning counterclockwise.

Poomsae Palgwae Oh Jang (5)

28. Moving the left foot, turn 270° into **right back stance** (oreun dwitkubi) and execute a **double knifehand low section block** (sonnal araemakki).

29. Step forward into **left back stance** (wen dwitkubi) and execute a **double knifehand block** (sonnal momtongmakki).

30. Slide the right foot back one step into **right back stance** (oreun dwitkubi) and execute a **palm heel middle section pressing block** (batangson momtong nullomakki).

31. Step forward into **right front stance** (oreun apkubi) and execute a **right reverse middle punch** (momtong bandaejireugi).

35. Step forward into **left front stance** (wen apkubi) and execute a **left reverse middle punch** (momtong bandaejireugi).

34. Slide the left foot back one step into **left back stance** (wen dwitkubi) and execute a **palm heel middle section pressing block** (batangson momtong nullomakki).

33. Step forward into **right back stance** (oreun dwitkubi) and execute a **double knifehand block** (sonnal momtongmakki).

32. Moving the right foot, turn 180° into **left back stance** (wen dwitkubi) and execute a **double knifehand low section block** (sonnal araemakki).

New Movements in Palgwae Oh Jang

Crane Stance
Hakdariseogi
First bend the knee of the standing leg as in horseriding stance. Place the arch of the other foot against the knee of the standing leg. Keep the legs close together and the raised knee pointed forward.

Scissors Block
Kawimakki
One hand makes low block and the other makes outward middle block. While making scissors block, the arms should cross in front of the chest and the hands should arrive at their stopping points simultaneously.

Palm Heel Middle Section Pressing Block
Batangson Momtong Nullomakki
The palm of the front hand presses downward and stops at the height of the solar plexus. The rear first rests on the side at belt level.

Double Punch
Dubeonjireugi
The double punch is performed by executing two punches in rapid succession, first punching with the front hand and then with the rear hand. The target for both punches is the solar plexus.

Elbow Target Strike
Palkup Pyojeokchigi
To execute the elbow target strike first stretch the target hand out, arm straight and hand open. Strike the elbow into the target hand, rather than slapping the target hand against the elbow. Keep the target hand open and do not place the thumb on the elbow.

Side Kick
Yopchagi
Begin the side kick by lifting the kicking leg, bending the knee then turning to the side. Once the body is facing sideways, pivot the supporting foot (on the ball of the foot) fully away from the direction of the target and extend the leg to kick. Strike the target with the foot blade and heel. The head and upper body should be raised so the body forms a Y shape at the pinnacle of the kick. The eyes should be on the target, which is the face or solar plexus.

PALGWAE
YUK JANG

Meaning of Palgwae Yuk Jang

The symbol of Palgwae Yuk Jang is Gam meaning water - the sustenance of life. Water symbolizes a constant flow and composure. There is nothing that water cannot overcome. When facing insurmountable obstacles, it waits patiently. No matter how the circumstances change, it never loses its intrinsic nature. Through practicing Palgwae Yuk Jang, the practitioner can develop self-confidence and self-control. This form is for the 3rd Gup. There are 19 movements.

Poomsae Line of Palgwae Yuk Jang

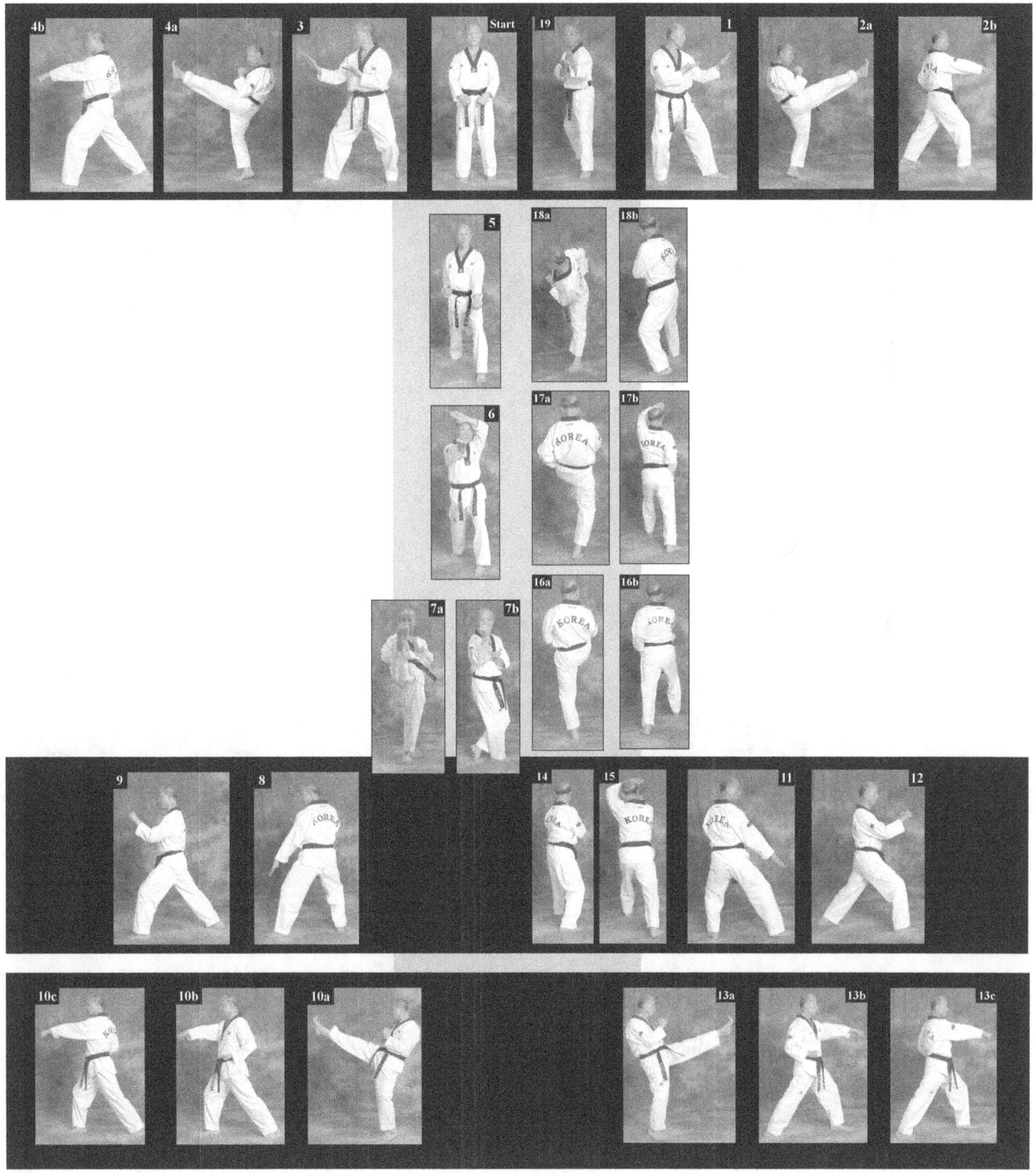

Palgwae Yuk Jang

Begin from **ready stance** (junbiseogi), eyes looking forward and feet shoulder width apart.

1. Move the left foot to the left into **right back stance** (oreun dwitkubi) and execute a **double knifehand block** (sonnal momtongmakki).

2a. With the left foot fixed, execute a **right front kick** (oreunbal apchagi).

2b. Set the right foot down in **right front stance** (oreun apkubi) and execute a **right reverse middle punch** (momtong bandaejireugi).

4b. Set the left foot down in **left front stance** (wen apkubi) and execute a **left reverse middle punch** (momtong bandaejireugi).

4a. With the right foot fixed, execute a **left front kick** (wenbal apchagi).

3. Moving the right foot, turn 180° clockwise into **left back stance** (wen dwitkubi) and execute a **double knifehand block** (sonnal momtongmakki).

Poomsae Palgwae Yuk Jang (6)

5. Moving the left foot, turn 90° into **left front stance** (wen apkubi) and execute a **left low section block** (arraemakki).

6. With feet fixed, execute a **swallow form knifehand strike** (jebipoom mokchigi).

7a. With the left foot fixed, execute a **right front kick** (oreunbal apchagi).

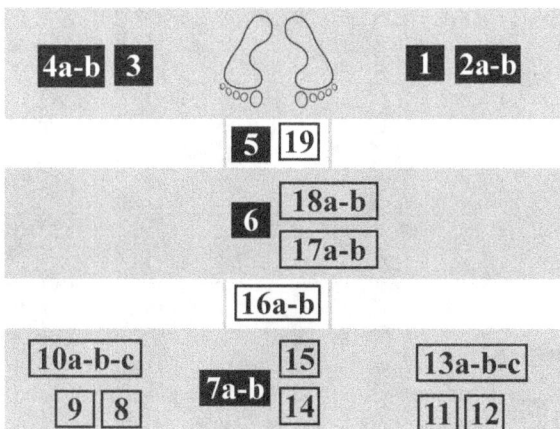

7b. Without setting the right foot down, jump forward into **rear cross stance** (dwi koaseogi) and execute a **right augmented high section backfist** (kodureo deungjumeok olgulchigi). **Kihap**.

278 Palgwae Poomsae

10b-c. Set the right foot down in **right front stance** (oreun apkubi) and execute a **double punch** (dubeonjireugi), punching first with the right hand and then with the left hand.

10a. With the right foot fixed, execute a **right front kick** (oreunbal apchagi).

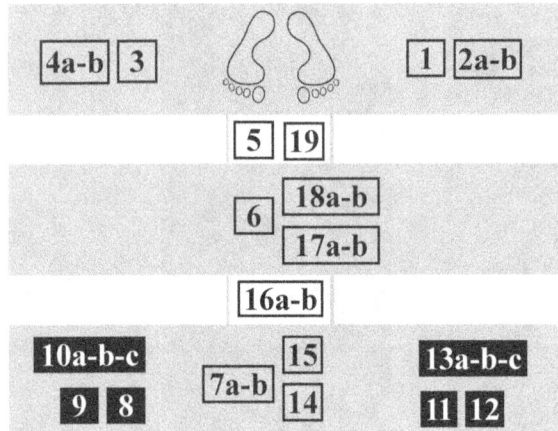

11. Moving the right foot, turn 180° clockwise into **left back stance** (wen dwitkubi) and execute a **double knifehand low section block** (sonnal arraemakki).

12. Slide the right foot forward into **right front stance** (oreun apkubi) and execute a **middle section opening block** (momtong hechomakki).

Poomsae Palgwae Yuk Jang (6)

9. Slide the left foot forward into **left front stance** (wen apkubi) and execute a **middle section opening block** (momtong hechomakki).

8. Moving the left foot, turn 270° counterclockwise into **right back stance** (oreun dwitkubi) and execute a **double knifehand low section block** (sonnal arraemakki).

13a. With the right foot fixed, execute a **left front kick** (wenbal apchagi).

13b-c. Set the left foot down in **left front stance** (wen apkubi) and execute a **double punch** (dubeonjireugi), punching first with the left hand and then with the right hand.

280　Palgwae Poomsae

16a. Without moving the left foot, execute a **right front kick** (oreunbal apchagi).

15. Slide the left foot forward into **left front stance** (wen abkubi) and execute a **swallow form palm strike to chin** (jebipoom teokchigi).

14. Moving the left foot, turn 90° counterclockwise into **right back stance** (oreun dwitkubi) and execute a **double knifehand block** (sonnal momtongmakki).

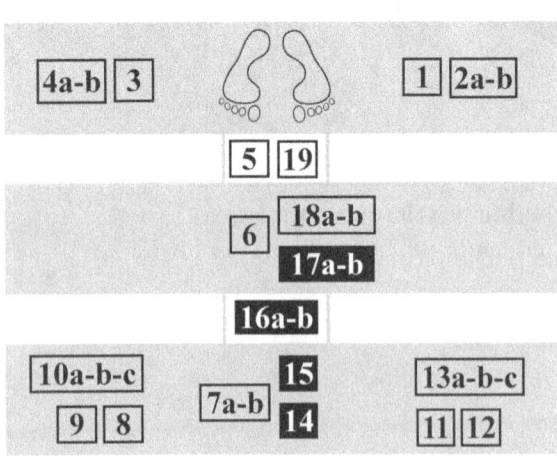

17b. Step down into **left front stance** (wen apkubi) and execute a **right high section block** (olgulmakki).

17a. Without moving the right foot, execute a **left front kick** (wenbal apchagi).

16b. Step down into **right front stance** (oreun apkubi) and execute a **right high section backfist strike** (deungjumeok olgulchigi). **Kihap**.

19. Pivot 180° counterclockwise into **right back stance** (oreun dwitkubi) and execute a **double knifehand block** (sonnal momtongmakki).

Moving the right foot, return to ready stance.

18b. Step down into **left back stance** (wen dwitkubi) and execute a **double knifehand block** (sonnal momtongmakki).

18a. Pivoting on the left foot, execute a **right side kick** (yopchagi).

New Movements in Palgwae Yuk Jang

Middle Section Opening Block
Momtong Hechomakki
Middle section opening block is two simultaneous outward middle blocks. The wrists should positioned no wider than the shoulders.

Swallow Form Knifehand Strike
Jebipoom Mokchigi
The front hand is held just above the forehead in a high section knifehand block. The rear hand executes a knifehand strike to the neck. Keep both wrists straight and fully extend the striking arm, twisting the upper body and hips into the strike.

Swallow Form Palm Strike to Chin
Jebipoom Teokchigi
The front hand is held just above the forehead in a high section knifehand block. The rear hand executes a palm strike to the chin. Fully extend the striking arm, twisting the upper body and hips into the strike.

PALGWAE

CHIL JANG

Meaning of Palgwae Chil Jang

The symbol of Palgwae Chil Jang is Gahn meaning mountain. A mountain is symbolic of majestic strength and immovable spirit. Through Palgwae Chil Jang, a student can improve stability of the mind and steadiness in movement: being dynamic in motion and still at rest. Increased inner muscular control builds inner confidence. Less is more in expressing controlled physical forces. This form is for the 2nd Gup. There are 23 movements.

Poomsae Line of Palgwae Chil Jang

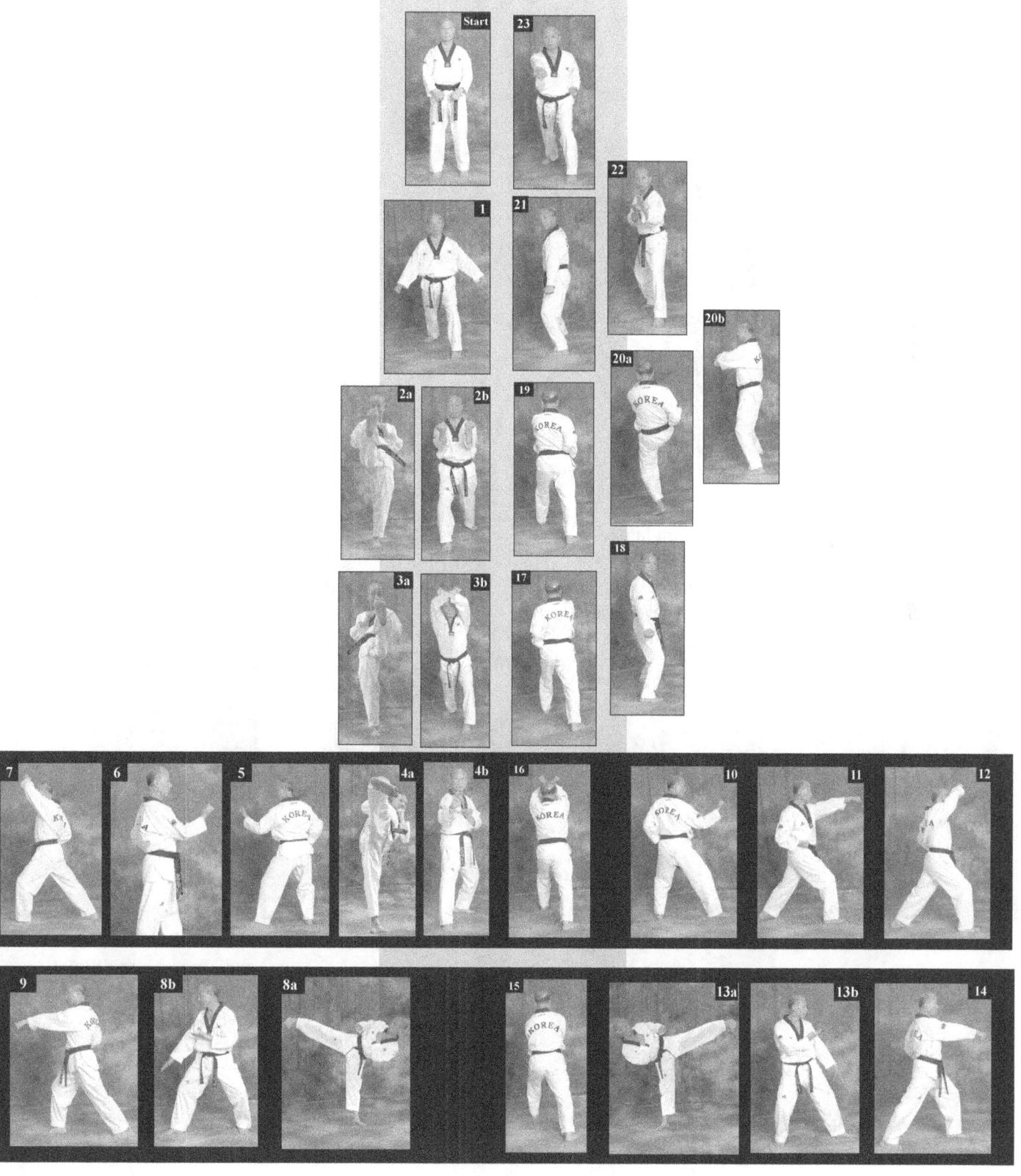

Palgwae Chil Jang

Begin from **ready stance** (junbiseogi), eyes looking forward and feet shoulder width apart.

1. Moving the left foot step forward into **left front stance** (wen apkubi) and execute a **low section opening block** (arae hechomakki).

2a. With the left foot fixed, execute a **right front kick** (oreunbal apchagi).

2b. Set the right foot down in **right front stance** (oreun apkubi) and execute a **middle section opening block** (momtong hechomakki).

Poomsae Palgwae Chil Jang (7)

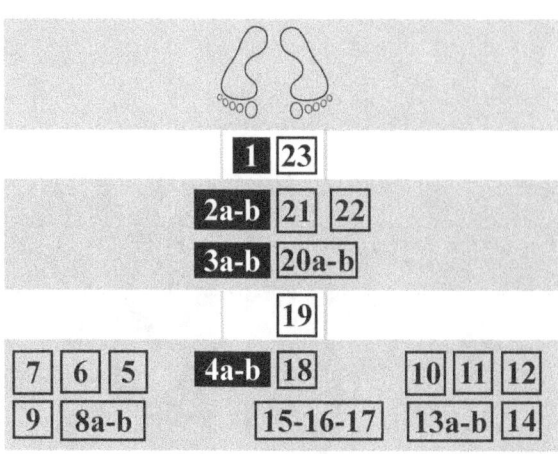

3a. With the right foot fixed, execute a **left front kick** (wenbal apchagi).

3b. Set the left foot down in **left front stance** (wen apkubi) and execute a **high section cross block** (otkoreo olgulmakki).

4a. With the left foot fixed, execute a **right side kick** (oreunbal yopchagi).

4b. Set the right foot down in **left back stance** (wen dwitkubi) and execute a **double knifehand block** (sonnal momtongmakki).

290 Palgwae Poomsae

9. Slide the right foot forward into **right front stance** (oreun apkubi) and execute a **left straight punch** (momtong barojireugi).

8b. Step down into **left back stance** (wen dwitkubi) and execute a **double knifehand low section block** (sonnal arraemakki).

8a. With the left foot fixed, execute a **right side kick** (oreunbal yopchagi).

7. Without moving the feet, execute a **left high section block** (olgulmakki).

10. Moving the right foot, turn 180° clockwise into **left back stance** (wen dwitkubi) and execute an **outward middle block** (momtong bakkatmakki).

11. Slide the right foot forward into **right front stance** (oreun apkubi) and execute a **left high section straight punch** (olgul barojireugi).

12. Without moving the feet, execute a **right high section block** (olgulmakki).

Poomsae Palgwae Chil Jang (7)   291

6. Slide the left foot forward into **left front stance** (wen apkubi) and execute **a right high section straight punch** (olgul barojireugi).

5. Moving the left foot, turn 270° counterclockwise into **right back stance** (oreun dwitkubi) and execute an **outward middle block** (momtong bakkatmakki).

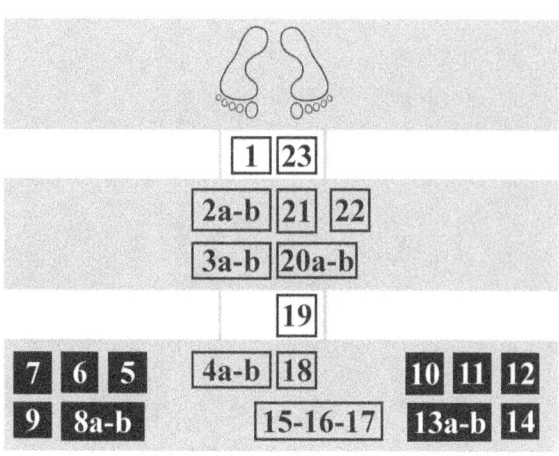

13a. With the right foot fixed, execute a **left side kick** (wenbal yopchagi).

13b. Step down into **right back stance** (oreun dwitkubi) and execute a **double knifehand low section block** (sonnal arraemakki).

14. Slide the left foot forward into **left front stance** (wen apkubi) and execute a **right straight punch** (momtong barojireugi).

292   Palgwae Poomsae

17. Without moving the feet, grab, twist and pull the blocking hands then execute a **high section straight punch** (olgul barojireugi).

16. Without moving the feet, execute a **high section cross block** (otkoreo oluglmakki).

15. Moving the left foot, turn 90° counterclockwise into **left front stance** (wen apkubi) and execute a **low section cross block** (otkoreo araemakki).

Poomsae Palgwae Chil Jang (7)   293

20a. Pivoting on the left foot, execute a **right target kick** (oreun pyojeokchagi).

19. Pivot 180° counterclockwise and slide the left foot forward into **left front stance** (wen apkubi), executing an **outward knifehand strike** (sonnal bakkatchigi).

18. Pivot 180° clockwise and slide forward into **horseriding stance** (juchumseogi), executing a **right low section side block** (arae yopmakki).

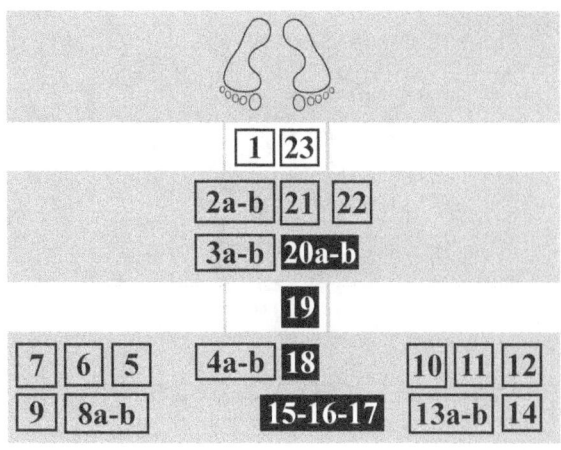

Moving the left foot, return to ready stance by stepping forward.

23. Slide the left foot forward into **left front stance** (wen apkubi) and execute a **right straight middle punch** (momtong barojireugi). **Kihap**.

22. Shift the body weight to the rear into **right back stance** (oreun dwitkubi) and execute a **double knifehand middle block** (sonnal momtongmakki).

21. Slide back a half step in horseriding stance and execute a **single mountain block** (waesanteulmakki).

20b. Set the right foot down in **horseriding stance** (juchumseogi) and execute a **right elbow target strike** (oreun palkup pyojeokchigi).

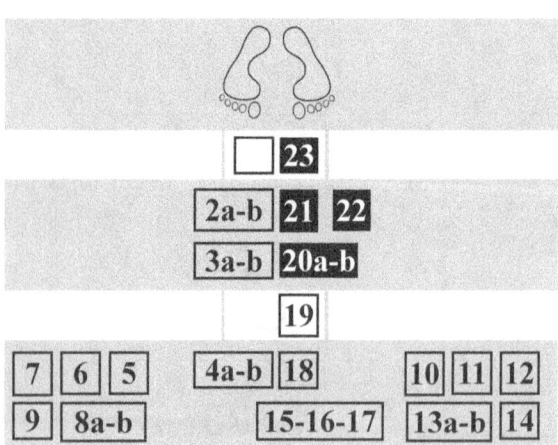

New Movements in Palgwae Chil Jang

Low Section Opening Block
Arae Hechomakki
When making low section opening block, use a slow controlled movement, exhaling forcefully for the duration of the execution. Look straight ahead throughout the movement. When the block is completed, each fist is held about 2 fists' distance from the thigh.

Low Section Cross Block
Otkoreo Arraemakki
The wrists are crossed and the palms face outward. When executing low section cross block, both fists are raised to the side of the rear foot and the block is delivered from the centerline of the body. The arm on the same side as the front leg is always on the bottom.

High Section Cross Block
Otkoreo Olgulmakki
The wrists are crossed and the palms face downward. When executing high section cross block, both fists are drawn to the rear side and the block is delivered from the centerline of the body. The arm on the same side as the front leg is always on the bottom.

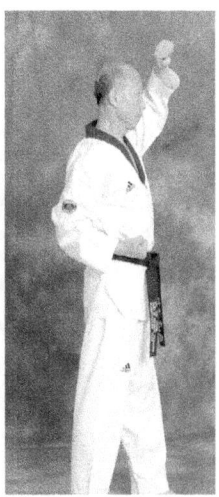

Single Mountain Block
Wesanteul Makki
The fist of the arm blocking the lower part of the body is held two fists' width from the thigh and the fist of the arm blocking the upper part of the body is aligned with the temple.

Target Kick
Pyojeokchagi

The instep of the foot strikes the fixed target of the open hand. Bend the kicking knee slightly at the moment of impact to adjust to the placement of the target hand.

PALGWAE
PAL JANG

Meaning of Palgwae Pal Jang

The symbol of Palgwae Pal Jang is Kohn meaning earth, where all things originate from and return to. Palgwae Pal Jang is the last form to be mastered before black belt. It means that the student should prepare for a new beginning: an end of a circle is the beginning of another. It is required, therefore, to perfect Palgwae Il Jang through Palgwae Pal Jang to be eligible for 1st Dan black belt. This form is required for the 1st Gup. There are 35 movements.

Poomsae Line of Palgwae Pal Jang

Palgwae Pal Jang

Begin from **ready stance** (junbiseogi), eyes looking forward and feet shoulder width apart.

1. Moving the left foot, step to the left into **left front stance** (wen apkubi) and execute an **left low section block** (arraemakki).

2. Sliding the left foot back into **left stance** (wenseogi), execute a **left hammerfist strike** (mejumeok naeryochigi).

3. Stepping forward into **right front stance** (oreun apkubi), execute a **right reverse middle punch** (momtong bandaejireugi).

6. Stepping forward into **left front stance** (wen apkubi), execute a **left reverse middle punch** (momtong bandaejireugi).

5. Sliding the right foot back into **right stance** (oreunseogi), execute a **right hammerfist strike** (mejumeok naeryochigi).

4. Moving the right foot, turn 180° clockwise into **right front stance** (oreun apkubi) and execute an **right low section block** (arraemakki).

Poomsae Palgwae Pal Jang (8)

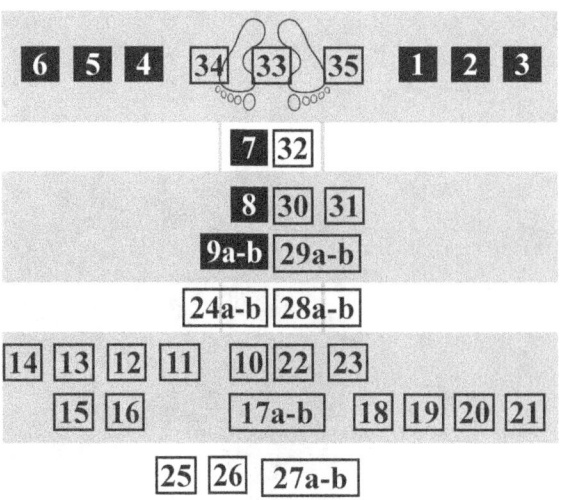

7. Moving the left foot, turn 90° counterclockwise into **right back stance** (oreun dwitkubi) and execute an **double knifehand middle block** (sonnal momtongmakki).

8. Step forward with the right foot into **right front stance** (oreun apkubi) and execute a **right vertical fingertip thrust** (pyonsonkkeut sewotzireugi).

9a. Push the right hand slightly forward and twist the body counterclockwise.

9b. Moving the left foot, turn 180° counterclockwise into **right back stance** (oreun dwitkubi) and execute a **left outward backfist strike** (deungjumeok bakkatchigi).

13. Slide the left foot slightly forward into **horseriding stance** (juchumseogi), executing a **left elbow strike** (palkup yopchigi).

14. Slide the left foot to the left into **left front stance** (wen apkubi) and execute a **left outward middle block** (momtong bakkatmakki).

15. Without moving the feet, execute a **right straight punch** (momtong barojireugi).

16. Turn the body clockwise and step the left foot into **horseriding stance** (juchumseogi), executing a **hinge block** (doltzeogi).

17a. Bring the left foot to right foot, making **close stance** (moaseogi).

17b. Slide the right foot forward into **left back stance** (wen dwitkubi) and execute a **right outward knifehand strike** (sonnal bakkatchigi).

12. Draw the left foot back slightly and bend the left arm to pull the left knifehand back to in front of the right shoulder.

11. Moving the left foot, turn 270° counterclockwise into **right back stance** (oreun dwitkubi) and execute a **left outward knifehand strike** (sonnal bakkatchigi).

10. Moving the right foot, step into **right front stance** (oreun apkubi) and execute a **right reverse high section punch** (olgul bandaejireugi). **Kihap**.

18. Draw the right foot back slightly and bend the right arm to pull the right knifehand back to in front of the left shoulder.

19. Slide the right foot slightly forward into **horseriding stance** (juchumseogi), executing a **right elbow strike** (palkup yopchigi).

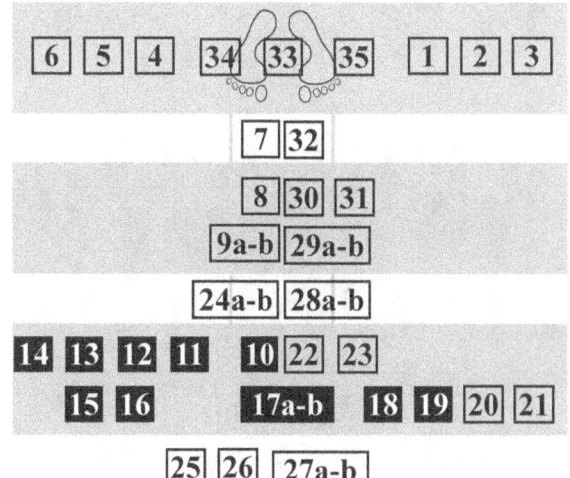

304 Palgwae Poomsae

20. Slide the right foot to the right into **right front stance** (oreun apkubi) and execute a **right outward middle block** (momtong bakkatmakki).

21. Without moving the feet, execute a **left straight straight punch** (momtong barojireugi).

22. Draw the right foot into **horseriding stance** (juchumseogi) and execute a **right hinge block** (doltzeogi).

23a. Bring the right foot to left foot, making **close stance** (moaseogi).

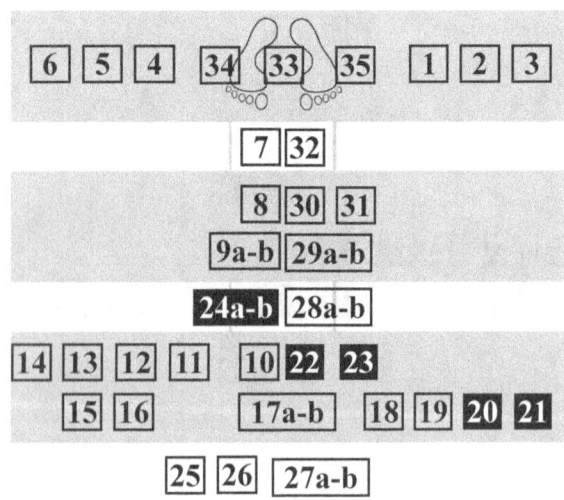

View from Front

Poomsae Palgwae Pal Jang (8) 305

24b. Step down into **left front stance** (wen apkubi) and execute a **right elbow target strike** (palkup pyojeokchigi).

24a. With the right foot fixed, execute a simultaneous **left punch** (jireugi) and **left side kick** (wenbal yopchagi).

23b. Raise the left foot into **right crane stance** (oreun hakdariseogi), continuing to execute a **right hinge block** (doltzeogi).

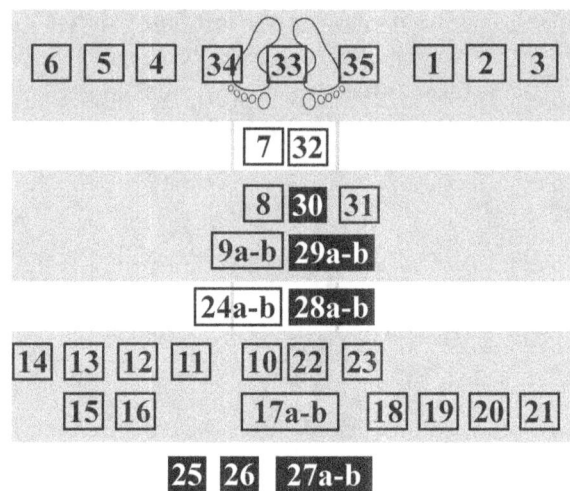

25. Moving the left foot, turn 180° clockwise into **horseriding stance** (juchumseogi) and execute an **left hinge block** (doltzeogi).

26. Raise the right foot into **left crane stance** (wen hakdariseogi), continuing to execute a **left hinge block** (doltzeogi).

27a. With the left foot fixed, execute a simultaneous **right punch** (jireugi) and **right side kick** (oreunbal yopchagi).

27b. Step down into **right front stance** (oreun apkubi) and execute a **left elbow target strike** (palkup pyojeokchigi).

29a. Stepping forward into **right front stance** (oreun apkubi), execute a **middle section opening block** (momtong hechomakki).

28b. With the feet fixed, execute a **double uppercut** (dujumeok jechojireugi).

28a. Moving the left foot, turn 180° counterclockwise into **left front stance** (wen apkubi) and execute a **middle section opening block** (momtong hechomakki).

308 Palgwae Poomsae

31. The left hand grabs and twists the opponent's wrist, pulling it to the waist. Moving the right foot, turn 180° clockwise into **horseriding stance** (juchumseogi), and execute a **rear elbow strike** (palkup dwitchigi).

30. Stepping forward into **right back stance** (oreun dwitkubi), execute a **left single knifehand middle section inward block** (hansonnal momtong anmakki).

29b. With the feet fixed, execute a **double uppercut** (dujumeok jechojireugi).

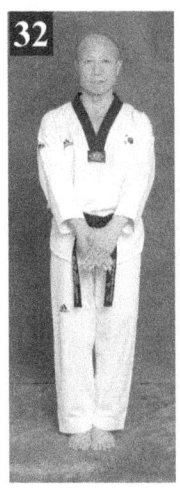

32. Slide the left foot to the right into **overlapping hands closed stance** (kyopson moaseogi).

33. Move the left foot to the left into **horseriding stance** (juchumseogi) and execute an **escape posture** (meongeppaegi).

34. Sliding the right foot slightly to the right, execute a **right rear punch** (dwitjireugi).

35. Sliding the left foot slightly to the left, execute a **left rear punch** (dwitjireugi). **Kihap**.

Moving the left foot, return to ready stance.

New Movements in Palgwae Pal Jang

Left or Right Stance
Wenseogi or Oreunseogi
From ready stance, turn the right foot outward 90° for right stance or the left foot outward 90° for left stance. This stance is used for hammerfist and backfist techniques in the Palgwae Poomsae.

Close Stance
Moaseogi
Stand upright with the feet touching and the knees straight. Tighten your Danjun and relax your shoulders. Tuck in your chin.

Overlapping Hands Close Stance
Kyopson Moaseogi
In Moaseogi, put the palm of the left knifehand on the back of the right open hand. Both hands are positioned at the vertical center of the body and both thumbs are bent and held against the side of the hands.

Escape Posture
Meongeppaegi
In horseriding stance, raise both shoulders, bringing the open hands up to chest level with the palms facing downward. The fingertips should point at each other and the hands should be on the same plane.

Downward Hammerfist Strike
Mejumeok Naeryochigi
In an in-to-out circular motion, strike vertically downward with the soft side of the clenched fist. At completion, the arm should be parallel to the floor.

Outward Knifehand Strike
Sonnal Bakkatchigi
The knifehand strikes from inward to outward, stopping at the outer line of the body. The thumb is bent alongside the knifehand. The other hand rests at the side at belt level.

Lateral Elbow Strike
Palkup Yopchigi
The fist of the striking arm is raised to shoulder level, then the elbow thrusts laterally. The arm should be tightly folded and the fist held close to the trunk.

Rear Elbow Strike
Palkup Dwitchigi
The elbow strikes to the rear and the hand of the striking hand is held open. The eyes look to the rear, at the target. The arm should be tightly folded and the hand held close to the trunk.

Double Uppercut
Dujumeok Jecheojireugi
From the waist, snap both fists upward. At completion, the fists should be aligned with each other, just below shoulder height. Tuck the elbows in close to the trunk.

Outward Backfist Strike
Deungjumeok Bakkatchigi
Strike outward using the two major knuckles. Align the fist with the height of the shoulder. Position the other hand at belt level.

Rear Punch
Dwitjireugi
The target for the punch is the face. The other elbow thrusts backward, while the body twists to the rear.

Hinge Block
Doltzeogi
Both arms begin on the opposite side of the body, rotating around the trunk to their stopping point. The upper arm guards the solar plexus and rests parallel to the flow. The other fist rests at the side at belt level.

Single Knifehand Middle Section Inward Block
Hansonnal Momtong Anmakki
The palm of the blocking hand faces the body at shoulder height. The elbow should be tucked close to the body but not touching it. The other fist rests on the side at belt level.

BLACK BELT
POOMSAE

BLACK BELT
KORYO

Meaning of Poomsae Koryo

Koryo is the name for an ancient Korean dynasty (AD 918-1392), which flourished with the spirits of the Seonbi (scholar) and Musa (warrior). Poomsae Koryo, therefore, symbolizes the spirit of the Seonbi warrior who was characterized by a strong martial spirit as well as a righteous character. The Junbiseogi (ready stance) for Poomsae Koryo is Tongmilgi, which promotes concentration by placing the hands between the upper and lower abdomen, the center of Ki in the body. The movement line of Koryo represents the Chinese character for Seonbi, a man of virtue. There are 30 movements in Poomsae Koryo. This form is for the 1st Dan.

Poomsae Line of Koryo

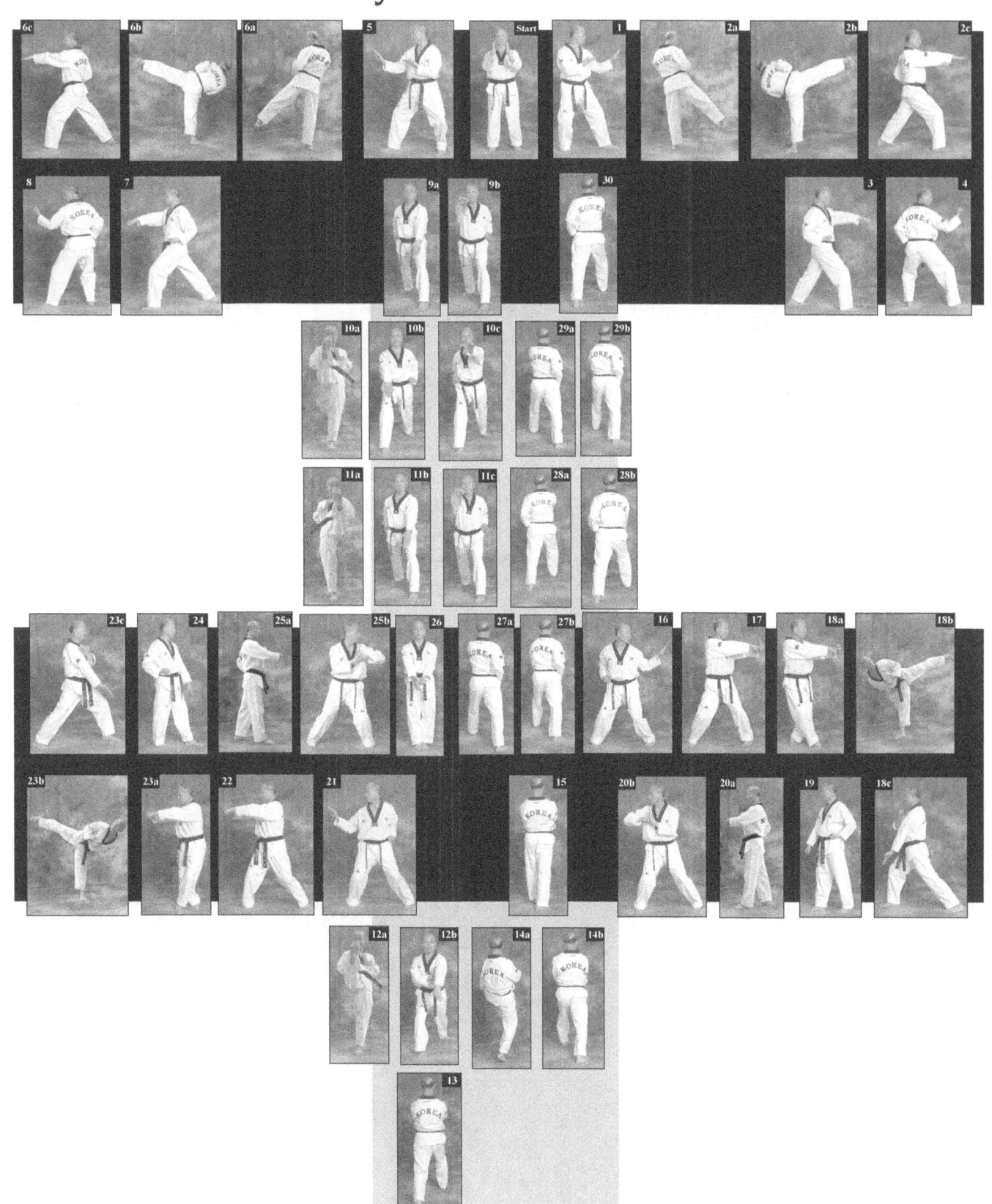

Koryo

Begin from **pushing hands ready stance** (tongmilgi junbiseogi), eyes looking forward and feet shoulder width apart.

1. Move the left foot to the left into **right back stance** (oreun dwitkubi) and execute a **double knifehand block** (sonnal momtongmakki).

2a. Pivoting on the left foot, execute a **right double side kick** (oreunbal keodup yopchagi), with first a low side kick (arae yopchagi) to the lower leg.

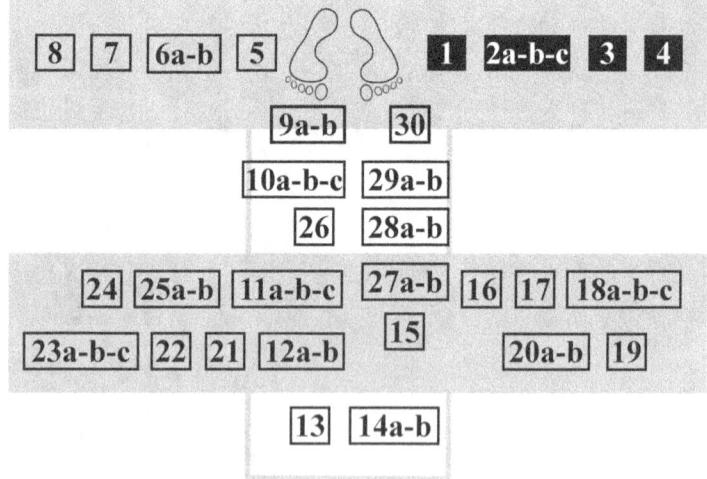

Poomsae Koryo

2b. Complete the **right double side kick** (oreunbal keodup yopchagi) with a middle section side kick (momtong yopchagi) to the trunk.

2c. Step down with the right foot into **right front stance** (oreun apkubi) and execute a **right outward knifehand strike** (sonnal bakkatchigi).

3. With the feet fixed, execute a **left straight middle punch** (momtong barojireugi).

4. Drawing the right foot back into **left back stance** (wen dwitkubi), execute an **inward middle block** (momtong anmakki).

6c. Step down with the left foot into **left front stance** (wen apkubi) and execute a **left outward knifehand strike** (sonnal bakkatchigi).

8. Drawing the left foot back into **right back stance** (oreun dwitkubi), execute an **inward middle block** (momtong anmakki).

7. With the feet fixed, execute a **right straight middle punch** (momtong barojireugi).

Poomsae Koryo

6b. Complete the **left double side kick** (wenbal keodup yopchagi) with a middle section side kick (momtong yopchagi) to the trunk.

6a. Pivoting on the right foot, execute a **left double side kick** (wenbal keodup yopchagi), with first a low side kick (arae yopchagi) to the lower leg.

5. Moving the right foot, turn 180° clockwise into **left back stance** (wen dwitkubi) and execute a **double knifehand block** (sonnal momtongmakki).

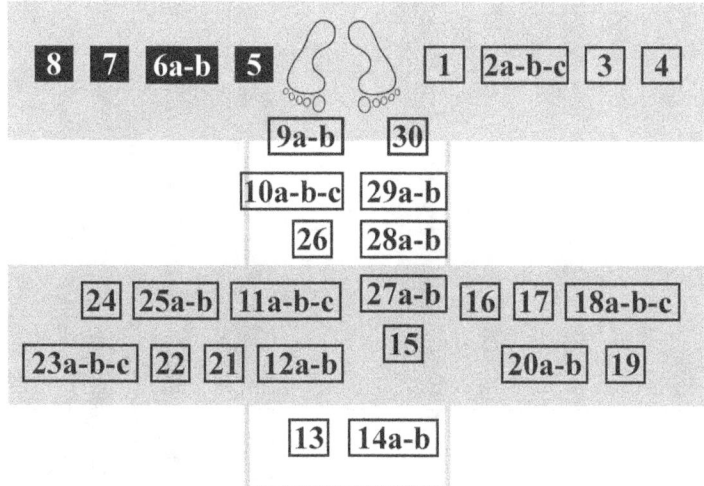

324 Black Belt Poomsae

9a. Moving the left foot, turn 90° counterclockwise into **left front stance** (wen apkubi) and execute a **left low section single knifehand block** (hansonnal araemakki).

9b. With the feet fixed, execute a **right arc hand strike** (agwison khaljaebi).

10a. With the left foot fixed, execute a **right front kick** (oreunbal apchagi).

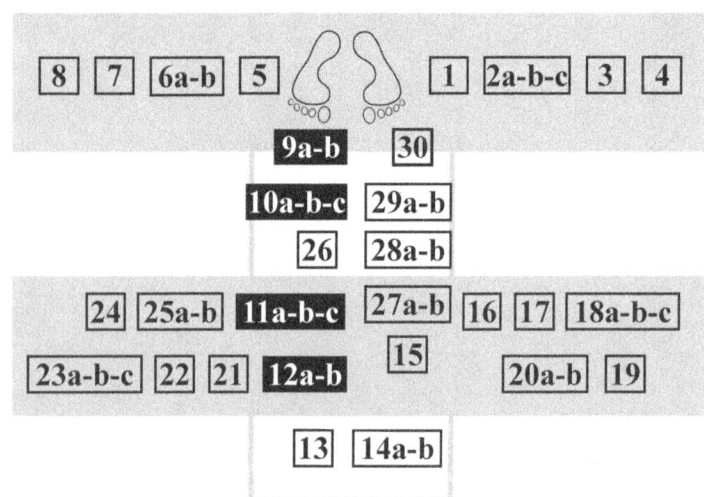

10b. Step down with the right foot into **right front stance** (oreun apkubi) and execute a **right low section single knifehand block** (hansonnal araemakki).

10c. With the feet fixed, execute a **left arc hand strike** (agwison khaljaebi).

Poomsae Koryo

11a. With the right foot fixed, execute a **left front kick** (wenbal apchagi).

11b. Step down with the left foot into **left front stance** (wen apkubi) and execute a **left low section single knifehand block** (hansonnal araemakki).

11c. With the feet fixed, execute a **right arc hand strike** (agwison khaljaebi). **Kihap.**

12a. With the left foot fixed, execute a **right front kick** (oreunbal apchagi).

12b. Step down with the right foot into **right front stance** (oreun apkubi) and execute a **left knee break** (murepkukki).

14b. Step down with the left foot into **left front stance** (wen apkubi) and execute a **right knee break** (murepkukki).

14a. With the right foot fixed, execute a **left front kick** (wenbal apchagi).

13. Moving the left foot, step forward and turn the body 180° clockwise into **right front stance** (oreun apkubi) and execute a **middle section inner forearm opening block** (anpalmok momtong hechomakki).

Poomsae Koryo 327

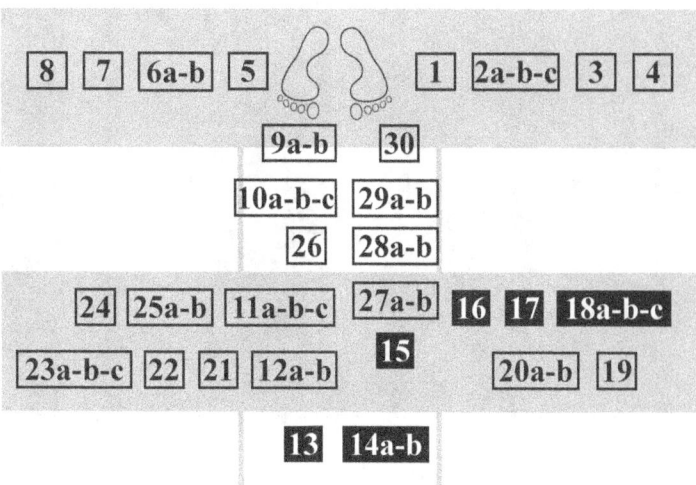

15. Draw the left foot back into **left walking stance** (wen apseogi) and execute a **middle section inner forearm opening block** (anpalmok momtong hechomakki).

16. Moving the right foot, turn the 270° clockwise into **horseriding stance** (juchumseogi) and execute a **left single knifehand middle section side block** (hansonnal momtong yopmakki).

17. With the feet fixed, execute a **right target punch** (jumeok pyojeokjireugi).

18a. Slide the right foot into **front cross stance** (apkoaseogi) while maintaining the position of the hands.

18b. Pulling the hands to the torso, execute a **left side kick** (wenbal yopchagi).

23b. Pulling the hands to the torso, execute a **right side kick** (oreunbal yopchagi).

23a. Slide the left foot into **front cross stance** (apkoaseogi) while maintaining the position of the hands.

22. With the feet fixed, execute a **left target punch** (jumeok pyojeokjireugi).

21. With the feet fixed, execute a **right single knifehand middle section side block** (hansonnal momtong yopmakki).

23c. Turning 180° counter-clockwise, set the right foot down in **left front stance** (wen apkubi) and execute a **left low section fingertip thrust** (pyonsonkkeut arae jeochotzireugi).

24. Draw the left foot back into **left walking stance** (wen apseogi) and execute a **left low section block** (araemakki).

25a. Step forward with the right foot and execute a **right palm heel pressing block** (batangson nullomakki).

25b. Step forward with the left foot into **horseriding stance** (juchumseogi) and execute a **left lateral elbow strike** (palkup yopchigi).

Poomsae Koryo 329

18c. Turning 180° clockwise, set the left foot down in **right front stance** (oreun apkubi) and execute a **left low section fingertip thrust** (pyonsonkkeut arae jeochotzireugi).

19. Draw the right foot back into **right walking stance** (oreun apseogi) and execute a **right low section block** (arraemakki).

20a. Step forward with the left foot and execute a **left palm heel pressing block** (batangson nullomakki).

20b. Step forward with the right foot into **horseriding stance** (juchumseogi) and execute a **right lateral elbow strike** (palkup yopchigi).

26. With the left foot fixed, draw the right foot into **close stance** (moaseogi) and execute a **left low section hammerfist target strike** (mejumeok arae pyojeokchigi).

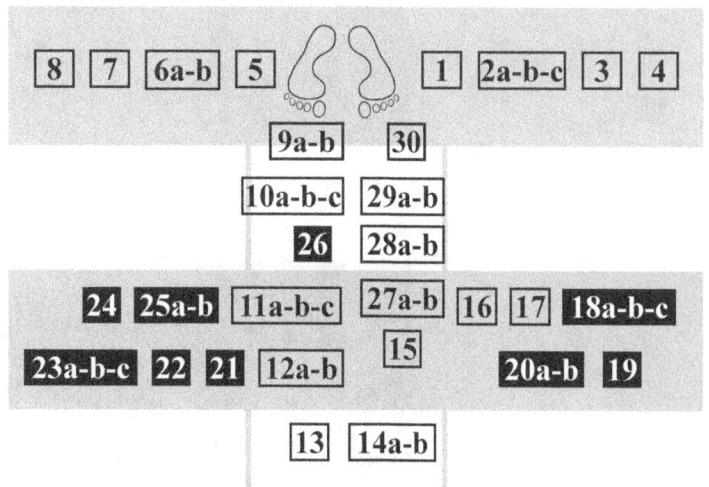

330 Black Belt Poomsae

28a. Step forward with the right foot into **right front stance** (oreun apkubi) and execute a **right single knifehand neck strike** (hansonnal mokchigi).

27b. With the feet fixed, execute a **left single low section knifehand block** (hansonnal araemakki).

27a. Moving the left foot, turn the body 180° counterclockwise into **left front stance** (wen apkubi) and execute a **left outward single knifehand strike** (hansonnal bakkatchigi).

29b. With the feet fixed, execute a **left single low section knifehand block** (hansonnal araemakki).

29a. Step forward with the left foot into **left front stance** (wen apkubi) and execute a **left single knifehand neck strike** (hansonnal mokchigi).

28b. With the feet fixed, execute a **right single low section knifehand block** (hansonnal araemakki).

Moving the left foot, turn the body 180° counterclockwise to return to **pushing hands ready stance** (tongmilgi junbiseogi).

30. Step forward with the right foot into **right front stance** (oreun apkubi) and execute a **right arc hand strike** (agwison khaljaebi). **Kihap.**

New Movements in Koryo

Pushing Hands Ready Stance
Tongmilgi Junbiseogi
Stand in parallel stance with the feet about shoulder width. The hands are held in knifehand form, with palms facing each other. Begin with the fingertips pointing downward and when the hands reach chest height, rotate them facing upward and push forward to the finish position.

Single Low Section Knifehand Block
Hansonnal Araemakki
Performed the same as low section block except the blocking hand is a knifehand with the palm facing downward. The elbow of the blocking arm should be held away from the body throughout the movement.

Middle Section Inner Forearm Opening Block
Anpalmok Momtong Hechomakki
The two fists are held at approximately shoulder height, with the palms facing the torso. The elbows are held close to but not touching the body.

Palm Heel Pressing Block
Batangson Nullomakki
The blocking hand is a knifehand with the palm facing downward. The hand is about 2 fists' distance from the torso at solar plexus height. The other hand is a fist held at belt level.

Low Section Fingertip Thrust
Pyonsonkkeut Arae Jeochotzireugi
The thrusting hand begins from the front of the chest and thrusts downward with the palm facing upward. The target is the groin. The other hand is a knifehand held just above the shoulder of the thrusting arm.

Arc Hand Strike
Agwison Khaljaebi
The striking hand is formed in an arc, with the four fingers held close together forming one side of the arc and the thumb making up the other side. The hand travels on a straight line to the target, as in punching.

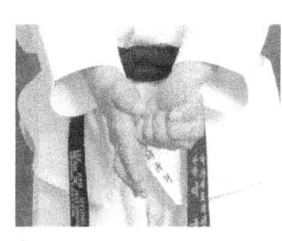

Target Punch
Jumeok Pyojeok Jireugi
Outstretch the target hand, keeping the elbow straight. When the punch strikes the target hand, the target hand should remain vertically flat. Do not grasp the punching fist with the target hand. The arms are held parallel to the floor and fully extended to the side of the body.

Low Section Hammerfirst Target Strike
Mejumeok Arae Pyojeokchigi
The left hand forms a fist with the palm facing away from the body. The hammerfist striking area of the left hand rests on the palm of the right knifehand, in front of the abdomen.

Poomsae Koryo

Outward Single Knifehand Strike
Hansonnal Bakkatchigi
The palm of the knifehand faces downward and the blade of the hand strikes the neck. The other hand is held in a fist at the belt level.

Single Knifehand Neck Strike
Hansonnal Mokchigi
The palm of the knifehand faces upward and the blade of the hand strikes the neck. The knifehand blade is slightly curved. The other hand is held in a fist at the belt level.

Double Side Kick
Keodup Yopchagi
The target for the first kick is the lower leg and the target for the second kick is the torso. Between kicks, fully retract and chamber the kicking leg. When the second kick is extended, the upper body should be raised so the body forms a "Y" shape.

Knee Break
Mureupkukki
The striking hand forms an arc hand strike to the knee. The other hand forms an arc hand pulling (palm up) toward the body and coming to rest just above the elbow of the striking arm.

BLACK BELT
KEUMGANG

Meaning of Poomsae Keumgang

Keumgang, meaning diamond, symbolizes hardness or the quality of being indestructible. The spiritual foundation of this form, Mount Keumgang, is the most magnificent mountain on the Korean peninsula and is regarded as the center of the national spirit and the origin of Keumgang Yuksa (a mighty warrior named by Buddha). Poomsae Keumgang, therefore, should be performed with the majestic, graceful and strong spirit of Keumgang. The line of movements symbolizes the Chinese character for mountain. The movements of the Poomsae should be performed powerfully and with good balance to demonstrate the dignity of the Keumgang spirit. There are 27 movements in Poomsae Keumgang. This form is for the 2nd Dan.

Poomsae Line of Keumgang

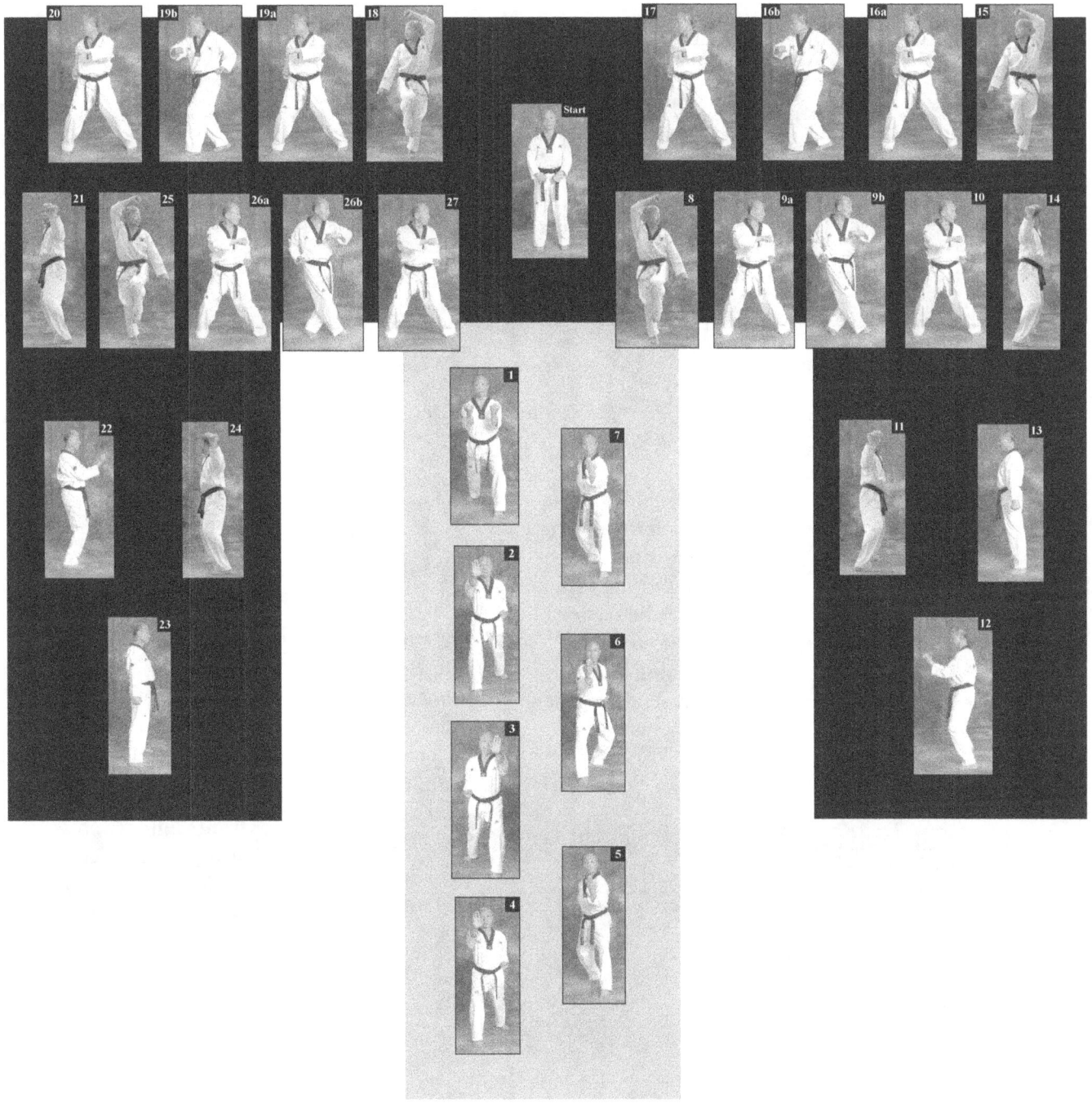

Keumgang

Begin from **ready stance** (junbiseogi), eyes looking forward and feet shoulder width apart.

1. Step forward with the left foot into **left front stance** (wen apkubi) and execute a **middle section inner forearm opening block** (anpalmok momtong hechomakki).

2. Step forward with the right foot into **right front stance** (oreun apkubi) and execute a **right palm heel jaw strike** (batangson teokchigi).

3. Step forward with the left foot into **left front stance** (wen apkubi) and execute a **left palm heel jaw strike** (batangson teokchigi).

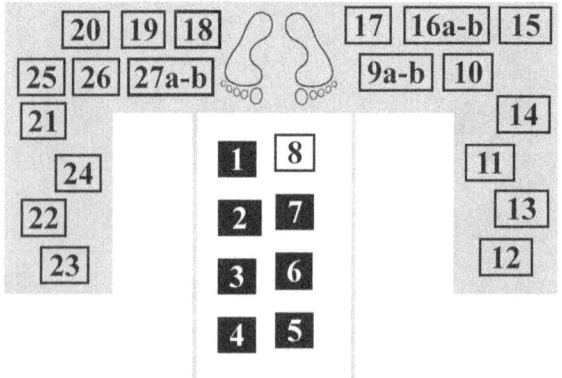

Poomsae Keumgang

4. Step forward with the right foot into **right front stance** (oreun apkubi) and execute a **right palm heel jaw strike** (batangson teokchigi).

5. Step backward with the right foot into **right back stance** (oreun dwitkubi) and execute a **left single knifehand middle section inward block** (hansonnal momtong anmakki).

6. Step backward with the left foot into **left back stance** (wen dwitkubi) and execute a **right single knifehand middle section inward block** (hansonnal momtong anmakki).

7. Step backward with the right foot into **right back stance** (oreun dwitkubi) and execute a **left single knifehand middle section inward block** (hansonnal momtong anmakki).

8. Pivoting on the right foot, look 90° to the left and slowly draw the left foot up into **right crane stance** (oreun hakdariseogi), executing a **diamond block** (keumgangmakki).

9a. Step down into **horseriding stance** (juchumseogi) and execute a **large hinge block** (kheun dolzteogi).

9b. Moving the right foot first turn 360° counterclockwise, maintaining the height of the body and the distance between the feet.

10. Finish the turn in **horseriding stance** (juchumseogi) and execute a **large hinge block** (kheun dolzteogi).

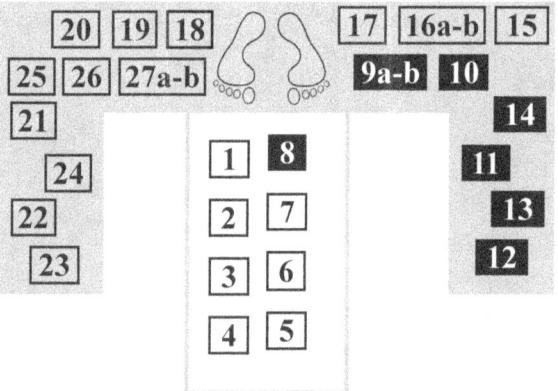

11. Pivoting 90° counterclockwise on the left foot, lift the right foot *(as in photo A)* then forcefully put it down in **horseriding stance** (juchumseogi) and execute a **mountain block** (santeulmakki). **Kihap**.

12. Pivoting 180° clockwise on the right foot, step into **horseriding stance** (juchumseogi) and execute a **middle section inner forearm opening block** (anpalmok momtong hechomakki).

13. With the right foot fixed, slide the left foot into **parallel stance** (naranhiseogi) and slowly execute a **low section opening block** (arae hechomakki).

14. Pivoting 180° clockwise on the right foot, lift the left foot then forcefully put it down in **horseriding stance** (juchumseogi) and execute a **mountain block** (santeulmakki).

18. Shift the weight onto the leftt foot and slowly draw the right foot up into **left crane stance** (wen hakdariseogi) and execute a **diamond block** (keumgangmakki).

19a. Step down into **horseriding stance** (juchumseogi) and execute a **large hinge block** (kheun dolzteogi).

19b. Moving the left foot first turn 360° clockwise, maintaining the height of the body and the distance between the feet.

20. Finish the turn in **horseriding stance** (juchumseogi) and execute a **large hinge block** (kheun dolzteogi).

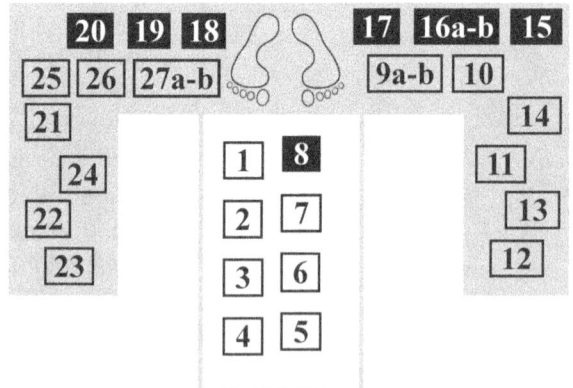

Poomsae Keumgang

17. Finish the turn in **horseriding stance** (juchumseogi) and execute a **large hinge block** (kheun dolzteogi).

16b. Moving the left foot first turn 360° clockwise, maintaining the height of the body and the distance between the feet.

16a. Step down into **horseriding stance** (juchumseogi) and execute a **large hinge block** (kheun dolzteogi).

15. Pivoting on the left foot, slowly draw the right foot up into **left crane stance** (wen hakdariseogi) and execute a **diamond block** (keumgangmakki).

21. Pivoting 90° clockwise on the right foot, lift the left foot then forcefully put it down in **horseriding stance** (juchumseogi) and execute a **mountain block** (santeulmakki). **Kihap.**

22. Pivoting 180° counterclockwise on the left foot, step into **horseriding stance** (juchumseogi) and execute a **middle section inner forearm opening block** (anpalmok momtong hechomakki).

23. With the left foot fixed, slide the right foot into **parallel stance** (naranhiseogi) and slowly execute a **low section opening block** (arae hechomakki).

24. Pivoting 180° counterclockwise on the left foot, lift the right foot then forcefully put it down in **horseriding stance** (juchumseogi) and execute a **mountain block** (santeulmakki).

Poomsae Keumgang

25. Pivoting on the right foot, look 90° to the left and slowly draw the left foot up into **right crane stance** (oreun hakdariseogi), executing a **diamond block** (keumgangmakki).

26a. Step down into **horseriding stance** (juchumseogi) and execute a **large hinge block** (kheun dolzteogi).

26b. Moving the right foot first turn 360° counterclockwise, maintaining the height of the body and the distance between the feet.

27. Finish the turn in **horseriding stance** (juchumseogi) and execute a **large hinge block** (kheun dolzteogi).

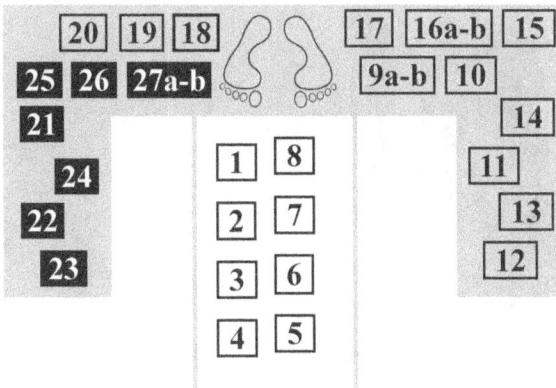

Moving the left foot, return to **ready stance** (junbiseogi).

New Movements in Keumgang

Diamond Block
Keumgangmakki
This block consists of a high section block with one arm and a low section block with the other. In Poomsae Keumgang, the fist of the low section block aligns with the raised foot. Look in the direction of the low section block.

Mountain Block
Santeulmakki
The fists are aligned with the temples, facing each other. The upper arms are held parallel to the floor and the elbows form ninety degree angles.

Large Hinge Block
Kheun Dolzteogi
The blocking arm is held away from the body, parallel to the ground, in front of the solar plexus. The fist faces palm downward. The other fist rests at the waist.

Palm Heel Jaw Strike
Batangson Teokchigi
The heel of the palm strikes at the jaw level, moving in a straight line like a punch. The fingertips face upward and slightly outward.

BLACK BELT
TAEBAEK

Meaning of Poomsae Taebaek

Taebaek means supreme brightness. It symbolizes the sacred spirit of the Mt. Baekdoo, from which Dangun, the founder of Korea, ruled the nation about 5,000 years ago as well as the humanitarian ideal of the founder, Hongik Ingan, who believed in Broad Salvation of Mankind. The line of movements follows the Chinese character meaning the bridge between heaven and Earth. It signifies that we human beings are created by Heaven's order and are the messengers between the two worlds. There are 26 movements in Poomsae Taebaek. This form is for the 3rd Dan.

Poomsae Line of Taebaek

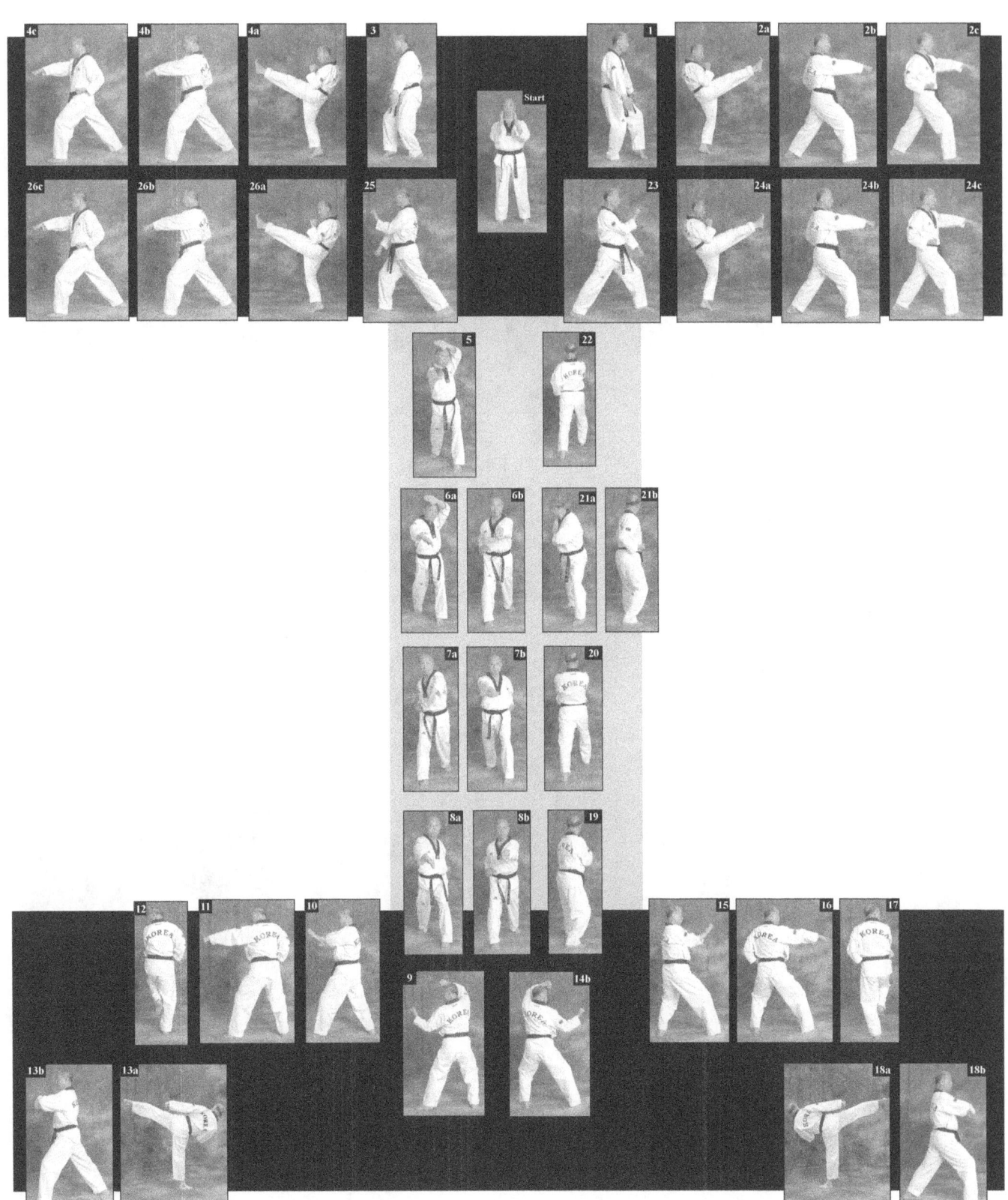

Taebaek

Begin from **ready stance** (junbiseogi), eyes looking forward and feet shoulder width apart.

1. Move the left foot to the left into **left tiger stance** (wen beomseogi) and execute a **double knifehand low section opening block** (sonnal arae hechomakki).

2a. With the left foot fixed, execute a **right front kick** (oreunbal apchagi).

4b-c. Step down with the left foot into **left front stance** (wen apkubi) and execute a **double punch** (dubeonjireugi), punching with the left hand first then the right.

2b-c. Step down with the right foot into **right front stance** (oreun apkubi) and execute a **double punch** (dubeonjireugi), punching with the right hand first then the left.

  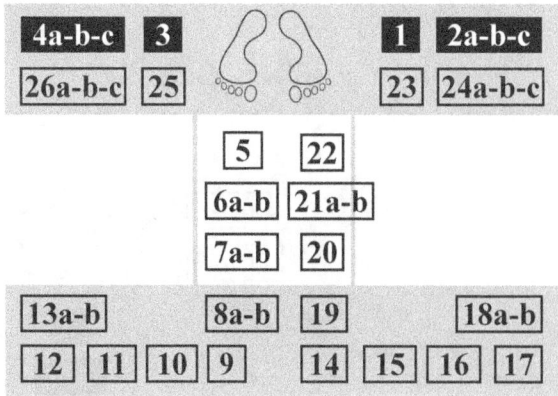

4a. With the right foot fixed, execute a **left front kick** (wenbal apchagi).

3. Turn 180° clockwise into **right tiger stance** (oreun beomseogi) and execute a **double knifehand low section opening block** (sonnal arae hechomakki).

354 Black Belt Poomsae

5. Moving the left foot, turn 90° counterclockwise into **left front stance** (wen apkubi) and execute a **swallow form knifehand strike** (jebipoom mokchigi).

6a. With the right hand, twist and grab the opponent's wrist.

6b. While pulling with the right hand, step forward into **right front stance** (oreun apkubi) and execute a **straight middle punch** (momtong barojireugi).

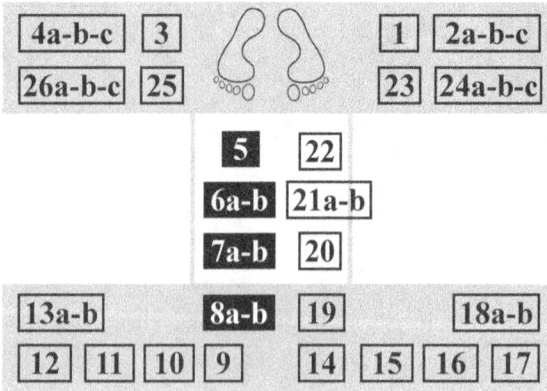

Poomsae Taebaek 355

7a. Open the left hand then twist outward, grabbing and pulling the opponent's wrist.

7b. While pulling with the left hand, step forward into **left front stance** (wen apkubi) and execute a **straight middle punch** (momtong barojireugi).

8a. Open the right hand then twist outward, grabbing and pulling the opponent's wrist.

8b. While pulling with the right hand, step forward into **right front stance** (oreun apkubi) and execute a **straight middle punch** (momtong barojireugi).

13b. Step down into **left front stance** (wen apkubi) and execute an **elbow target strike** (palkup pyojeokchigi).

13a. Pivoting on the right foot, execute a **left side kick** (wenbal yopchagi).

12. Raise the left foot into **right crane stance** (hakdariseogi), and execute a **small hinge block** (jageun doltzeogi).

14a. Turn 180° clockwise into **feet together close stance** (modumbal moaseogi) and execute a **small hinge block** (jageun doltzeogi).

14b. Slide the right foot into **left back stance** (wen dwitkubi) and execute a **diamond middle section block** (keumgang momtong makki).

15. With the feet fixed, execute a **pulling high section uppercut** (dangkyo teokjireugi).

16. With the feet fixed, execute a **middle section side punch** (momtong yopjireugi).

Poomsae Taebaek

11. With the feet fixed, execute a **middle section side punch** (momtong yopjireugi).

10. With the feet fixed, execute a **pulling high section uppercut** (dangkyo teokjireugi).

9. Moving the left foot, turn 270° counterclockwise into **right back stance** (oreun dwitkubi) and execute a **diamond middle section block** (keumgang momtong makki).

17. Raise the right foot into **left crane stance** (hakdariseogi), and execute a **small hinge block** (jageun doltzeogi).

18a. Pivoting on the left foot, execute a **right side kick** (oreunbal yopchagi).

18b. Step down into **right front stance** (oreun apkubi) and execute an **elbow target strike** (palkup pyojeokchigi).

20. Step forward with the right foot into **right front stance** (oreun apkubi) and execute a **left pressing block** (nullomakki) and **right vertical fingertip thrust** (pyonsonkkeut sewotzireugi).

19. Bring the right foot to the left foot then slide the left foot forward into **right back stance** (oreun dwitkubi), executing a **double knifehand block** (sonnal momtongmakki).

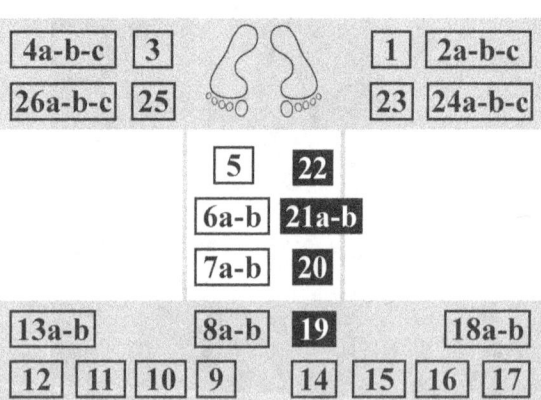

22. Step forward with the right foot into **right front stance** (oreun apkubi) and execute a **right reverse punch** (momtong bandaejireugi).

21b. Moving the left foot turn 180° into **right back stance** (oreun dwitkubi) and execute a **left outward backfist strike** (deungjumeok bakkatchigi).

21a. Pivot the body 180° counterclockwise, and bring the right hand to the rear waist.

23. Moving the left foot turn 270° counterclockwise into **left front stance** (wen apkubi) and execute a **scissors block** (kawimakki).

24a. With the left foot fixed, execute a **right front kick** (oreunbal apchagi).

Moving the left foot, return to **ready stance** (junbiseogi).

26b-c. Step down with the left foot into **left front stance** (wen apkubi) and execute a **double punch** (dubeonjireugi), punching with the left hand first then the right.

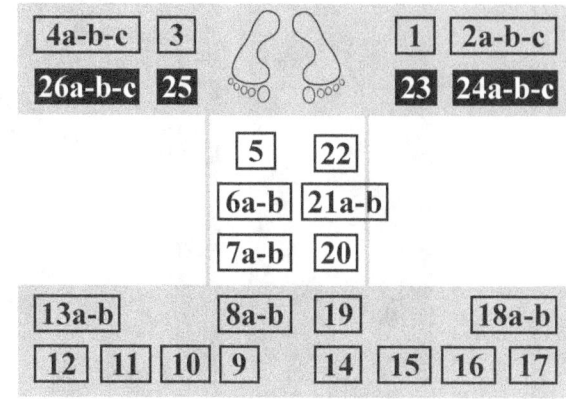

24b-c. Step down with the right foot into **right front stance** (oreun apkubi) and execute a **double punch** (dubeonjireugi), punching with the right hand first then the left.

26a. With the right foot fixed, execute a **left front kick** (wenbal apchagi).

25. Moving the right foot turn 270° clockwise into **right front stance** (oreun apkubi) and execute a **scissors block** (kawimakki).

New Movements in Taebaek

Small Hinge Block
Jageun Dolzteogi
The blocking arm is positioned directly above the other fist, which is held at the waist. The palm of the fist of the blocking arm faces the body.

Double Knifehand Low Section Opening Block
Sonnal Arae Hechomakki
The open hands are held with the palms facing down. The arms should be positioned symmetrically at about a forty-five degree angle to the body. Keep the upper body erect and slightly round the shoulders.

BLACK BELT
PYONGWON

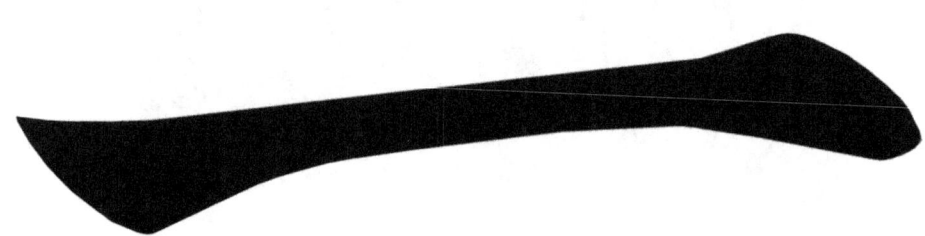

Meaning of Poomsae Pyongwon

Pyongwon means a plain or a vast field of land. It is the foundation of life for all creatures and the place from which all creatures gain sustenance. Pyongwon is based on the idea of peace and struggle resulting from the principles of origin and use. The Kyopson Junbiseogi (overlapping hands ready stance) requires a concentration of force in the Danjun (lower abdomen), the source of all strength, much like the land is the source of strength for all life. The line of movements symbolizes the origin and transformation of the plain. There are 25 movements in Poomsae Pyongwon. This form is for the 4th Dan.

Poomsae Line of Pyongwon

Pyongwon

Begin from **overlapping hands ready stance** (kyopson junbiseogi), eyes looking forward and feet together.

1. Move the left foot to the left into **parallel stance** (naranhiseogi) and execute a **double knifehand low section opening block** (sonnal arae hechomakki).

2. With the feet fixed, execute **pushing hands** (tongmilgi).

3. Moving the right foot, pivot 90° clockwise into **left back stance** (wen dwitkubi) and execute a **single low section knifehand block** (hansonnal araemakki).

4. Pivot 180° counterclockwise into **right back stance** (oreun dwitkubi) and execute a **single knifehand middle section outward block** (hansonnal momtong bakkatmakki).

Poomsae Pyongwon 367

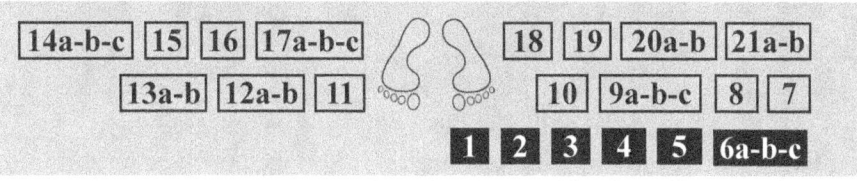

5. Slide the left foot forward into **left front stance** (wen apkubi) and execute a **right elbow uppercut** (palkup ollyochigi).

6a. With the left foot fixed, execute a **right front kick** (oreunbal apchagi).

6b. Set the right foot down, pivoting on it to execute a **left turning side kick** (wenbal momdollyo yopchagi).

9a. In place, twist the body and raise the right leg.

9b. Stomp the right foot down into **horseriding stance** (juchumseogi) and execute a **right pulling backfist strike** (deungjumeok dangkyo teokchigi). **Kihap**.

9c. With the feet fixed, execute a **left pulling backfist strike** (deungjumeok dangkyo teokchigi).

11. Step with the right foot into **horseriding stance** (juchumseogi) and execute an **opening mountain block** (hecho santeulmakki).

12a. Raise the right foot into **crane stance** (hakdarkiseogi) and execute a **diamond block** (keumgangmakki).

12b. With the feet fixed, execute a **left small hinge block** (jageun doltzeogi).

Poomsae Pyongwon

6c. Turn 180° clockwise and set the left foot down in **left back stance** (wen dwitkubi) and execute a **double knifehand block** (sonnal momtongmakki).

7. With the feet fixed, execute a **low section knifehand block** (sonnal araemakki).

8. In place, shift the feet into **horseriding stance** (juchumseogi) and execute an **augmented high section side block** (kodureo olgul yopmakki).

10. Step the left foot in front of the right foot into **front cross stance** (apkoaseogi) and execute a **double elbow strike** (meongechigi).

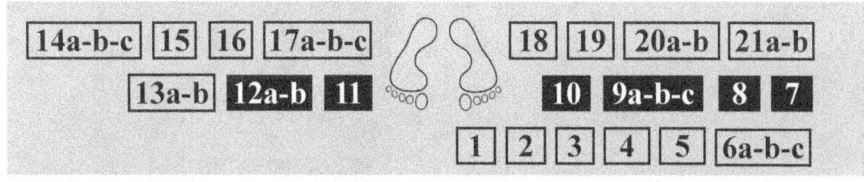

14c. Turn 180° counter-clockwise and set the right foot down in **right back stance** (oreun dwitkubi), executing a **double knifehand block** (sonnal momtongmakki).

14b. Set the left foot down, pivoting on it to execute a **right turning side kick** (oreunbal momdollyo yopchagi).

15. With the feet fixed, execute a **low section knifehand block** (sonnal araemakki).

16. In place, shift the feet into **horseriding stance** (juchumseogi) and execute an **augmented high section side block** (kodureo olgul yopmakki).

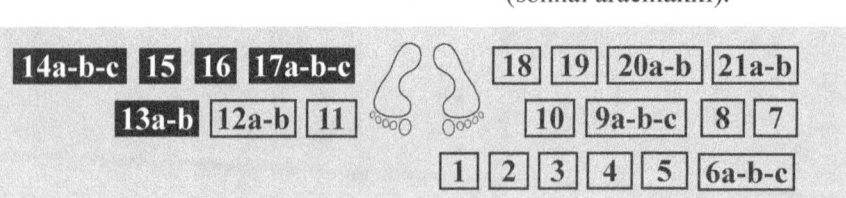

Poomsae Pyongwon 371

14a. With right foot fixed, execute a **left front kick** (wen apchagi).

13b. Set the right foot down in **right front stance** (oreun apkubi) and execute a **left elbow uppercut** (palkup ollyochigi).

13a. Pivoting on the left foot, execute a **right side kick** (oreunbal yopchagi).

17a. In place, twist the body and raise the left leg.

17b. Stomp the left foot down into **horseriding stance** (juchumseogi) and execute a **left pulling backfist strike** (deungjumeok dangkyo teokchigi). **Kihap**.

17c. With the feet fixed, execute a **right pulling backfist strike** (deungjumeok dangkyo teokchigi).

18. Step the right foot in front of the left foot into **front cross stance** (apkoaseogi) and execute a **double elbow strike** (meongechigi).

19. Step with the left foot into **horseriding stance** (juchumseogi) and execute an **opening mountain block** (hecho santeulmakki).

20a. Raise the left foot into **crane stance** (hakdarkiseogi) and execute a **diamond block** (keumgangmakki).

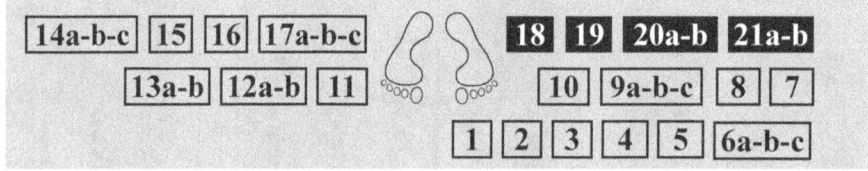

Poomsae Pyongwon

20b. With the feet fixed, execute a **right small hinge block** (jageun doltzeogi).

21a. Pivoting on the right foot, execute a **left side kick** (wenbal yopchagi).

21b. Set the left foot down in **left front stance** (wen apkubi) and execute a **right elbow target strike** (palkup pyojeokchigi).

Moving the left foot, return to **overlapping hands ready stance** (kyopson junbiseogi).

New Movements in Pyongwon

Overlapping Hands Ready Stance
Kyopson Junbiseogi
The feet are kept together, as in close stance and the body is held erect. Place the left open hand on top of the right open hand. The hands should be firmly aligned but not touching each other.

Augmented High Section Side Block
Kodureo Olgul Yopmakki
The blocking arm defends the upper side area of the body with the inside forearm. The palm of the fist faces the head. The augmenting arm is positioned in front of the solar plexus with the palm of the fist facing downward.

Opening Mountain Block
Hecho Santeulmakki
The fists should be aligned with the temples and the palms facing each other. The arms should be held symmetrically, with the upper arms parallel to the floor. In blocking, the fists rise from the belt level, in an outward direction.

Elbow Uppercut
Palkup Ollyochigi
The elbow is brought upward, close to the body, in a twisting motion to strike a high section target. The back of the fist faces away from the body, with the palm side of the closed fist facing the ear.

Pulling Backfist Jaw Strike
Deungjumeok Dangkyo Teokchigi
The supporting hand pulls the opponent while the striking hand delivers a backfist strike to the jaw. The elbow of the striking hand rests on the downward turned fist of the other hand.

Double Elbow Strike
Meongechigi
With both fists clenched, simultaneously strike outward with the elbows. The front of the fists face each other and are aligned with the solar plexus, but do not rest on the body.

Turning Side Kick
Momdollyo Yopchagi
This is a side kick to the front direction, executed by turning the body 180°. Begin by turning the body counterclockwise then bring the rear foot up next to the standing leg. Look over the shoulder on the raised leg side and execute the side kick. Align the head, hip and foot at the moment of impact.

BLACK BELT
SIPJIN

Meaning of Poomsae Sipjin

The word Sipjin is derived from the principle of longevity which maintains there are ten natural entities symbolic of long life: sun, moon, mountain, water, stone, pine tree, herb of eternal youth, turtle, deer and crane. This Poomsae symbolizes the longevity humans derive from these everlasting elements of nature. The line of movements follows the Chinese character for ten, symbolizing the infinitely multiplying nature of the decimal system and the endless development of life forms in nature. In Taekwondo practice, ten is a sign of progress and growth systematically cultivated according to the rules and discipline of the art. There are 31 movements in Poomsae Sipjin. This form is for the 5th Dan.

Poomsae Line of Sipjin

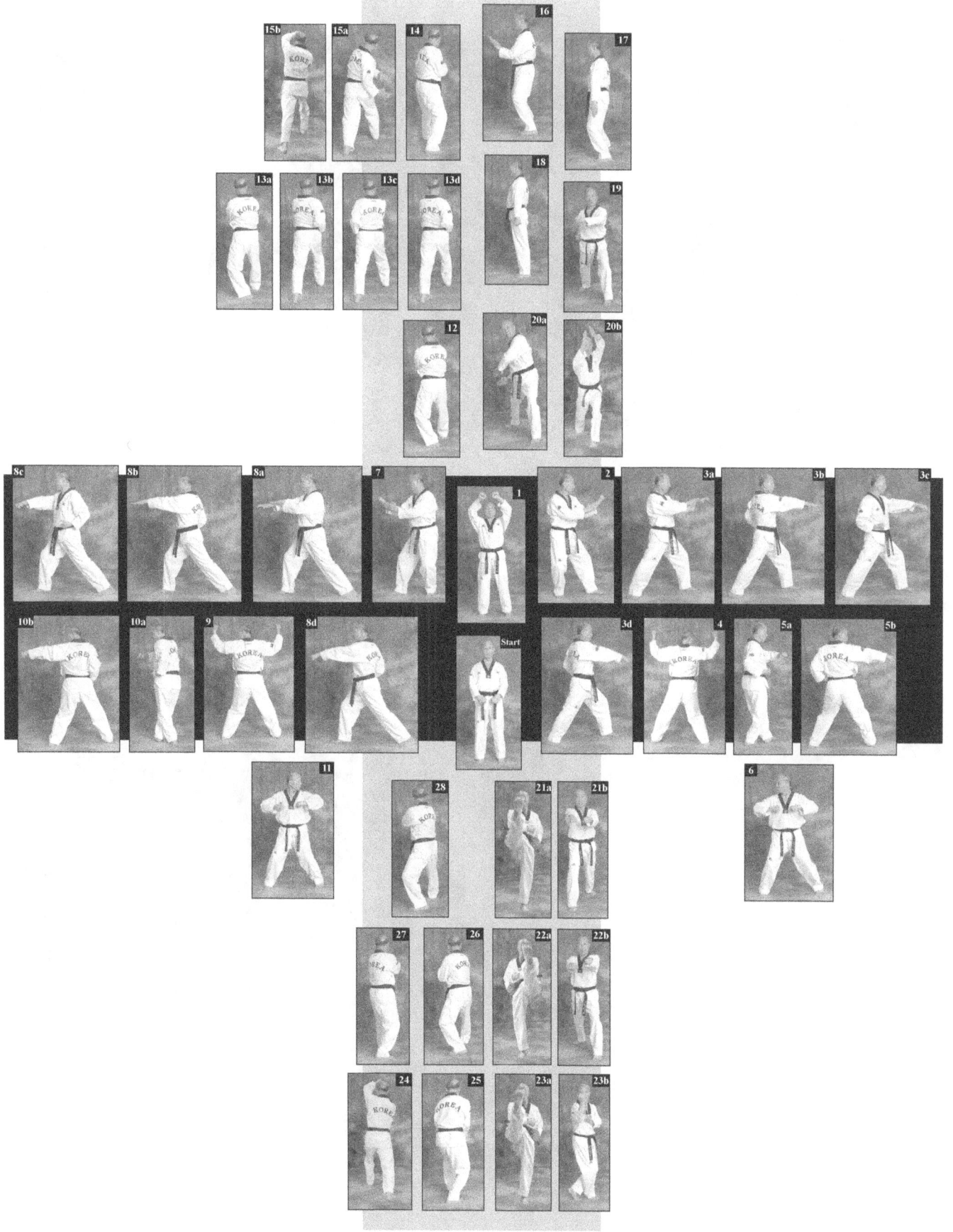

Sipjin

Begin from **ready stance** (junbiseogi), eyes looking forward and feet shoulder width apart.

1. With the feet fixed, execute a **bull block** (hwangsomakki).

2a. With the feet fixed, open the arms and pause briefly.

2b. Move the left foot into **right back stance** (oreun dwitkubi) and execute a **left palm augmented outward middle section block** (sonbadak kodureo momtong bakkatmakki).

3c-d. With the feet fixed, execute a **double punch** (dubeonjireugi), punching first with the left hand and then with the right.

Poomsae Sipjin 381

3a. Slowly open the left fist. When the fingers are nearly open, begin twisting the left wrist inward. The right hand continues to firmly support the left throughout. Simultaneously slide the left foot into **left front stance** (wen apkubi).

3b. From **left front stance** (wen apkubi), complete the movement begun in 3a by executing a **right horizontal fingertip thrust** (pyonsonkkeut upeo tzireugi).

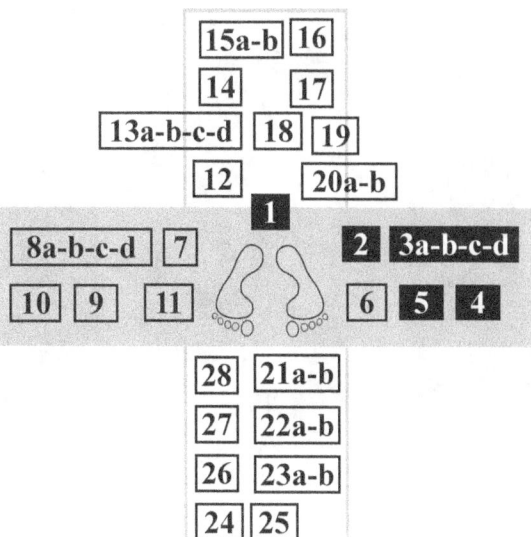

4. Step forward with the right foot into **horseriding stance** (juchumseogi) and execute an **opening mountain block** (hecho santeulmakki).

5a. Step the left foot in front of the right into **front cross stance** (apkoaseogi). The left hand grabs the opponent and the right chambers for the side punch.

5b. Continue moving in the same direction, stepping with the right foot into **horseriding stance** (juchumseogi) and execute a **right side punch** (yopjireugi).

8c-d. With the feet fixed, execute a **double punch** (dubeonjireugi), punching first with the right hand and then with the left.

8b. From **right front stance** (oreun apkubi), complete the movement begun in 8a by executing a **left horizontal fingertip thrust** (pyonsonkkeut upeo tzireugi).

10b. Continue moving in the same direction, stepping with the left foot into **horseriding stance** (juchumseogi) and execute a **left side punch** (yopjireugi). **Kihap**.

10a. Step the right foot in front of the left into **front cross stance** (apkoaseogi). The right hand grabs the opponent and the left chambers for the side punch.

9. Step forward with the left foot into **horseriding stance** (juchumseogi) and execute an **opening mountain block** (hecho santeulmakki).

Poomsae Sipjin

8a. Slowly open the right fist. When the fingers are nearly open, begin twisting the right wrist inward. The left hand continues to firmly support the right throughout. Simultaneously slide the right foot into **right front stance** (oreun apkubi).

7. Bring the left foot to the right foot then move the right foot into **left back stance** (wen dwitkubi) and execute a **left palm augmented outward middle section block** (sonbadak kodureo momtong bakkatmakki).

6. Stepping with the right foot, turn 180° counterclockwise into **horseriding stance** (juchumseogi) and execute a **double elbow strike** (meongechigi).

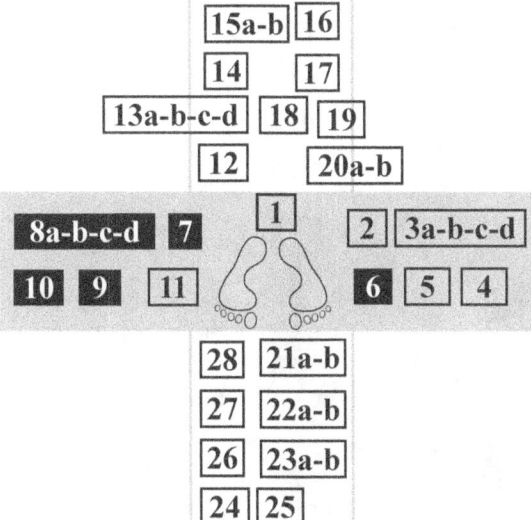

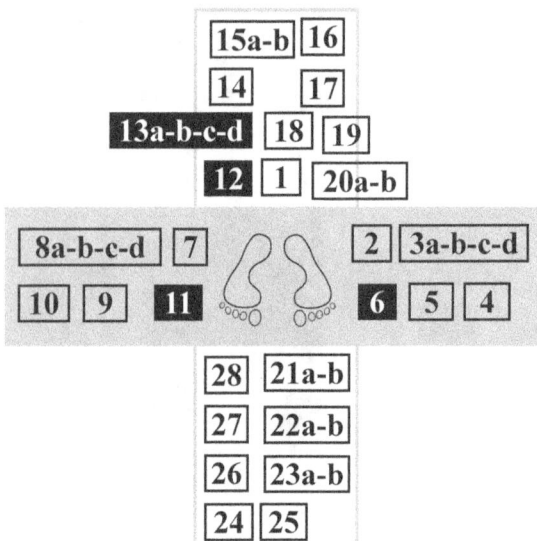

13a. Slowly open the right fist. When the fingers are nearly open, begin twisting the right wrist inward. The left hand continues to firmly support the right throughout. Simultaneously slide the right foot into **right front stance** (oreun apkubi).

12. Stepping with the right foot, turn 90° clockwise into **left back stance** (wen dwitkubi) then execute a **right palm augmented outward middle section block** (sonbadak kodureo momtong bakkatmakki).

11. Stepping with the left foot, turn 180° clockwise into **horseriding stance** (juchumseogi) and execute an **double elbow strike** (meongechigi).

Poomsae Sipjin

13c-d. With the feet fixed, execute a **double punch** (dubeonjireugi), punching first with the right hand and then with the left.

13b. From **right front stance** (oreun apkubi), complete the movement begun in 13a by executing a **left horizontal fingertip thrust** (pyonsonkkeut upeo tzireugi).

15b. With the feet fixed, execute **boulder pushing** (bawimilgi), with the eyes looking straight ahead between the two hands.

15a. Step forward with the right foot into **right front stance** (oreun apkubi) simultaneously bringing the hands to the right side of the waist, with the palms open and the thumbs pointing toward each other.

14. Stepping forward with the left foot into **right back stance** (oreun dwitkubi), execute a **double knifehand low section block** (sonnal araemakki).

Poomsae Sipjin

18. Slowly, powerfully close the fists to form **low section opening block** (arae hechomakki). When the hands are almost closed, straighten the legs into **wide stance** (nolpke bollyoseogi).

17. With the feet fixed, slowly execute a **double knifehand low section opening block** (sonnal arae hechomakki).

16. Turn the body 90° counterclockwise while sliding the left foot back into **horseriding stance** (juchumseogi), executing a **ridgehand middle section opening block** (sonnaldeung momtong hechomakki).

19. Pivoting 90° counterclockwise, step the left foot into **left front stance** (wen apkubi) and **pull up** (kureo olligi).

20a. With the feet fixed, bring the hands to the right side of the waist, with the palms open and the thumbs pointing toward each other.

20b. With the feet fixed, execute **boulder pushing** (bawimilgi), with the eyes looking straight ahead between the two hands.

21a. With the left foot fixed, execute a **right front kick** (oreunbal apchagi).

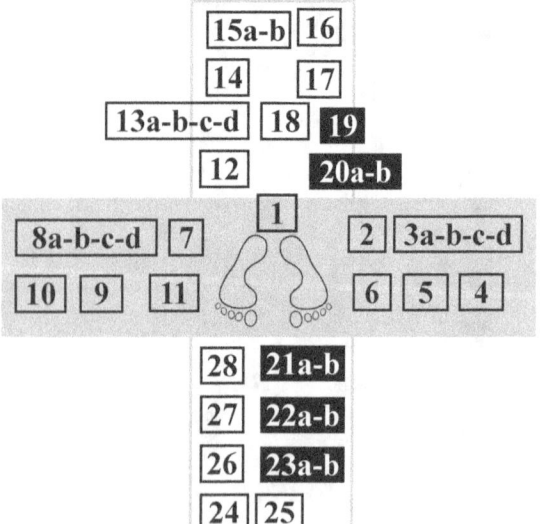

21b. Set the right foot down in **right front stance** (oreun apkubi) and execute a **simultaneous punch** (chetdarijireugi).

22a. With the right foot fixed, execute a **left front kick** (wenbal apchagi).

22b. Set the left foot down in **left front stance** (wen apkubi) and execute a **simultaneous punch** (chetdarijireugi).

23a. With the left foot fixed, execute a **right front kick** (oreunbal apchagi).

23b. Setting the right foot down (pounding the ground) in **left rear cross stance** (dwikoaseogi), execute an **augmented high section backfist strike** (kodureo deungjumeok olgul apchigi). **Kihap**.

26. Step forward with the right foot into **left back stance** (wen dwitkubi) and execute a **ridgehand middle section block** (sonnaldeung momtongmakki).

25. Slide the left foot back into **right tiger stance** (oreun beomseogi) and execute a **knifehand low section cross block** (sonnal otkoreo araemakki).

24. Turning 180° counterclockwise step with the left foot into **left front stance** (wen apkubi), and execute **boulder pushing** (bawimilgi).

Moving the right foot, return to **ready stance** (junbiseogi).

28. Step forward with the right foot into **left back stance** (wen dwitkubi) and execute a **simultaneous punch** (chetdarijireugi).

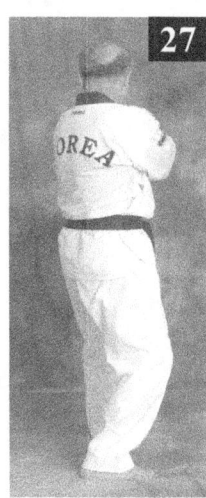

27. Step forward with the left foot into **right back stance** (oreun dwitkubi) and execute a **simultaneous punch** (chetdarijireugi).

New Movements in Sipjin

Wide Stance
Nolpke Bollyoseogi
Place the feet parallel to each other and slightly wider than shoulder width. Center your weight between the two feet.

Boulder Pushing
Bawimilgi
Bring the hands to the right side of the waist, with the palms open and the thumbs pointing toward each other, then slowly, as if pushing a large boulder, press the hands up to eye level. The eyes look straight forward, through the gap in the hands.

Pulling Up
Kureo Olligi
The blocking arm is pulled slightly across the body and then firmly upward to end at solar plexus level. The arm should be held one fist's distance away from the body and parallel to the floor.

Bull Block
Hwangsomakki
The arms are raised, simultaneously passing directly in front of the face and ending just above the head. There should be one fist's distance between the hands and one fist's distance between the hands and head.

Palm Augmented Outward Middle Section Block
Sonbadak Kodureo Momtong Bakkatmakki
When in motion, the support hand pushes the blocking hand to increase its force. The middle finger of the support hand rests on the outer edge of the blocking forearm. When the block is completed, the support hand rests firmly next to, but not touching the blocking arm.

Ridgehand Middle Section Block
Sonnaldeung Momtongmakki
With both fists clenched, simultaneously strike outward with the elbows. The front of the fists face each other and are aligned with the solar plexus, but do not rest on the body.

Ridgehand Middle Section Opening Block
Sonnaldeung Momtong Hechomakki
The palms of the open hands face upward. The fingertips should be aligned at the same height, just about shoulder level and the elbows held close to the body.

Knifehand Low Section Cross Block
Sonnal Otkoreo Araemakki
Cross the knifehands at the wrist, with the front arm beneath the rear arm. The wrists should be touching and the blades of the hands are facing downward. The hands are held at groin height.

Horizontal Fingertip Thrust
Pyonsonkkeut Upeo Tzireugi
In Sipjin, the horizontal fingertip thrust is made by sliding the thrusting hand over the other hand as it twists out of palm augmented outward middle section block. The thrust should be made swiftly and end at shoulder height. The arm is aligned vertically with the front leg.

Simultaneous Punch
Chetdarijireugi
The fists simultaneously punch the opponent's torso. The arms form a "U" shape. The rear shoulder should be turned slightly forward and the elbow of the front arm slightly bent. There should be approximately one fist's distance between the rear fist and front arm.

Augmented High Section Backfist Strike
Kodureo Deungjumeok Olgul Apchigi
The striking fist is aligned with the bottom of the nose and the back of the fist faces outward. The augmented arm is held in front of the solar plexus with the palm of the fist facing upward.

BLACK BELT
JITAE

Meaning of Poomsae Jitae

Jitae means a man standing on the earth looking at the sky. This represents a variety of human activities, particularly surviving the hardships we face from birth through death. From the earth, we take the energy and vigor for life, strengthening our bodies; when the body becomes strong, the mind is in harmony. Thus Poomsae Jitae signifies that one should stand for himself and by himself to survive on the earth and leave something significant behind when he dies. The line of movement symbolizes a man standing on the earth preparing to spring up toward the heaven. There are 28 movements in Poomsae Jitae. This form is for the 6th Dan.

Poomsae Line of Jitae

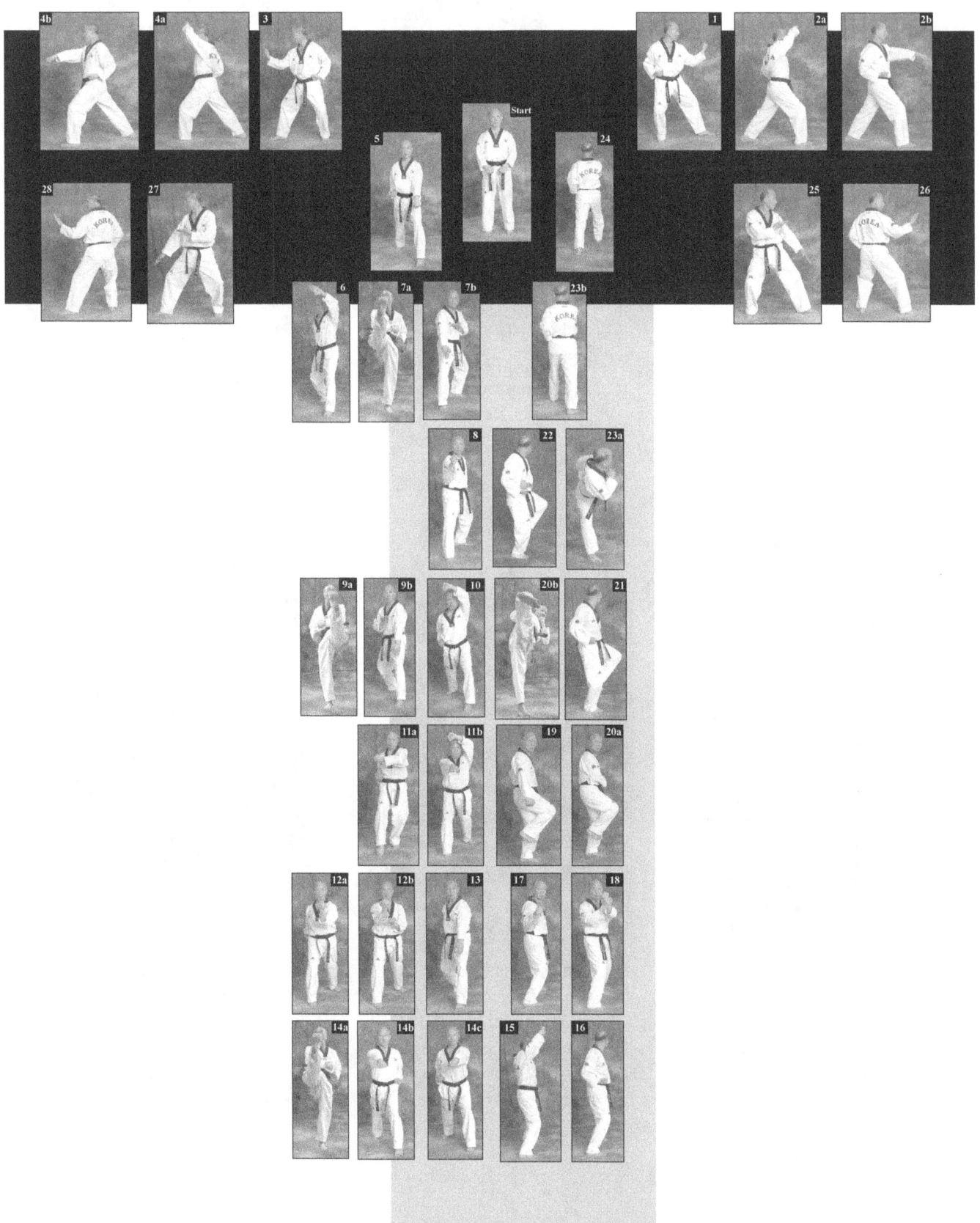

Jitae

Begin from **ready stance** (junbiseogi), eyes looking forward and feet shoulder width apart.

1. Move the left foot into **right back stance** (oreun dwitkubi) and slowly execute a **left outward middle block** (momtong bakkatmakki).

4a. Slowly step forward with the left foot into **left front stance** (wen apkubi) and slowly and powerfully execute a **left high section block** (olgulmakki).

4b. With the feet fixed, slowly and powerfully pull the opponent with the left hand while executing a **right straight punch** (momtong barojireugi).

5. Turn 90° counterclockwise moving the left foot into **left front stance** (wen apkubi) and execute a **left low section block** (araemakki).

Poomsae Jitae

2a. Slowly step forward with the right foot into **right front stance** (oreun apkubi) and slowly and powerfully execute a **right high section block** (olgulmakki).

2b. With the feet fixed, slowly and powerfully pull the opponent with the right hand while executing a **left straight punch** (momtong barojireugi).

3. Turning 180° clockwise move the right foot into **left back stance** (wen dwitkubi) and slowly execute a **right outward middle block** (momtong bakkatmakki).

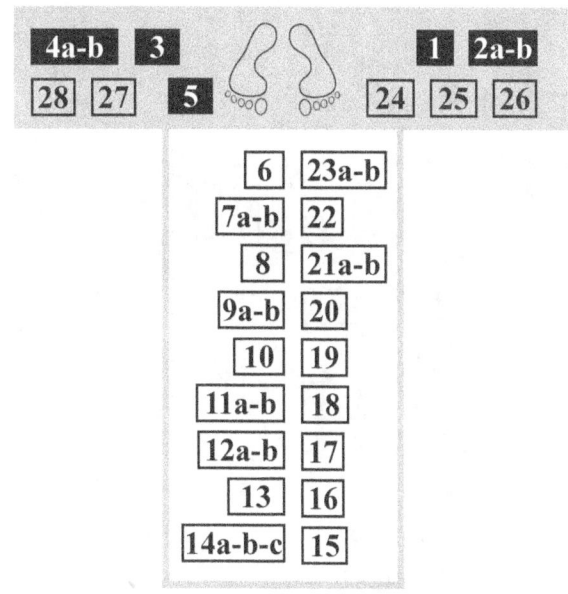

6. Slide the left foot back into **right back stance** (oreun dwitkubi) and execute a **single knifehand high section block** (hansonnal olgulmakki). Movements 5 and 6 should be done in quick succession.

7a. With the left foot fixed, execute a **right front kick** (oreunbal apchagi).

7b. Set the right foot down in **left back stance** (wen dwitkubi) and execute a **double knifehand low section block** (sonnal araemakki).

8. With the feet fixed, slowly and powerfully execute an **outward middle block** (momtong bakkatmakki).

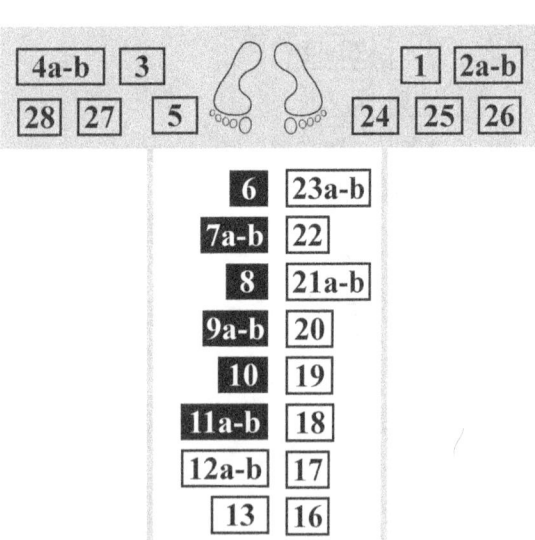

9a. With the right foot fixed, execute a **left front kick** (wenbal apchagi).

9b. Set the left foot down in **right back stance** (oreun dwitkubi) and execute a **double knifehand low section block** (sonnal araemakki).

10. Slide the left foot back into **left front stance** (wen apkubi) and slowly execute a **high section block** (olgulmakki).

11a. Stepping forward with the right foot, lower the left arm to prepare for **diamond front punch** (keumgang apjireugi).

11b. Complete the step forward into **right front stance** (oreun apkubi) and execute a **diamond front punch** (keumgang apjireugi).

12a. With the feet fixed, execute a **left inward middle block** (momtong anmakki).

12b. With the feet fixed, quickly execute a **right augmented middle block** (kodureo momtongmakki).

13. Step back with the right foot into **right back stance** (oreun dwitkubi) and execute a **left single knifehand low section block** (hansonnal araemakki).

14a. With the left foot fixed, execute a **right front kick** (oreunbal apchagi).

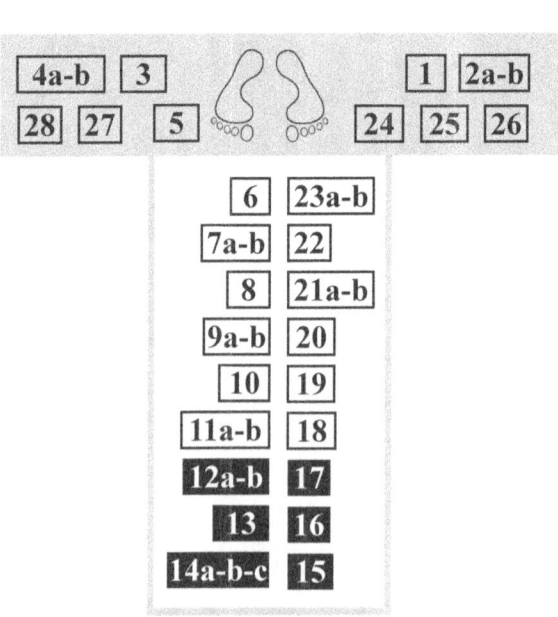

Poomsae Jitae

14b-c. Set the right foot down to the rear in **left front stance** (wen apkubi) and execute a **double punch** (momtong dubeonjireugi), punching first with the right hand and then with the left.

15. Turning 180° counterclockwise move the left foot into **horseriding stance** (juchumseogi) and slowly execute a **bull block** (hwangsomakki).

16. With the feet fixed, execute a **left low section side block** (arae yopmakki).

17. With the feet fixed, rotate the upper body 180° and execute a **right single knifehand middle section side block** (hansonnal momtong yopmakki).

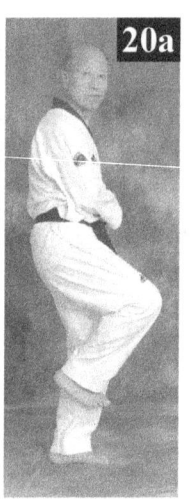

18. With the feet fixed, execute a **left hammerfist target strike** (mejumeok pyojeokchigi). **Kihap**.

19. Lift the right leg into **left crane stance** (wen hakdariseogi) and execute a **right low section side block** (arae yopmakki).

20a. With the feet fixed, execute a **small hinge block** (jageun doltzeogi).

20b. Pivoting on the left foot, execute a **right side kick** (oreunbal yopchagi).

Poomsae Jitae

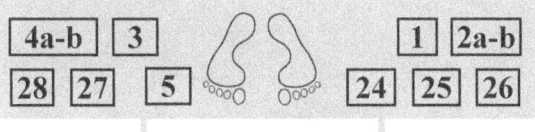

21. Set the right foot down beside the left, then lift the left leg into **right crane stance** (oreun hakdariseogi) and execute a **left low section side block** (arae yopmakki).

22. With the feet fixed, execute a **small hinge block** (jageun doltzeogi).

23a. Pivoting on the right foot, execute a **left side kick** (wenbal yopchagi).

23b. Set the left foot down in **left front stance** (wen apkubi) and execute a **right straight punch** (momtong barojireugi).

24. Step forward with the right foot into **right front stance** (oreun apkubi) and execute a **right reverse punch** (momtong bandaejireugi). **Kihap.**

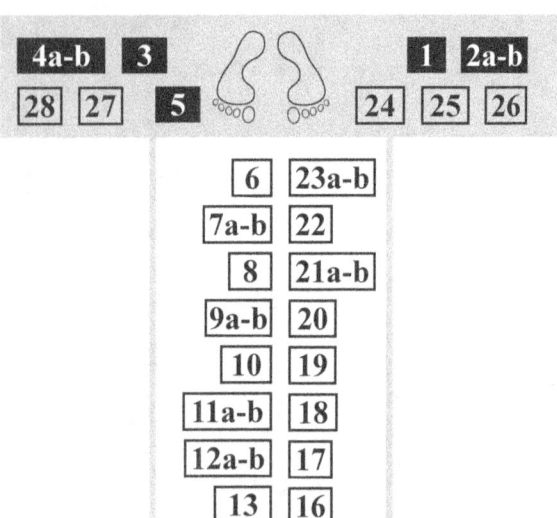

25. Turning 270° counterclockwise, move the left foot into **right back stance** (oreun dwitkubi) and execute a **double knifehand low section block** (sonnal araemakki).

26. Step forward with the right foot into **left back stance** (wen dwitkubi) and execute a **double knifehand middle section block** (sonnal momtongmakki).

Moving the left foot, return to **ready stance** (junbiseogi).

28. Step forward with the left foot into **right back stance** (oreun dwitkubi) and execute a **double knifehand middle section block** (sonnal momtongmakki).

27. Turning 180° clockwise, move the right foot into **left back stance** (wen dwitkubi) and execute a **double knifehand low section block** (sonnal araemakki).

New Movements in Jitae

Augmented Middle Block
Kodureo Momtongmakki
The inside of the forearm blocks outward and the palm of the fist faces the body. The augmented fist is held next to the elbow of the blocking arm, in front of the solar plexus. The palm of the fist faces upward.

Single Knifehand High Section Block
Hansonnal Olgulmakki
The blocking arm begins from the opposite side of the waist, crosses the body and ends in front of the forehead. The palm of the knifehand faces away from the body. The other fist rests at the waist.

Hammerfist Target Strike
Mejumeok Pyojeokchigi
The hammerfist strikes the palm of the open target hand. The target hand should remain fixed at chest height, allowing the hammerfist to travel to the target.

Diamond Front Punch
Keumgang Apjireugi
One arm executes a high section block and the other executes a straight punch. In executing the diamond front punch, the arms should move together, completing their movements simultaneously.

BLACK BELT
CHEONKWON

천 권

Meaning of Poomsae Cheonkwon

Cheonkwon literally means Heavenly Fist or Heavenly Might. Its infinite nature signifies creation, change and completion. According to Korean mythology, the founding ancestor of the Korean people was called Hwanin. Hwanin settled down in a heavenly place to spread heavenly thought and actions. For this reason, Cheon (meaning heaven) was the subject of awe and fear for the Han people (Koreans). Thus Poomsae Cheonkwon signifies the mythical history and sublime thoughts of the founding fathers of Korea. The characteristics of the movements are circular arm movements, which express the greatness and inclusiveness of the Cheonkwon concept. The line of movements symbolizes a man descending to Earth from the heavens, being empowered by the heavens and attaining oneness between the Earthly world (body) and the heavenly world (mind). There are 27 movements in Poomsae Cheonkwon. This form is for the 7th Dan.

Poomsae Line of Cheonkwon

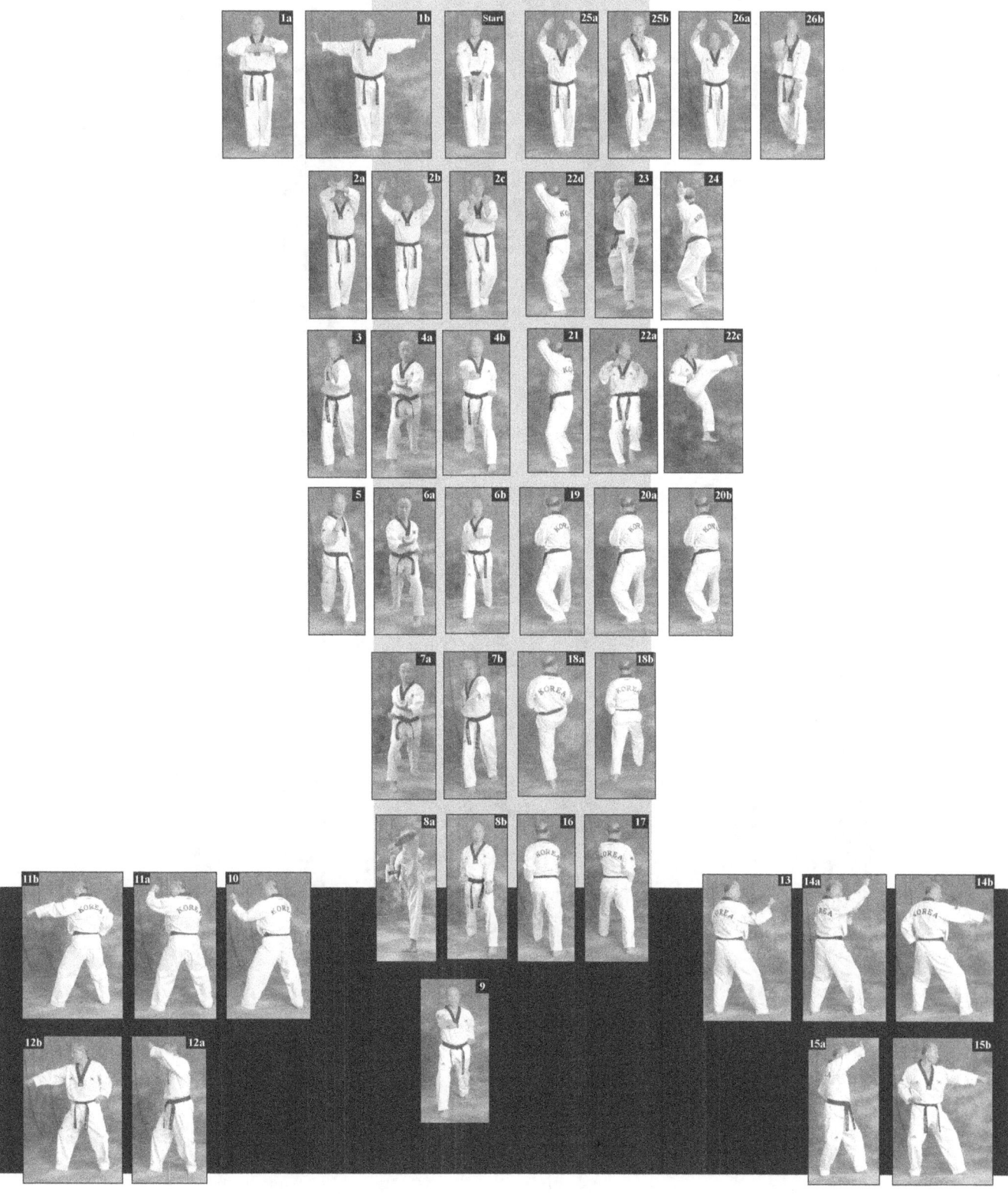

Cheonkwon

Begin from **overlapping hands ready stance** (kyopson junbiseogi), eyes looking forward and feet together.

1a. With the feet fixed, inhale while raising the two hands to the chest, with the left hand on top of the right.

1b. With the feet fixed, exhale while executing a **wingspreading posture** (nalgaepyogi) by twisting the palms outward.

2a. Quickly bring the two hands down to the abdomen then raise them up past the chest and head.

2b. Continue circling the arms outward, forming the hands into knuckle fists as they reach the bottom of the circle.

2c. Complete the movement in **right tiger stance** (oreun beomseogi) and quickly execute a **double knuckle uppercut** (sosumjireugi).

Poomsae Cheonkwon 413

3. In place, pivot the feet into **right front stance** (oreun apkubi) and execute a **left single knifehand twist block** (hansonnal bitureomakki).

4a. Slowly and powerfully twist and pull the opponent's wrist with the left hand.

4b. Continue pulling and step forward with the left foot into **left front stance** (wen apkubi) and slowly and powerfully execute a **right straight punch** (momtong barojireugi).

5. With the feet fixed, execute a **right single knifehand twist block** (hansonnal bitureomakki).

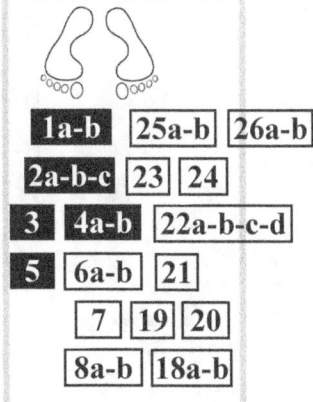

414 Black Belt Poomsae

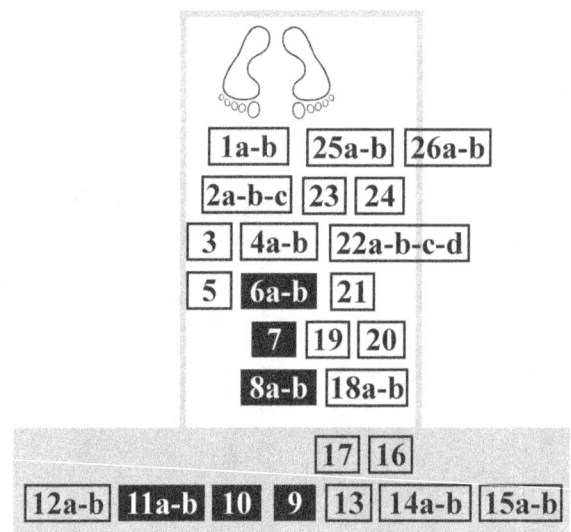

11b. With the feet fixed, execute a **left side punch** (momtong yopjireugi).

11a. Raise the left arm and circle it up above the head then outward, breaking the opponent's grip on the wrist. Then chamber the fist at the waist for the side punch.

10. Turning 270° counter-clockwise, move the left foot into **right back stance** (oreun dwitkubi) and execute a **left augmented outward middle section block** (kodureo momtong bakkatmakki).

9. Step forward with the right foot into **right front stance** (oreun apkubi) and execute a **right reverse punch** (momtong bandaejireugi).

6a-b. In place, slowly twist and pull the opponent's wrist with the right hand. Continue pulling and step forward with the right foot into **right front stance** (oreun apkubi) and flow slowly and powerfully execute a **left straight punch** (momtong barojireugi).

7a-b. With the feet fixed, execute a **left single knifehand twist block** (hansonnal bitureomakki). In place, slowly twist and pull the opponent's wrist with the left hand.

8a-b. Pivoting on the right foot, execute a **left side kick** (wenbal yopchagi) with **Kihap**. Set the left foot in **left front stance** (wen apkubi) and execute a **left low section block** (araemakki).

12a. Raise the left arm up and outward, breaking the opponent's grip on the wrist, simultaneously stepping forward with the right foot.

12b. Complete the step forward into **left back stance** (wen dwitkubi), executing a **right side punch** (momtong yopjireugi).

13. Turning 180° clockwise, move the right foot into **left back stance** (wen dwitkubi) and execute a **right augmented outward middle section block** (kodureo momtong bakkatmakki).

14a. Raise the right arm and circle it up above the head then outward, breaking the opponent's grip on the wrist. Then chamber the fist at the waist for the side punch.

14b. With the feet remaining fixed, execute a **right side punch** (momtong yopjireugi).

Poomsae Cheonkwon 417

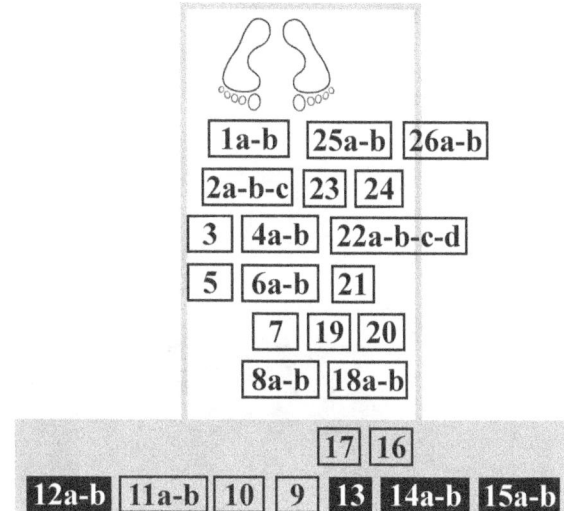

15a. Raise the right arm up and outward, breaking the opponent's grip on the wrist, simultaneously stepping forward with the left foot.

15b. Complete the step forward into **right back stance** (oreun dwitkubi), executing a **left side punch** (momtong yopjireugi).

418 Black Belt Poomsae

16. Moving the left foot, turn 90° counterclockwise into **left front stance** (wen apkubi) and execute a **right inner forearm twisting middle section block** (anpalmok momtong bitureomakki).

17. With the feet fixed, execute a **left reverse punch** (momtong bandaejireugi).

18a. With the left foot fixed, execute a **right front kick** (oreunbal apchagi).

18b. Set the right foot down in **right front stance** (oreun apkubi) and execute a **right reverse punch** (momtong bandaejireugi).

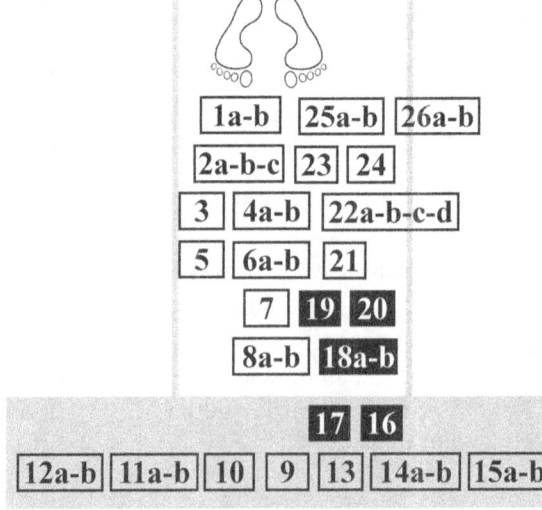

20b. Continue quickly shuffling forward, again moving the right foot into **left back stance** (wen dwitkubi) while executing a **right augmented low section block** (kodureo araemakki). Slap the right forearm with the left palm as the arms cross.

20a. Shuffle quickly forward by shifting the weight onto the left foot then moving the right foot a half step then the left, while simultaneously executing a **right middle block** (bakkatmakki). Slap the right forearm with the left palm as the arms cross.

19. Slide the right foot back into **left back stance** (wen dwitkubi) and execute a **double knifehand low section block** (sonnal araemakki).

22b. As the body rotates in the air, the left leg begins to drop and the right leg raises for the kick. At the same time, the left arm extends to make the target.

22a. To begin the **jumping turning target kick** (pyojeokchagi), shift the weight onto the right foot. Lift the left leg and rotate the body counterclockwise.

21. Slide the right foot forward into **horseriding stance** (juchumseogi) and execute a **right diamond side punch** (keumgang yopjireugi).

23. In place, turn 180° counterclockwise into **right back stance** (oreun dwitkubi) and execute a **left single knifehand mountain block** (sonnal waesanteulmakki).

22d. Having turned 360° in the air, land with the right foot forward in **horseriding stance** (juchumseogi) and execute a **right diamond side punch** (keumgang yopjireugi).

22c. The left foot lands first, but before it touches the ground the right foot must strike the target. The left foot should not touch the ground before the foot strikes the target.

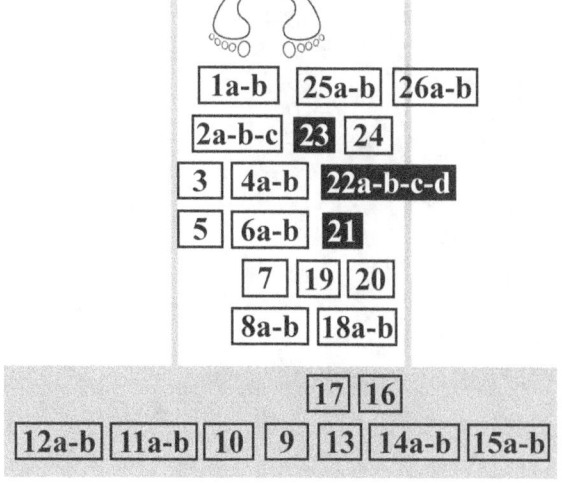

24. In place, turn 180° clockwise into **left back stance** (wen dwitkubi) and execute a **right single knifehand mountain block** (sonnal waesanteulmakki).

25a. Slide the left foot into **close stance** (moaseogi) and bring the hands to overlap in front of the lower abdomen. Continue raising the hands in front of the chest, face and over the head, circling outward.

25b. As the hands reach the height of the trunk, step the right foot forward into **right tiger stance** (oreun beomseogi), executing a **mountain pushing posture** (taesanmilgi).

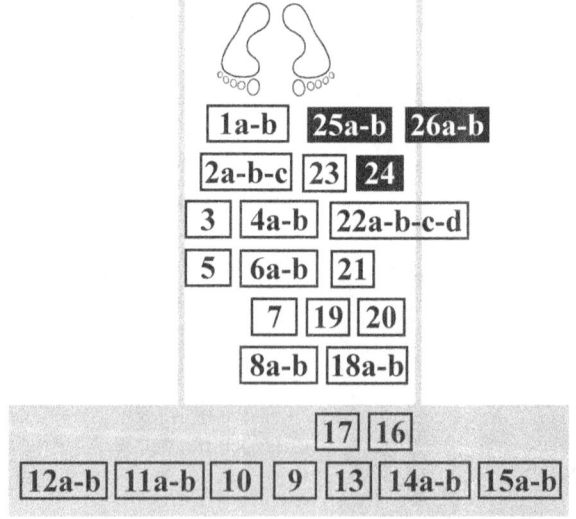

 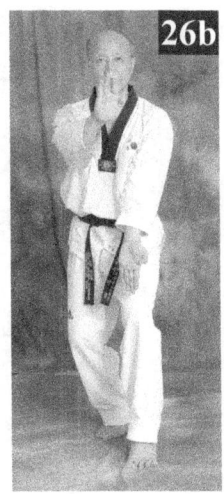 

26a. Slide the right foot back into **close stance** (moaseogi) and bring the hands to overlap in front of the lower abdomen. Continue raising the hands in front of the chest, face and over the head, circling outward.

25b. As the hands reach the height of the trunk, step the left foot forward into **left tiger stance** (wen beomseogi), executing a **mountain pushing posture** (taesanmilgi).

Moving the left foot, return to **overlapping hands ready stance** (kyopson junbiseogi).

New Movements in Cheonkwon

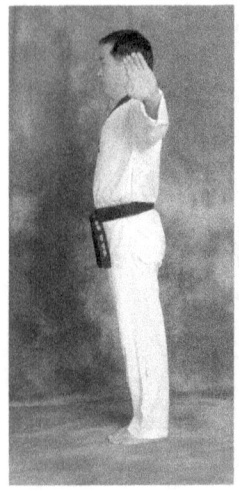 

Wingspreading Posture
Nalgaepyogi
Spread your arms to the sides with the palms facing outwards and the fingertips pointing upward. The hands, shoulders and head should be aligned on the same vertical plane. The arms should be extended on the horizontal plane.

Mountain Pushing Posture
Taesanmilgi
The hands are in palm-hand formation. The upper hand is held at eye level and the lower hand is held at the lower abdomen. This movement should be done slowly and powerfully.

Inner Forearm Twisting Middle Section Block
Anpalmok Momtong Bitureomakki
The blocking arm travels outward, blocking with the inner forearm. The body is twisted approximately 45° into the block with the upper torso held erect.

Single Knifehand Mountain Block
Sonnal Waesanteulmakki
The hands are open, with the palm of the raised hand facing the head and the palm of the other hand facing the leg. The fingertips of the raised hand are aligned with the top of the head and the arm is bent at a 90° angle.

Double Knuckle Uppercut
Sosumjireugi
The middle knuckles of each hand protrude from the fist to strike the sides of the jaw in an upward motion. The fists should be aligned at the same height and the elbows held close to the body.

Diamond Side Punch
Keumgang Yopjireugi
The diamond side punch begins from a small hinge block on the opposite side of the body. One arm performs a high section block and the other arm performs a middle section punch. Look toward the punching target.

BLACK BELT
HANSOO

Meaning of Poomsae Hansoo

Hansoo means water, which is the source of sustenance and growth. The nature of water, characterized by unbreakability and flexibility, is the basis for Poomsae Hansoo. As water forms rivers and seas from a single drop, Hansoo symbolizes the birth of a life followed by growth, strength, weakness, harmony, loftiness, and adaptability over a lifespan. This Poomsae should be performed with fluidity and graceful power. The line of movements follows the Chinese character for water. There are 27 movements in Poomsae Hansoo. This form is for the 8th Dan.

Poomsae Line of Hansoo

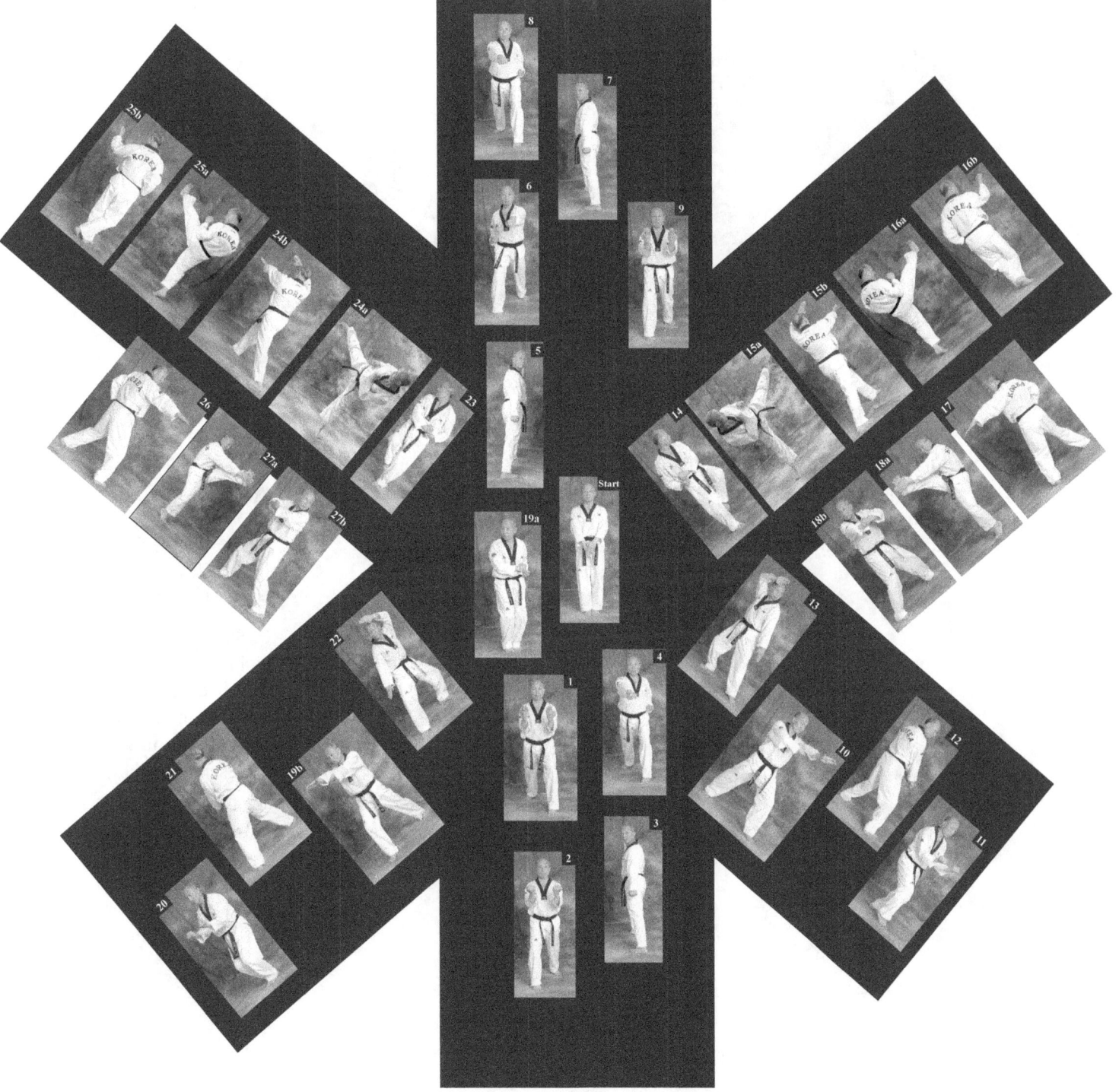

Hansoo

Begin from **overlapping hands ready stance** (kyopson junbiseogi), eyes looking forward and feet together.

1. Step forward with the left foot into **left front stance** (wen apkubi) and execute a **ridgehand middle section block** (sonnaldeung momtong hechomakki).

2. Step forward with the right foot into **right front stance** (oreun apkubi) and execute a **double hammerfist side strike** (dumejumeok yopkurichigi).

3. Step back with the right foot into **right front stance** (oreun apkubi) and execute a **single mountain block** (waesanteulmakki).

Poomsae Hansoo 431

4. In place, shift the weight and pivot the feet into **left front stance** (wen apkubi) and execute a **right straight punch** (momtong barojireugi).

5. Step back with the left foot into **left front stance** (wen apkubi) and execute a **single mountain block** (waesanteulmakki).

6. In place, shift the weight and pivot the feet into **right front stance** (oreun apkubi) and execute a **left straight punch** (momtong barojireugi).

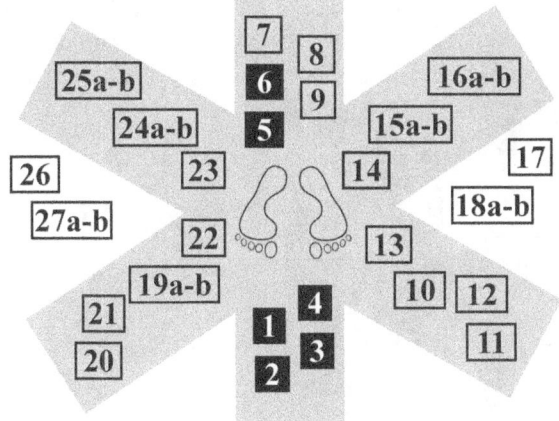

7. Step back with the right foot into **right front stance** (oreun apkubi) and execute a **single mountain block** (waesanteulmakki).

8. In place, shift the weight and pivot the feet into **left front stance** (wen apkubi) and execute a **right straight punch** (momtong barojireugi).

9. Step forward with the right foot into **right front stance** (oreun apkubi) and execute a **ridgehand middle section block** (sonnaldeung momtong hechomakki).

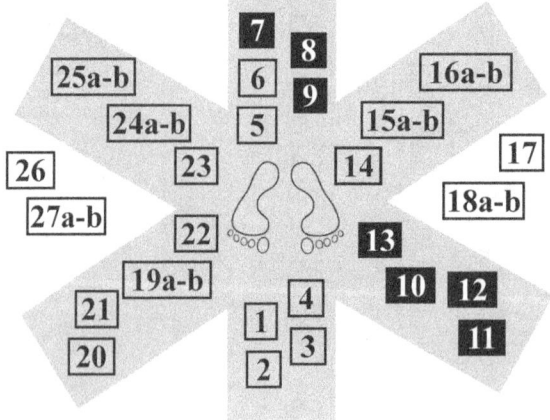

Poomsae Hansoo

10. Moving the left foot, step 45° to the left into **left front stance** (wen apkubi) and execute a **left arc hand strike** (agwison khaljaebi).

11. Jump forward with the right foot into **right assisting stance** (oreun kyotdariseogi) and execute a **double uppercut** (dujumeok jecheojireugi).

12. Slide the left foot back into **horseriding stance** (juchumseogi) and execute a **target low section block** (pyojeok araemakki).

13. Step back with the right foot into **right back stance** (oreun dwitkubi) and execute a **knifehand diamond block** (sonnal keumgangmakki).

16a-b. With the left foot fixed, execute a **right front kick** (oreunbal apchagi). Set the right foot down in **left rear cross stance** (wen dwikoaseogi) and execute a **right backfist strike** (deungjumeok apchigi).

15a-b. Pivoting on the right foot, execute a **left side kick** (wenbal yopchagi). Set the left foot down in **left front stance** (wen apkubi) and execute a **swallow form knifehand strike** (jebipoom mokchigi).

14. Pivoting on the right foot, turn 90° clockwise into **right crane stance** (oreun hakdariseogi) and execute a **small hinge block** (jageun doltzeogi).

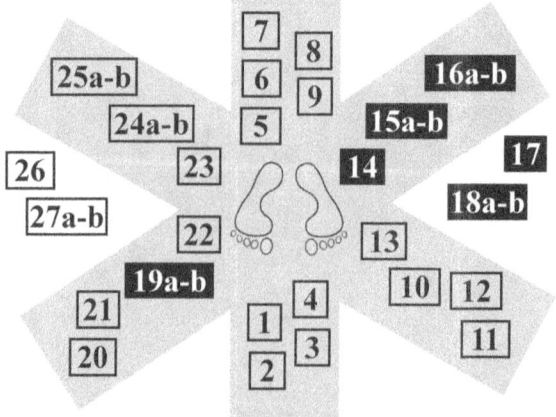

Poomsae Hansoo 435

17. Turning 180° counterclockwise, set the left foot down to the rear in **horseriding stance** (juchumseogi) and execute a **left knifehand side strike** (sonnal yopchigi).

18a. Pivoting on the left foot execute a **right target kick** (oreunbal pyojeokchagi).

18b. Set the right foot down in **horseriding stance** (juchumseogi) and execute a **right elbow target strike** (palkup pyojeokchigi).

19a. Bring the left foot to the right in **feet together close stance** (modumbal moaseogi), chambering the hands for the **arc hand strike** (agwison khaljaebi).

19b. Immediately step forward with the right foot into **right front stance** (oreun apkubi), executing a **right arc hand strike** (agwison khaljaebi).

20. Jump forward with the left foot into **left assisting stance** (wen kyotdariseogi) and execute a **double uppercut** (dujumeok jecheojireugi).

21. Slide the right foot back into **horseriding stance** (juchumseogi) and execute a **target low section block** (pyojeok araemakki).

22. Step back with the left foot into **left back stance** (wen dwitkubi) and execute a **knifehand diamond block** (sonnal keumgangmakki).

Poomsae Hansoo 437

25b. Set the left foot down in **right rear cross stance** (oreun dwikoaseogi) and execute a **left backfist strike** (deungjumeok apchigi).

25a. With the right foot fixed, execute a **left front kick** (wenbal apchagi).

24b. Set the right foot down in **right front stance** (oreun apkubi) and execute a **swallow form knifehand strike** (jebipoom mokchigi).

24a. Pivoting on the left foot, execute a **right side kick** (oreunbal yopchagi).

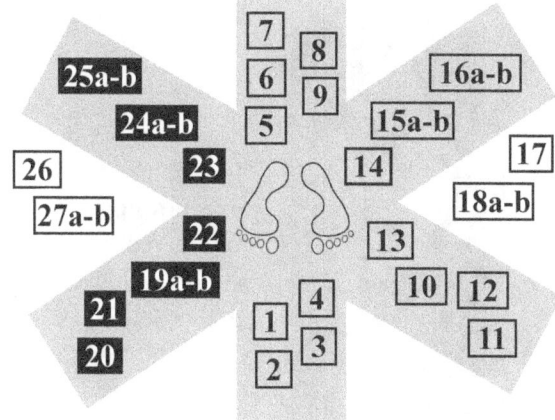

23. Pivoting on the left foot, turn 90° clockwise into **left crane stance** (wen hakdariseogi) and execute a **small hinge block** (jageun doltzeogi).

26. Moving the right foot turn 180° clockwise into **horseriding stance** (juchumseogi) and execute a **knifehand side strike** (sonnal yopchigi).

27a. Pivoting on the right foot execute a **left target kick** (wenbal pyojeokchagi).

27b. Set the left foot down in **horseriding stance** (juchumseogi) and execute a **left elbow target strike** (palkup pyojeokchigi).

Moving the right foot, return to **overlapping hands ready stance** (kyopson junbiseogi).

New Movements in Hansoo

Assisting Stance
Kyotdariseogi
The first toe of the assisting (rear) foot touches the arch of the front foot. Bend the knees to lower the body. The weight is supported on the front foot. Only the ball of the front foot is touching the ground, assisting with maintaining the balance.

Target Low Section Block
Pyojeok Araemakki
The arc of one hand forms the target for the inner wrist of the blocking hand. The hands are positioned in front of the lower abdomen and the eyes look toward the open hand side.

Knifehand Diamond Block
Sonnal Keumgangmakki
The raised arm makes a high section block and the other arm makes a low section block. Both hands are knifehands. Align the low section block with the front thigh.

Double Hammerfist Side Strike
Dumejumeok Yopkurichigi
The inner wrists face each other, using the soft side of the fist to strike the opponent's kidneys. The elbows are bent at the time of the strike. In the process of striking, the arms move toward each other, beginning from outside the shoulders.

Knifehand Side Strike
Sonnal Yopchigi
The strike begins on the opposite side of the body, with the palm facing the body. The knifehand then rotates to palm-down on contact with the target. Align the head, hand and shoulder on the same plane. The other fist rests at the waist.

BLACK BELT
ILYEO

Meaning of Poomse Ilyeo

Ilyeo symbolizes oneness as formulated by the great monk Wonhyo of the Silla Dynasty (57 BC - 976 AD). Wonhyo (617 - 686) was one of the leading thinkers, writers and teachers of the Korean Buddhist tradition. His philosophy includes the "consciousness-only" enlightenment experience, the concept that everything in the universe is either a point, a line or a circle, which eventually end up as one. Poomsae Ilyeo represents the harmonization of the body, mind, spirit and substance, which is the culmination of martial arts practice. This concept begins from the first movement of Bojumeok Moaseogi (covered fist close stance). Through practicing Poomsae Ilyeo, the Taekwondo practitioner purifies all worldly thoughts and concentrates on every moment of existence to reach the final phase of training—the world of oneness. The line of movements follows the Buddhist mark, meaning a state of perfect selflessness where origin, substance and service come into congruity. There are 23 movements in Poomsae Ilyeo. This form is for the 9th Dan.

Poomsae Line of Ilyeo

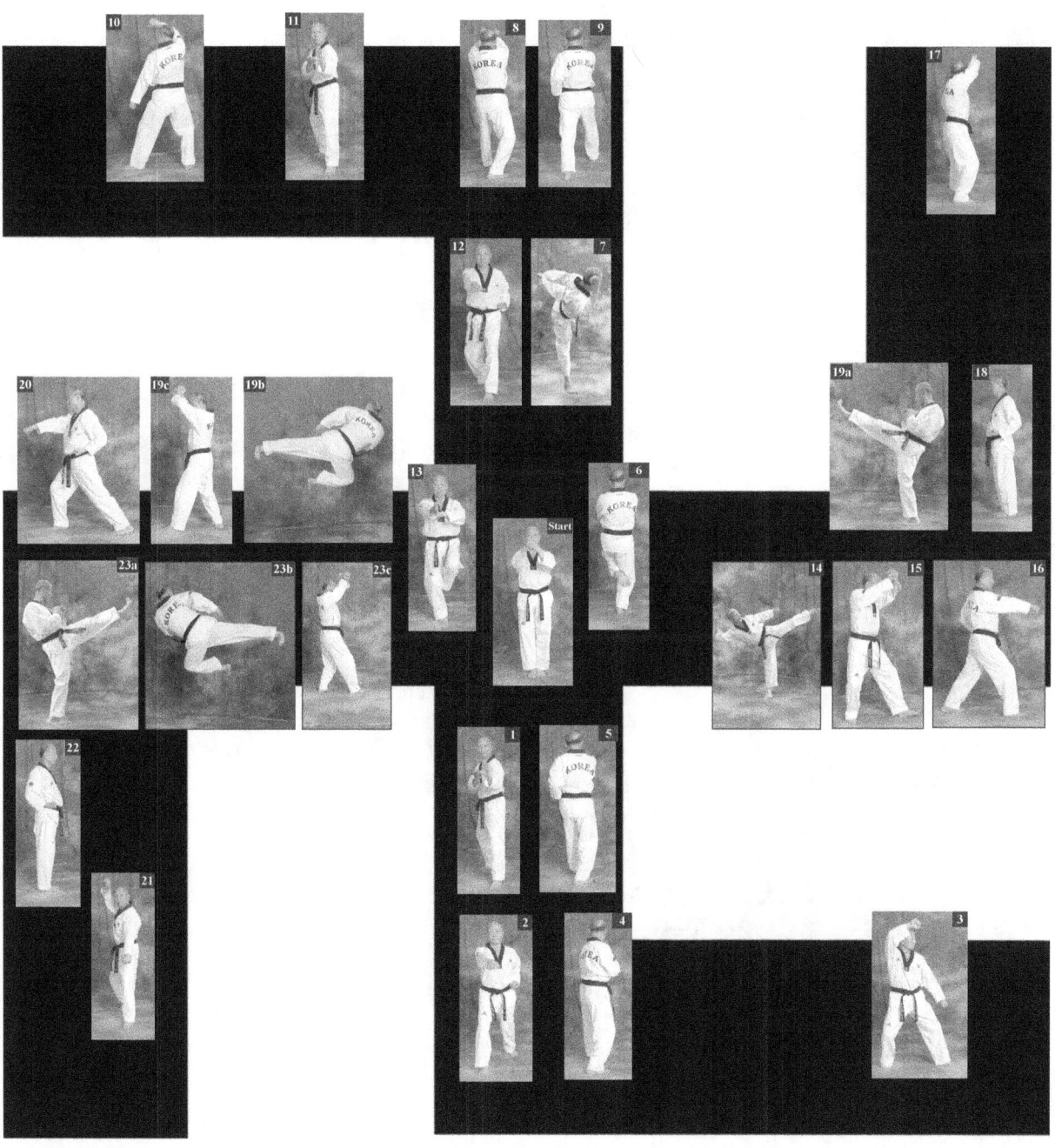

Ilyeo

Begin from **covered fist ready stance** (bojumeok junbiseogi), eyes looking forward and feet together.

1. Step forward with the left foot into **right back stance** (oreun dwitkubi) and execute a **double knifehand block** (sonnal momtongmakki).

2. Step forward with the right foot into **right front stance** (oreun apkubi) and execute a **right reverse punch** (momtong bandaejireugi).

3. Stepping with the left foot, turn 90° counterclockwise into **right back stance** (oreun dwitkubi) and execute a **diamond block** (keumgangmakki).

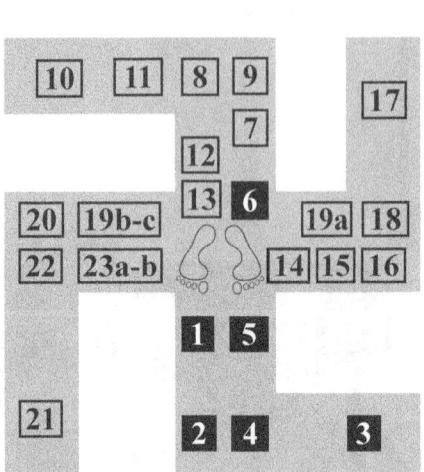

6. Jump forward with the right foot into **right crane back stance** (oreun ogeumseogi) and execute a **right vertical fingertip thrust** (pyonsonkkeut sewotzireugi). **Kihap**.

5. With the feet fixed, execute a **right straight punch** (momtong barojireugi).

4. Stepping with the left foot, turn 90° counterclockwise into **right back stance** (oreun dwitkubi) and execute a **double knifehand block** (sonnal momtongmakki).

12. With the feet fixed, execute a **right straight punch** (momtong barojireugi).

11. Stepping with the left foot, turn 90° counterclockwise into **right back stance** (oreun dwitkubi) and execute a **double knifehand block** (sonnal momtongmakki).

10. Stepping with the left foot, turn 90° counterclockwise into **right back stance** (oreun dwitkubi) and execute a **diamond block** (keumgangmakki).

13. Jump forward with the right foot into **right crane back stance** (oreun ogeumseogi) and execute a **right vertical fingertip thrust** (pyonsonkkeut sewotzireugi). **Kihap**.

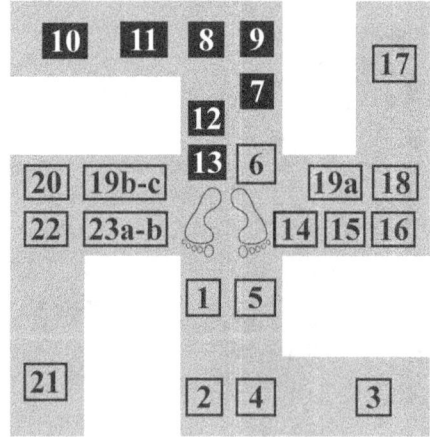

Poomsae Ilyeo 447

9. The hands twist and draw the opponent's wrist while the right foot steps forward into **right front stance** (oreun apkubi) and execute a **right reverse punch** (momtong bandaejireugi).

8. Set the left foot down in **right back stance** (oreun dwitkubi) and quickly execute a **high section cross block** (otkoreo olgulmakki).

7. Pivoting on the right foot in **right single leg stance** (oreun wedariseogi), slowly execute a **left side kick** (wenbal yopchagi) while simultaneously executing a **single mountain block** (waesanteul makki).

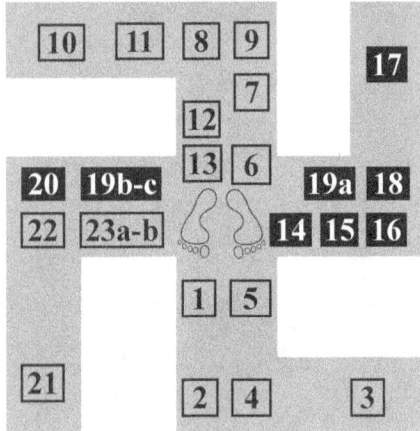

14. Pivoting on the right foot in **right single leg stance** (oreun wedariseogi), slowly execute a **left side kick** (wenbal yopchagi) while simultaneously executing a **single mountain block** (waesanteul makki).

20. The hands twist and draw the opponent's wrist while the right foot steps forward into **right front stance** (oreun apkubi) and execute a **right reverse punch** (momtong bandaejireugi).

19c. Set the left foot down in **right back stance** (oreun dwitkubi) and execute a **high section cross block** (otkoreo olgulmakki).

15. Set the left foot down in **right back stance** (oreun dwitkubi) and execute a **high section cross block** (otkoreo olgulmakki).

16. The hands twist and draw the opponent's wrist while the right foot steps forward into **right front stance** (oreun apkubi), then execute a **right reverse punch** (momtong bandaejireugi).

17. Stepping with the left foot, turn 90° counterclockwise into **right back stance** (oreun dwitkubi) and execute a **diamond block** (keumgangmakki).

19b. Set the right foot down one step further in front then execute a **left jump side kick** (wenbal twio yopchagi).

19a. With the left foot fixed, execute a **right front kick** (oreunbal apchagi).

18. Stepping with the left foot, turn 180° counterclockwise into **feet together close stance** (modumbal moaseogi) and bring the **fists to the waist** (dujumeok heoriseogi).

21. Stepping with the left foot, turn 90° counterclockwise into **right back stance** (oreun dwitkubi) and execute a **diamond block** (keumgangmakki).

22. Stepping with the left foot, turn 180° counterclockwise into **feet together close stance** (modumbal moaseogi) and bring the **fists to the waist** (dujumeok heoriseogi).

23a. With the right foot fixed, execute a **left front kick** (wenbal apchagi).

23b. Set the left foot down one step further in front then execute a **right jump side kick** (oreunbal twio yopchagi).

Poomsae Ilyeo

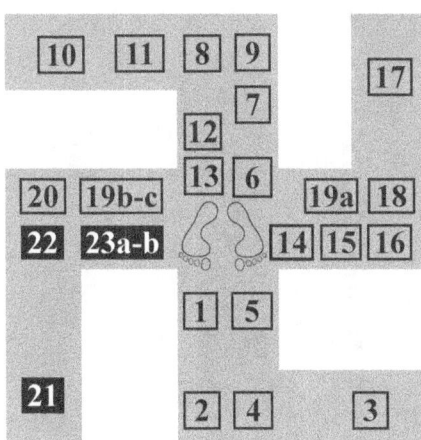

23c. Set the right foot down in **left back stance** (wen dwitkubi) and execute a **high section cross block** (otkoreo olgulmakki).

Moving the right foot, return to **covered fist ready stance** (bojumeok junbiseogi).

New Movements in Ilyeo

Crane Back Stance
Ogeumseogi
Crane back stance is similar to crane stance except the lifted leg is placed behind the knee rather than beside the leg. The raised foot wraps around the back of the knee, assisting with balance and acting as a brake on forward movement.

Two Hands at Waist in Close Stance
Dujumeok Heoriseogi
Stand with the feet together. The fists rest at the waist facing upward and the elbows are pulled back. The chest is open and the chin naturally tucked in.

Jump Side Kick
Twio Yopchagi
Before jumping, squat slightly, hop up and chamber the kicking leg. At the apex of the jump, execute the side kick while pulling the other leg up beneath the thigh of the kicking leg. Look at the target and hold the arms close to the body.

About Dr. Sang H. Kim

Dr. Sang H. Kim (Sang-hwan Kim, 7th Dan) was born in Daegu, South Korea. He began Taekwondo training at the age of four. At 15, he entered Yuga Buddhist temple to deepen his training and earned his 4th Dan at 16. During college, he taught Taekwondo to CID agents of the US Army at Camp Walker. As a special agent during his military service, he developed tactical combat methods for hand-to-hand and hand-to-weapon combat.

To advance his education, he traveled to the United States to study in 1985 and has since traveled to Europe, North and South America and Asia to present seminars on Taekwondo and motivational skills. He holds an MS degree in Sports Science and Ph.D. in Sports Media Studies.

He taught Taekwondo at Trinity College from 1987 to 1994 and was a technical advisor for the Taekwondo programs at Wesleyan University and the University of Connecticut. He has spoken on Sports Philosophy, Fighting Strategy and Motivation at Yale University, Gordonstoun School in Scotland, Brunell University in London, and private and public organizations in Bermuda, Ireland, Spain, Austria, and the United Kingdom.

He has been featured in magazines including *Black Belt, Taekwondo Times, Taekwondo People, WTF Magazine, Combat, Fighter's Magazine, Delta Sky, Vitality,* and *Bottom Line Business.*

His books and films have been reviewed in the *Dallas Observer, Hartford Courant, Worcester Telegram, El Nacional (Oklahoma), The Herald News, Inner-self Magazine, Memphis Business Journal, The Observer, San Francisco Sun Reporter, The Star Gazette, The Times,* and 90 more publications.

He authored 10 books including the bestsellers *Ultimate Flexibility, Ultimate Fitness Through Martial Arts, Teaching: the Way of The Master, Taekwondo Kyorugi, Instructor's Desk Reference, Martial Arts After 40* and *1,001 Ways To Motivate Yourself and Others* (translated into more than 20 languages). He also starred in over 100 martial arts training films and DVDs including *Encyclopedia of Self-defense, Taegeuk Poomsae, Beginner Taekwondo, Ultimate Fitness for Martial Arts, Complete Kicking, Complete Sparring* and *Taekwondo Hand Skills.*

His close relationships with US Federal agencies and the CT State Police lead him to develop Law Enforcement Safety & Survival training DVDs. He has also produced over a dozen documentaries on international subjects including *The Real Royal Trip, Ki: the Science of Energy, Zen for Martial Arts, 100 Years of Tradition,* and *Admiral Yi Sun-shin and the Turtle Boat.*

He wrote, produced and directed *Zen Man,* his first martial arts feature film, in 2006 and is currently producing and directing his second feature film in Santa Fe, New Mexico.

About Dr. Kyu Hyung Lee

Grandmaster Taekwondo 9th Degree Black Belt

Dr. Kyu Hyung Lee is one of the highest-ranking Taekwondo masters in the world and one of the most revered Poomsae instructors in the history of Taekwondo. He was the head of the 1988 Olympic Taekwondo Demonstration team and the Korean Team manager for the First World Taekwondo Poomsae Competition. From 1973 to 2005, he was the head of the internationally famous Midong Elementary School Demonstration team who has performed for royalty and heads of state around the world. From 1989 to 2005, he was the head of the Korean National Taekwondo Demonstration team. He holds a Ph.D. in physical education, 9th Dan black belt in Taekwondo and a WTF International Referee S (Special) class license. Currently he is a professor at Keimyung University in Daegu, South Korea.

Experience

Head of the Kukkiwon and Korean National Taekwondo Demonstration Team and Korean National Junior Taekwondo Demonstration Team which have performed at major national and international events

1973 - Present	Head of Korean National Junior Taekwondo Demonstration Team
1978 - Present	Head of the Kukkiwon & Korean National Demonstration Team

Designed and planned Taekwondo demonstrations for youth and adult teams

- "LEAP" For the 1986 Asian Games
- "Over the Wall" for the 1988 Seoul Olympic Games
- Opening Ceremonies for the 1988 Paralympics
- 50th Anniversary of the Army, October 1998
- Opening Ceremony of the 1999 Grand PrixWorld Fencing Games
- Special Presentation for Queen Elizabeth II, April 1999
- Special Presentation for the 109th IOC Congress in Seoul, June 1999
- Special Presentation for First lady of Ukraine, March 28, 2001
- Special Presentation for Zhu Lin, the wife of Li Peng, the chairman of the National People's of Congress of China, May 26, 2001
- Opening ceremony of The 2nd World Broadcasting Congress, December 2, 2001
- Special Presentation for Pyongyang in North Korea, September 14-17, 2002
  Taekwondo demonstration team interchange by mutual agreement of the 7th North and South of Korea Minister Congress
- Design and present 40 youth and 40 adult Taekwondo demonstrations annually

Teach traditional Taekwondo, including its theoretical background and practices enabling students to develop their minds, bodies and spirits

1983 - Present	Instructor at Taekwondo Teachers Training Center of the Kukkiwon
1992 - June 2001	Martial Arts Instructor of the Sports Department of the Korea Military Academy

1999 - Present	Concurrent Professor of the Sports Major at Kyemyoung University
2003 - Present	Chairman of Demonstration committee of World Taekwondo Federation

Education

August 1985	Graduated from Yongin University
February 1988	Masters Degree in Sports Education, Yonsei University
August 11, 1999	THE HONORARY DOCTOR OF EDUCATION (No.238) Russia National University of Education of Kkomsamolsky-Na-Amure
August 20, 2002	THE DOCTOR OF SCIENCE (No.079) Title : *A study on the Relationship between Taekwondo practice and the Development of Personality on elementary students* Keimyoung University

Licenses

Feb. 24, 1974	Licensed a referee's license from the Korea Taekwondo Association (First Degree Referee No. 80).
Sept. 1, 1975	Licensed an international referee's license from the World Taekwondo Federation (Special Degree International Referee No. 002-0088).
Mar. 9, 1975	Licensed an international master's license from the World Taekwondo Federation (No. 1094).
Feb. 29, 1988	Licensed a teacher's license (No. 203569, second class teacher's license for middle or high school - for physical education) by the Ministry of Education.
Mar. 2, 1999	Concurrent professor of the Sports Major of Kyemyoung University (No. 99-5)
June 9, 2001	Licensed the official 9th Dan Blackbelt of Taekwondo (No. 05000110 from Kukkiwon)
Sept. 17, 2003	Licensed a Promotion test committee's 1st class member of Kukkiwon. (No.0501081)
Nov. 7, 2003	Licensed a Chairman of World Taekwondo Federation Demonstration committee. (No.2003-054)
Nov. 25, 2003	Licensed an International Referee's license from the Kukkiwon. (First degree referee No.001008)

Teaching Experience

1973 - present	Teacher of the Korean National Junior Taekwondo Demonstration Team
1983 - present	Instructor of Taekwondo Teachers Training Center of the KUKKIWON
1989 - present	Teacher of the Korean National Taekwondo Demonstration Team
1992 - June 30, 2001	Martial arts instructor of the Sports Department of the Korea Military Academy
1998 - 2001	Instructor of Taekwondo Department of Korea National University of Physical Education
1999 - 2002	Concurrent professor of the Sports Major of Kyemyoung University
1999 - present	Instructor of Institute of Taekwondo Masters of Yonsei University
2002	Instructor for participants of Kukkiwon High Dan Examination(6-9 Dan)

Overseas Activities

July 20 1993	Appointed as the honorary ambassador of the Arkansas State Government of the U.S.
April 12, 1998	Appointed as chairman of the technical committee of Russia Taekwondo Federation.
May 8 - Jun 4, 1990	Initiator of WTF Taekwondo diffusion in the Union of Soviet Socialist Republics
1973 - present	Technical guidance and Demonstration worldwide (about 200 countries) (Asia, Southeast Asia, Oceania, North and South America, Europe, Africa etc,)

International Awards

Dec. 19, 1995   Award from the U.S. President (for sportsmen given by the President Bill Clinton)
Jun. 2, 2001   Award from the U.S. President (for sportsmen given by the President George W. Bush)

Awards and Recognitions

Feb. 24, 1983   Award from the President of the World Taekwondo Federation
                           (for the spreading of Taekwondo around the world)
Oct. 27, 1986   Award from the Seoul Asian Games Organization Committee
                           (for excellent demonstration of duties and contributions to the operation of
                           games)
Dec. 31, 1986   Award from the Minister of the Sports Ministry (for the successful Taekwondo
                           demonstration for the opening ceremony of the 10th Asian Games)
April 4, 1989   Award from the Minister of the Sports Ministry
                           (for contributions to the 24th Olympic Games)
Dec. 31, 1990   Award from the Minister of the Sports and Youth Ministry
                           (for excellent demonstration of duties, promotion of national sports
                           and youth training)
Sept. 16, 1994   'Noonsol' award from the Noonsol Committee (for children's education)
Dec. 23, 1996   Award for citizens with good deeds from Mayor of Seoul City
                           (for contributions to the community and municipal development)
Dec. 12, 1997   Award from the President of the Korea Taekwondo Association
                           (for Taekwondo development and enhancement of the national prestige)
Dec. 24, 1998   Award from the Minister of the National Defense Ministry
                           (for contributions to the 50th anniversary of the national army)
Dec, 20, 2002   Awarded a WORLDCUP Medal from the Minister of Culture & Tourism
                           (No.20427, 2002FIFA KOREA/JAPAN FIFA WORLDCUP)
Oct. 31, 2003   Award from the Minister of the National Defense Ministry
                           (for contributions to Taekwondo Championship of the Minister
                           of the National Defense Ministry)

Publications:

Master's Thesis, Yeonsei University, 1987
        The Effect of The Practice of Taekwondo on Children's Mental Education
        Dept. of Physical Education The Graduate School of Yonsei University

Doctoral Thesis, Keimyung University, 2001
        A study on the Relationship between Taekwondo practice and the Development of Personality on el
        elementary students
          Department of Physical Education Graduate School Keimyung University

And 10 more articles for national and international publications.

Books:

Taekwondo, 1983, Japanese Text Book
The Theory and Practical Knowledge of Taekwondo: I-Poomsae, II-Demonstration, 1999, Yeonsei University
Today's Taekwondo, 2002, Co-authored with Bae Yung-sang, Song Hyung-suk, Emun Publication, Korea

Also Available from Turtle Press:

Martial Arts Injury Care and Prevention
Armlock Encyclopedia
Championship Sambo
Timing for Martial Arts
Strength and Power Training
Complete Kickboxing
Ultimate Flexibility
Boxing: A 12 Week Course
The Fighter's Body: An Owner's Manual
The Science of Takedowns, Throws and Grappling for Self-defense
Fighting Science
Martial Arts Instructor's Desk Reference
Solo Training
Solo Training 2
Fighter's Fact Book
Conceptual Self-defense
Martial Arts After 40
Warrior Speed
The Martial Arts Training Diary for Kids
Teaching Martial Arts
Combat Strategy
The Art of Harmony
Total MindBody Training
1,001 Ways to Motivate Yourself and Others
Ultimate Fitness through Martial Arts
Taekwondo Kyorugi: Olympic Style Sparring

For more information:
Turtle Press
1-800-778-8785
e-mail: orders@turtlepress.com

http://www.turtlepress.com

www.ingramcontent.com/pod-product-compliance
Lightning Source LLC
Chambersburg PA
CBHW082020300426
44117CB00015B/2287